THE ACTON—NEWMAN RELATIONS

THE
ACTON–NEWMAN RELATIONS

The Dilemma of Christian Liberalism

by

Hugh A. MacDougall, O.M.I.

FORDHAM UNIVERSITY PRESS

NEW YORK · 1962

To my mother

Contents

Preface

In the history of the development of Christian thought in the nineteenth century two names stand out in the English-speaking world: Lord Acton and Cardinal Newman. Both men, highly endowed intellectually, thought hard and deeply about the relevance of Christianity to the rapidly changing society of their day. Both were men of vision and were profoundly concerned about the apparent drift of Western Christendom toward a totally secularized society. Though differing considerably in their approach to many questions, they were agreed that only in a religious culture could freedom flourish. Many of the problems which disquieted them, with heightened accents, perplex us today. Catholics, in particular, will find the controversies in which they were involved strangely topical. Far from being an exercise in mere antiquarianism, a study of their relations should be of vital interest to the twentieth-century reader.

The story of the Acton-Newman relations is known to the majority of readers solely from Wilfrid Ward's accounts in his great biographies of Newman, Wiseman and W. G. Ward and from Cardinal Gasquet's *Lord Acton and His Circle*. No subsequent writer has added substantially to Ward's or Gasquet's narratives. Yet as a history of the relations of two of the greatest men of the last century both are far from adequate. Ward's account covers only one period of their relations: the *Rambler* and *Home and Foreign* period. But even here he omits important details and is inaccurate in some others.[1] Gasquet's work, also primarily concerned with the early journalistic period, while carrying a useful introduction, is marred by a very faulty transcription of the Acton-Simpson correspondence. There is avail-

---

[1] Since the above was written an excellent work covering this period has appeared: *The Liberal Catholic Movement in England (1848–1864)* by Dr. Josef Altholz (London, 1962).

able a mass of material which for various reasons was not
utilized by either Ward or Gasquet and from which one may
present a much fuller and more coherent history of the Acton-
Newman relations than has hitherto appeared.

In this study the many printed works of Acton and Newman
themselves form a basic source of information. While I have
constantly availed myself of letters printed in Ward's and
Gasquet's books and in the published volumes of Acton's
correspondence, viz., *Letters of Lord Acton to Mary Gladstone*
and *Lord Acton's Correspondence*, I have in almost all instances
first consulted the original manuscripts. My debt to other
authors, while indeed great, is chiefly for background matter.

Probably the richest source of manuscript material is found
in the Newman archives of the Birmingham Oratory.[2] There one
comes upon a great many letters and notes that have never been
used by any of Newman's numerous biographers. Thus, for
instance, there is Newman's correspondence with Monsell (Lord
Emly) which only came into the possession of the Oratory Fathers
after Ward's biography and was not used by him. This collection
is probably the most important single one in the archives.
"Indeed," Newman once told Father Neville, "I have written
more confidentially to Lord Emly about myself than to any other
person."[3] The large collection of Acton manuscripts in the
Cambridge University Library provides another important
source. Though several students of Acton have spent long hours
working their way through this formidable collection none can
claim to have exhausted its wealth. Mr. Douglas Woodruff is in
possession of a second valuable collection of Acton papers. Of
special importance here are Newman's letters to Acton (partly
used by Ward in his biography of Newman) and Acton's correspondence with Döllinger. This latter correspondence, Acton's
most important, is presently being prepared for publication by
Victor Conzemius of Luxembourg, through whose great kindness
I have been permitted to utilize the typed transcripts he has
prepared. At Downside Abbey is found the Acton-Simpson
correspondence. Although Gasquet's volume contains a con-

---

[2] A definitive edition of the *Letters and Diaries of John Henry Newman* is presently
being published by Thomas Nelson and Son. The assiduous editorial work done
by C. Stephen Dessain of the Oratory is a model of its kind.

[3] A report, dated 15 Oct. 1876, of a conversation Newman held with Father
Neville is filed with the Monsell correspondence at the Oratory.

siderable portion of these letters an even larger portion remains unpublished. In addition to the above sources useful information was also discovered in the Blennerhasset papers in the Cambridge University Library, the William Gladstone and Mary Gladstone letters in the British Museum, the Manning papers in the archives of the parish of St. Mary of the Angels, Bayswater, and the Wiseman papers in the archives at Archbishop's House, Westminster.

I am indebted to all those who so generously placed the above materials at my disposal and who in discussions helped me better understand my subject. In particular I must acknowledge a great debt to the sympathetic guide under whose direction I pursued this study, Professor Herbert Butterfield, Master of Peterhouse, Cambridge. I hold it a privilege to have worked under so distinguished a scholar. Among others who helped me in various ways I must also mention Professor D. W. Brogan, Professor Dudley Edwards, Gerald Fitzgerald, William Greenway, Aubrey Gwynn, S. J., Professor David Knowles, Archbishop David Mathew and Edward Stewart.

THE ACTON—NEWMAN RELATIONS

Introduction

In no period in history has the age-old problem of reconciling new knowledge with long-held belief appeared in a more acute form than in the nineteenth century. In almost every field of investigation new discoveries tended to throw doubt on existing beliefs. The scientific revolution, the development of critical history with its momentous repercussions on biblical studies in particular, the new speculations which threatened to overthrow the philosophical basis of the mediaeval Christian synthesis, all combined to present to Christian intellectuals a Herculean task of assimilation and reconciliation if the educated mind of Europe was not to be lost to Christianity.

The Catholic Church, having emerged from the Napoleonic era gravely weakened, was ill-prepared to meet the challenge. With its monastic organization reduced to impotency and all its universities secularized, never in its history was enlightened leadership more demanded. But it was not forthcoming. The first five popes of the century were zealously devoted to their office but in mentality they belonged to an age that had passed away and were incapable of understanding the new one that had arrived. The history of official Catholicism in the first three-quarters of the century is mainly one of retreat and entrenchment behind traditional defenses that no longer were equal to the demands placed upon them.

Yet, within the Catholic body there was a strong unofficial movement led by men keenly alive to the seriousness of the challenge facing Christianity. Favoring toleration and free inquiry, they boldly urged Catholics to adopt a new approach more suited to the changed circumstances. Generally designated

1

as *liberal* Catholics they represented the most vital intellectual force within the Church. It was something of their spirit that Newman and Acton were to attempt to introduce into English Catholicism.

The picture presented by the Catholic Church in England in the early years of the nineteenth century was a dismal one. After centuries of proscription it stood stripped of all social significance within the English community. "Its members," to quote Elliott-Binns, "were regarded by most Englishmen as followers of an obscure foreign religious sect, and its priests, who often dressed as laymen, as aliens, and undesirable at that."[1] Newman, in his famous sermon, *The Second Spring*, related his own memories of

the utter contempt into which Catholicism had fallen by the time that we were born. . . No longer the Catholic Church in the country; nay, no longer, I may say, a Catholic community;—but a few adherents of the Old Religion, moving silently and sorrowfully about, as memorials of what had been. 'The Roman Catholics;'—not a sect, not even an interest, as men conceived of it,—not a body, however small, representative of the Great Communion abroad,—but a mere handful of individuals, who might be counted, like the pebbles and *detritus* of the great deluge, and who, forsooth, merely happened to retain a creed which, in its day indeed, was the profession of a Church.[2]

By mid-century the character of English Catholicism had radically altered. Heavy Irish immigration during the famine years combined with the converts following in the wake of the Oxford Movement to increase Church membership from "a mere handful" to a community numbering some 700,000.[3] Rome acknowledged the new status by establishing a hierarchy in 1850.

By far the largest group was made up of Irish working-class families. Ill-paid, ill-housed, and poorly educated, at the very

[1] L. E. Elliott-Binns, *Religion in the Victorian Era* (London, 1936), p. 114.
[2] *Sermons Preached on Various Occasions* (Burns and Oates, London, 1887), p. 171. Unless otherwise indicated all further references to Newman's works are to the standard edition (1874–1921) published by Longmans Green and Co.
[3] Philip Hughes, "The English Catholics in 1850," *English Catholics 1850–1950* (edited by G. A. Beck, London, 1950), p. 45. Father Hughes bases his estimate on the census returns of 1851 which gave the number of persons present at church services on Sunday, 30 March 1851. Any estimate of church membership formed from such figures can, of course, be only a rough approximation.

bottom of the social scale, this body presented bishops and priests with special problems far removed from those which were to gain the attention of Newman and Acton.

The native English Catholics, the Old Catholics, formed another distinct group. They belonged almost exclusively to the landed class, "intermarried with each other, lived on their estates, or, if they came to London, in a narrow circle of their own."[4] They had little contact with or knowledge of continental Catholicism; and in their desire, born of past persecutions, to avoid conspicuousness, eschewed the outward non-liturgical expressions of piety and devotion usually associated with continental worship. They disliked the enthusiasm of Wiseman and did not favor the decided encouragement he gave to the newly returned religious orders. They had, "in spite of the suspicion with which they were regarded, become more English than Catholic."[5] Excluded, as other nonconformists, from university life,[6] and accustomed to living on the periphery of society, they remained isolated from the various cultural currents of the day and were little influenced by the new thought which so disturbed educated society in general. Too often the new converts, fresh from the universities, mistook their unobtrusiveness and dislike of display for ignorance or apathy. Still, in spite of their small numbers, they could boast of a fair measure of scholarly achievement by such men as Milner, Butler and Lingard. However, as the century progressed no other writers of equal calibre appeared in their ranks.

A further group was formed by the converts who left the Oxford Movement. The earlier converts had quietly assumed the ways of the Old Catholics and were more or less indistinguishable from them, but the new Oxford converts displayed an excessive zeal which was viewed with the utmost distaste by many of the old school. Some of them were inclined to regard themselves as bearers of light to a community sunk in intellectual darkness. But their erudition was not always appreciated. *Prima facie* one

[4] F. W. Cornish, *The English Church in the Nineteenth Century* (London, 1910), vol. i, p. 338.

[5] E. Halévy, *A History of the English People in the Nineteenth Century* (London, 1951), vol. iv, p. 373.

[6] They might go to Cambridge as undergraduates but they could not proceed to a degree without subscribing to a religious test. At Oxford the test was exacted at matriculation.

would expect them to have exercised a liberalizing influence on the isolated Catholic community. But more often than not the exact opposite proved true. Most of them had rebelled against the liberal victory within the Anglican Church and were content to fight against liberalism in any form. Paradoxically, it was with the Old Catholic group that Newman eventually found himself most in sympathy, and his fellow Oxford converts such as Ward, Manning and Faber were as perpetual thorns in his side.

The historian of the Pontificate of Pius IX has concluded that he failed to give the leadership necessary to meet the intellectual challenge of the day.[7] The results of this default were reflected in English Catholicism. No official leader made any serious effort to face the difficulties introduced by the intellectual revolution. The findings of the higher criticism were too often dismissed as emanations from perverse (if not diabolical) minds. Many priests, blind to the problems of sincere Christian intellectuals, either condemned them as semi-infidel or ignored them. English Catholics, on the whole, whether through ignorance or a stubborn opposition born of the conviction that the new thought was fundamentally anti-Christian, remained in revolt against everything the new age stood for, against the new England.

It is against this background that the efforts of Acton and Newman to introduce a more scholarly spirit into English Catholicism must be seen. They were both concerned with the fundamental problem of subsuming into the Christian system all in modern thought that was not unalterably hostile to it. Both refused to admit that there could be any *real* opposition between traditional Christianity and what was of permanent value in the new thought. The God of religion was the God of science, and the progress of science, if rightly understood, could constitute no danger to religion. Deeply conscious of history in its profounder sense, they alone among English Catholics perceived the true nature of the danger facing Christianity: the evolution of modern civilization along non-Christian principles, due to the default of Christian intellectuals.

Catholic education, the Italian revolution, the decline of Liberal Catholicism, the Vatican Council and its aftermath, these were the main topics that united or divided Catholics in the 60's and 70's. And it is with these subjects that the first phase of the

---

[7] R. Aubert, *Le Pontificat de Pie IX* (Paris, Bloud et Gay, 1952), p. 500. This is volume 21 of the *Histoire de l'Eglise* edited by A. Fliche and V. Martin.

Acton-Newman relations is principally occupied. The large measure of sympathy existing between them throughout this period has never been given due recognition. But by the 1880's, Acton, the earlier champion of Catholicism and friend of Newman, is found condemning the Papacy in terms reminiscent of Luther, and rejecting Newman's thought as a system of infidelity. The latter part of this inquiry is mainly concerned with gaining an understanding of this second phase.

I. The Early Years

John Emerich Edward Dalberg-Acton was born in Naples on January 10, 1834, just four months after a thirty-three-year-old Oxford clergyman, John Henry Newman, had inaugurated a series of *Tracts for the Times* destined to stir a complacent Anglican Church to its foundations. Not even the most fertile of imaginations would have conceived it probable that the new-born Roman Catholic and the greatest Anglican divine of the century would one day be found working together toward common ends. Yet within twenty-five years such was to be the case.

At the age of three, upon the death of his father, the infant Acton succeeded to a baronetcy in England, and, with his German mother as guardian, was brought to his estate at Aldenham. At the age of eight he spent a year at St. Nicholas, a preparatory seminary near Paris. He was then enrolled as a student at St. Mary's College, Oscott, at the time under the presidency of Dr. Nicholas Wiseman, the future Cardinal. On the completion of four years' studies at Oscott he continued at Edinburgh under the private tuition of Dr. Logan, a former Vice-President of Oscott. Unable to gain admission to a college in Cambridge, he went to Munich in 1850 to become the pupil and travelling companion of Dr. Ignatius Döllinger, Professor of Canon Law and Church History in the University of Munich and the pride of German Catholic scholarship.

Dr. Döllinger took a warm interest in his gifted student and in the course of his six years at Munich introduced him to many of the leading scholars and politicians of Catholic Europe. At this period Munich was pre-eminently the intellectual center of the Catholic world. The work of such men as Döllinger, Hefele, Görres, Phillips, Höfler, Lasaulx, all scholars alive to the various intellectual currents of the day yet intensely devoted to the cause of Catholicism, must have made a profound impression on the young English student. The self-effacing character of the Catholicism he had known as a young boy would compare unfavorably with the intellectual vigor of South-German Catholicism. Associations formed during his Munich sojourn were to play an important role in developing the broadness of vision which characterized his approach to history. His training had a distinctly historical bent, with the emphasis on ecclesiastical history—this due in no small measure to the special interests of his priest-mentor. His total lack of insularity of outlook, while of undoubted value to the scholar, was not necessarily conducive to sympathetic relations with the people with whom he eventually hoped to work. Lord Granville, who had married Lady Acton in 1840, recognizing the difficulties that might result from his stepson's unusual background, wrote to him in 1852:

> I should regret extremely your adoption of English prejudices, but unless at your critical age, you imbibe some sympathy with the peculiar feelings of the people with whom you are to act thro' life, I am afraid that you will not obtain that sympathy from them, without which your powers of being useful must be determined.[1]

Newman's thoroughly English background formed a strong contrast to Acton's cosmopolitan training. "I had rather be an Englishman (as indeed I am) than belong to any other race under heaven,"[2] he proclaimed to the world in his *Apologia* and no one who knew him doubted for an instant. Born in 1801 he had already crowded into his life an immense activity and productivity by the time Acton had attained his majority. His memorable career at Oxford came to an end with his conversion to Catholicism in 1845. Though compelled to abandon Oxford and the work of his most fruitful years he never ceased to regard Oxford with anything but the profoundest affection.

In temperament the contrast with Acton was even greater. Highly sensitive by nature and exceedingly refined in his tastes, Newman was never wholly at ease outside a small circle of intimate friends. In his personal relations he was keenly aware of

[1] Granville to Acton (copy), July 1852, Blennerhasset Papers C[ambridge] U[niversity] L[ibrary], Add. Mss. 7486, Item 56.

[2] *Apologia* [*Pro Vita Sua*], preface, p. xvi.

every changing mood, and in his subtle efforts to be fair to himself as well as to others he exposed himself to the charge of disingenuousness. Acton, on the other hand, though a shy man, was at home in any company. He had the outspokenness of a somewhat arrogant youth, and eschewed the refinements, both in literature and personal relations, which were so much a part of Newman's genius. It is the delicate artist, matured by years of tribulations, contrasted with an eager youth in whom were united great intellectual gifts and a fundamentally generous nature. The artist recognized the sterling qualities in the raw youth, and he, not insensitive to rare genius, responded to a friendship which could never be intimate but promised to be none the less real.

Acton first made acquaintance with Newman at Oscott, the year of the latter's conversion. Undoubtedly the eleven-year-old boy would have been impressed at meeting the much talked about Mr. Newman, and forty-five years later we find him recalling the meeting.[3] With Dr. Dollinger he visited Newman at his Oratory in May, 1851.[4] There is no record of the topics discussed at this meeting but it may be assumed that problems associated with Catholic education were discussed; for in the previous month Dr. Paul Cullen, Catholic Primate of Ireland, had written to Newman seeking advice on the best way of setting about establishing a Catholic University in Ireland and requesting him to deliver a set of lectures in Dublin "against Mixed Education."[5] Soon after the meeting John Acton returned to Munich, leaving Newman at the threshold of one of the most important ventures of his career, and one in which the young student was intensely interested.

The vision of a "Catholic University to spread religion, science, and learning, wherever the English language is spoken"[6] fired Newman's imagination and he threw all his energies into the new enterprise. Within six months of Cullen's initial request Newman was named President of the proposed University. At last (it seemed to Newman) his period of oblivion was coming

[3] Acton to W. Neville, 25 Dec. 1890, Orat[ory] P[ersonal] C[orrespondence].

[4] [Wilfrid] Ward. [*The Life of John Henry Cardinal*] *Newman* (London, 1912), vol. i, 264; See Acton's Notebook under 'Itinerary of 1851,' CUL Add. Mss. 5645, 15.

[5] F. McGrath, *Newman's University*: [*Idea and Reality*], (London, 1951), p. 104.

[6] *Historical Sketches*, iii, p. 148.

to an end. After seven years in the Catholic Church he was finally to undertake a great work under the banner of the Pope.

Although three years were to elapse before the new institution opened its doors Newman did not remain idle. In a series of lectures delivered in the Spring of 1852 before a select Dublin audience, he put forward his idea of a University. It was an imposing ideal and has since become a classic, but it could only have been proposed as a realizable one in the Ireland of the 1850's by a convert totally ignorant of Irish conditions.

"Are we to suppose," asked Mark Pattison, "that this magnificent ideal of a national institute, embracing and representing all knowledge, and making this knowledge its own end, was the wisdom of riper years?"[7] One has only to compare his University lectures to the writings of his earlier years to conclude that it was. Dread of modern intellectual developments gave way to the conviction that truth would prevail. He who had once considered that "troublers of the Christian community would in a healthy state of things be silenced or put out of it,"[8] now championed free discussion. And rather than grieve at the *open* development of unbelief, he accepted it as a healthier state of affairs than one where it made its way under the guise of faith as in earlier centuries:

It is one great advantage of an age in which unbelief speaks out, that Faith can speak out too; that, if falsehood assails Truth, Truth can assail falsehood. In such an age it is possible to found a University more emphatically Catholic than could be set up in the middle ages, because Truth can entrench itself carefully, and define its own profession severely, and display its colours unequivocally, by occasion of that very unbelief which so shamelessly vaunts itself. And a kindred advantage to this is the confidence which, in such an age, we can place in all who are around us, so that we need look for no foes but those who are in the enemy's camp.[9]

He lamented the needless antagonism which sometimes existed in fact "between the divines and the cultivators of the Sciences generally," and with admirable moral courage demanded complete freedom for the scholar in his own field:

[7] M. Pattison, *Memoirs* (London, 1885), p. 95.

[8] *The Via Media of the Anglican Church* (Basil Montagu Pickering, London, 1877), vol. i, p. 4 (p. 5, 1837 ed.). Volume i of *The Via Media* first was published in 1837 under the title *Lectures on the Prophetical Office of the Church, viewed relatively to Romanism and popular Protestantism*.

[9] *The Idea of a University* (Longmans, 1947), p. 288.

I am making no outrageous request, when in the name of a University, I ask religious writers, jurists, economists, physiologists, chemists, geologists, and historians, to go on quietly, and in a neighbourly way, in their own respective lines of speculation, research, and experiment, with full faith in the consistency of that multiform truth, which they share between them, in a generous confidence that they will be ultimately consistent, one and all, in their combined results, though there may be momentary collisions, awkward appearances, and many forebodings and prophecies of contrariety, and at all times things hard to the Imagination, though not, I repeat, to the Reason. It surely is not asking them a great deal to beg of them,—since they are forced to admit mysteries in the truths of Revelation, taken by themselves, and in the truths of Reason, taken by themselves,—to beg of them, I say, to keep the peace, to live in good will, and to exercise equanimity, if when Nature and Revelation are compared with each other, there be, as I have said, discrepancies,— not in the issue, but in the reasonings, the circumstances, the associations, the anticipations, the accidents, proper to their respective teachings.[10]

Acton followed with a lively interest Newman's efforts to build an improved Oxford in Dublin. He could find in Newman's University discourses the same bold and scholarly spirit that made the work of the Munich scholars so impressive to him. Like them, Newman stoutly defended the sovereignty of truth and reprobated the cowardly spirit manifested by those who stood in fear and trembling before scientific research. No doubt in Acton's mind there arose visions of a new Munich circle in Dublin.

He believed there was something he could do to help forward Newman's work. In the course of a visit to America in the summer of 1853 he had met Orestes Brownson, the vociferous convert-philosopher, and was struck by his "extraordinary force and originality, his rare, natural capacity, his heartiness, and the disadvantage of his isolation."[11] He was convinced that Brownson would make an invaluable addition to Newman's University and urged that he be offered a post.

Despite warnings that Brownson would be sure to lecture against him (he had already savagely attacked Newman's *Essay on Development*) Newman felt that it would be for the good of the new institution to have as guest lecturer such a well-known American.[12] He wrote to Brownson asking him to accept for one

[10] *Ibid.*, pp. 341–42.
[11] CUL Add. Mss. 4987, 221.
[12] *My Campaign in Ireland* (A. King & Co. Aberdeen, 1895), pp. xxii–xxxiii.

year "the office of Lecturer-Extraordinary."[13] The proposed subject was, in the instance, a surprising one. In Newman's own words:

The subject which I should propose to your acceptance would be one of such surpassing interest and breadth that I am often surprised that it is not put more prominently forward in Collegiate establishments. We never omit a professorship of astronomy, but how much more fertile a subject of thought is the province of geography! Viewed under its different heads, as physical, moral, and political, it gives scope to a variety of profound philosophical speculations, which will at once suggest themselves to your mind. It treats of the very stage and field of all history; of the relation of that field to the characters of nations, to social institutions, and to forms of religion, of the migrations of tribes, the direction and course of conquests and empires, the revolutions and extension of commerce, and the future destinies of the human race. This is the subject I offer to your acceptance.[14]

But not even Newman's magic was equal to the task of clothing geography with sufficient charm to beguile Brownson. Geography was not to his taste. Yet he was not disinclined to come to Dublin to lecture on a subject more suited to his studies.[15]

Acton learned of the unsatisfactory state of affairs from Brownson's son, who had come to Munich to study under Dr. Döllinger. He decided to take a bold hand in the matter. He immediately wrote a long letter to Brownson presenting him with a solution to his difficulty, as well as proffering some sage counsel (Acton was twenty, Brownson fifty-one) as to the course Brownson's future work should take.[16] "I will undertake in the first place," promised Acton,

to remove your difficulty about the subject-matter of your lectures, for I am quite certain that they would be too happy to let you lecture on opossums if you chose to communicate your good things in that way. The vast field of philosophy will be yours, and you will have an opportunity of making philosophical questions familiar to a nation hitherto barely acquainted with them, and I thank God for the good fortune of my countrymen in being initiated in that magnificent science by you of all men living. I am sure you will see how much may here be done for the glory of God, and I do most sincerely hope that nothing will prevent its being done. I can speak with perfect confidence of the facilities which

---

[13] H. F. Brownson, [Orestes A.] Brownson's Middle Life (Detroit, 1899), p. 470.
[14] Ibid.
[15] Ibid.
[16] H. F. Brownson, Brownson's Middle Life, pp. 471–78.

will be given you to choose your own subject, for I am intimately acquainted with Newman's closest friends, and I know the immense price they attach to the prospect of an alliance with you in this work. I will write at once to them on this point, and this obstacle, if not already removed, as I know not what communications you have had with Newman, will at once disappear. It is very probable that this University may be exceedingly effective in promoting Catholic learning and Catholic literature in England and Ireland. Nobody can give it such an impulse as you.[17]

Brownson eventually reached agreement with Newman and decided to come to Dublin. So anxious was Newman to make full use of his undoubted intellectual gifts that he arranged to provide rooms for him in his own house and planned for a table "in common with himself for Dr. Brownson and two or three others."[18] However, rising hostility in Dublin circles to Brownson's appointment compelled Newman to write to him in September asking him to defer his coming indefinitely. To save Newman from further embarrassment, Brownson withdrew altogether.[19]

Newman, aware of Acton's interest in the University, first wrote to him on June 5, 1854 asking permission to put his name down on the University Books.[20] "This involves nothing at all," he explained to Acton, "except your goodwill to an Institution which the Church has sanctioned and which is now commenced, since I took the oaths yesterday, the feast of Pentecost." There were other names he desired: "I also wish to be allowed to enter on the book in like manner the names of Dr. Döllinger [he had declined an extraordinary professorship],[21] Dr. *Windishman*[22] (I know I do not spell his name rightly) and Dr. Phillips[23]; and should be much obliged to you to obtain them for me." The young student was keenly gratified by such a request. In his

---

[17] *Ibid.*, pp. 472–73.

[18] *My Campaign in Ireland*, pp. xxxiv–xxxv.

[19] F. McGrath, *Newman's University*, p. 218.

[20] Newman to Acton, 5 June 1854, Orat. P. C. Newman had apparently forgotten that Acton had accompanied Döllinger on his 1851 visit to the Oratory, for his opening sentence read: "I hope you will allow me to write to you without more introduction than that of having seen you at Oscott, and of your having shown interest in our University in a letter you wrote to Mr. Badeley."

[21] F. McGrath, *Newman's University*, p. 215; Newman to Acton, 5 June 1854, Orat. P. C.

[22] F. H. Windischmann (1811–1861), a German theologian.

[23] George Phillips (1804–1872), a convert German canonist.

reply he expressed his "deep gratitude" for the opportunity of being some use to the University, and concluded with a reference to his own future:

The opening you have given me towards making your acquaintance, which has long been my most earnest wish, I shall not readily lose sight of, and I trust you will allow me to make use of it hereafter in order frequently to consult you and speak to you, always with the greatest confidence and respect on my own plans and proceedings.[24]

Newman, however, soon learned that sound ideas fortified by the blessing of a Pope were not sufficient for the successful erection of a University. He went to Ireland as "a poor innocent,"[25] unfamiliar with the hard realities that made his enterprise almost impossible of fulfillment. It is an unsatisfactory task to attempt to apportion blame for the failure of Newman to realize his plans; given the conditions that prevailed in Ireland he could not succeed. With the wisdom of hindsight he recognized this. Writing in 1870 he observed:

Universities are not brought into existence every day, and the primary difficulty in originating one, is that commonly they have no deliberate origination, and, as Oxford, are the slow growth and random issue of personal and private exertions, or, if erected on set purpose, they are the work of the State executive. But, in the case of that to be established in Dublin private men were to dispense with time and circumstance, and to create it in a day, not only without, but against the civil Government, and in a population, Catholic indeed, but indifferent to the undertaking [,] under a Catholic hierarchy, divided as to its expediency, before a Catholic public viewing all things in a mere political aspect, and for the sake of a Catholic gentry both suspicious and hopeless of Episcopal enterprises.[26]

Add to the above reasons adduced by Newman the general poverty of the Irish, and the fact that "English Catholics felt no interest at all in the University scheme and had no intention to make use of it, should it get into shape,"[27] and the reasons for the relative failure of the enterprise become apparent.

Newman's rectorship had begun on November 12, 1851, and after three years of varied frustrations the new University opened on November 3, 1854 to a group of twenty students.

[24] Acton to Newman, 15 July 1854, Orat. P. C.
[25] *Autobiographical Writings* (London, 1956), p. 320.
[26] *Autobiographical Writings*, pp. 285–286.
[27] *Ibid.*, pp. 329–330.

Though the numbers increased slowly it was plain to Newman that his dream of a Catholic University in Dublin serving as a vigorous center of thought for the English-speaking Catholic world could not be realized. His rectorship ended on November 12, 1858. Four days earlier he had returned to England, crossing St. George's Channel for the fifty-sixth and last time.[28]

The failure of Newman to achieve all he had hoped for must have come as a serious disappointment to Acton. He had once intimated to Brownson that he hoped to work for the enlightenment of English-speaking Catholics through the medium of history,[29] and the existence of a Catholic University would have provided the ideal field of operation for his work. Yet, although Newman's inspired ideas failed to be realized in Ireland, why (Acton asked himself) should not an attempt be made in England? A journal he kept during the course of a visit to Rome with Döllinger in 1857 reveals the direction in which his thoughts were running.[30] The title of an entry dated June 24, 1857 reads: "Project of printing a letter to Newman on the foundation of a Catholic University in England."[31] The long entry abounds with interesting observations and reflections on English Catholicism and on the desirability of a Catholic University:

The Catholic body wants two things: to be internally united and to be externally strong and able.

We require first to see, feel, and know our own strength. Then only we can prove it, and tell as a power in England.

This can be done only by an institution which shall combine together our intellectual resources. They are lost and useless by dispersion, and gradually fade. Union alone could foster, nourish, and promote learning among our scholars, and introduce it among our youth. It would be the Bewusstseyn of the English Catholics. It would first unite and amalgamate our native and converted Catholics, and destroy the incipient disagreement. Our young men have no higher studies, except in divinity. But this is of no use to our laity, and to them we must most address our efforts. Some go to Cambridge, or to London, or abroad, or to private tutors, most do nothing. The real love of learning inspired only by the union of studies wt an [sic] university.

[28] *Autobiographical Writings*, p. 333.
[29] H. F. Brownson, *Brownson's Middle Life*, p. 474.
[30] CUL Add. Mss. 5751. See H. Butterfield, "Journal of Lord Acton: Rome 1857," *Cambridge Historical Journal*, vol. viii, No. 3, 1946.
[31] There is no record of such a letter having been sent.

It would be the beginning of learning among us. We have every other internal advantage: an excellent priesthood and a faithful flock, and also political liberty.

But withal we have not the weight we deserve because we have so little literature, or at least so few contributors to the national literature.

We do little to prevent its tone from being entirely protestant. Yet this is a duty to ourselves, to our religion, and to our country.

It would be a bond of union separate from political agitation, and would be a greater title to respect than our political proceedings.

It would combine with the plan of a general seminary, for a university is nothing without a faculty of theology, and ecclesiastical studies are lame without connexion with the universalities of studies.

In this way it would be a bond between clergy and laity.

No moment so favourable as the present when we have so many converts, whose strength will die with them if not used for the good of the Church during their prime.

Religion is not a sufficient link, because it does not give conformity enough in many things.

That can only be by a common education, which shall also unite in ideas, and therefore more perfectly than has been the case in action, the clergy and the laity.

Students coming from many places have various and discordant opinions. We have many examples of that.

Thereby the experience of the converts will become the common property of the Catholic body.

It will do no harm to Dublin because no English will go to Dublin, as is pretty clear. If they went not in Newman's time, still less will they go later.

Dublin takes a more and more Irish character, and will stand when it has beaten the colleges.[32]

The English University will be supported by all the Catholic laity of England, and by all the bishops who greatly want a seminary with higher studies.

It will not meet with the difficulties that beset Dublin, as there will be no opposition.

It will relieve the colleges, and make their proper course better by removing the necessity of attempting higher studies.

It will give no umbrage to government, but will rather be encouraged by it.

Total inactivity of the Catholic laity with regard to Dublin.

So many Irish continue to come to England that perhaps some of

[32] Belfast, Cork, and Galway, Colleges of Queen's University established in 1849 and 1850.

them too would go to it, and it might save some from the Godless colleges as it would not be in opposition to anything.[33]

It would raise the studies at our colleges by giving them a higher aim and object.

It might very well be without medicine.[34]

The practicality of attempting the foundation of a Catholic University in England excepted, these jottings could be paralleled with passages from Newman's writings. They reveal nothing of the arrogance so prominent a feature of Acton's later references to his co-religionists. Rather they express sentiments one might expect from a high-minded, intelligent, rather idealistic Catholic enthusiast about to return to his own country and work for the cause of a religion he dearly loved. Fully aware of the serious shortcomings in the Catholic body, he was sanguine that they could be overcome. He was eager to join forces with his fellow-Catholics and above all with Newman.

At this period Acton had before him an admirable statement of the dispassionate approach necessary for his future work. "It is enough," we read in his *Roman Journal* (had he recorded Döllinger's warning?),

to say decidedly what we are persuaded is true, and in time it will bear fruit of itself. The absence of any prejudice or object in view must remove the chief objection to the opinions of such a person. In historical matters it is hard, because 99/100 of mankind know history only by party statements—wait to influence them till you have the authority which learning gives. To hear a view calmly but decidedly stated must make some impression and shake prejudice. As to discussing German works it must not be done as to show the intention of accusing people of neglect and ignorance.

Unhappily for the success of his future work it cannot be claimed that Acton's actions were always in accord with these wise cautions.

Acton returned to England in the autumn of 1857 to take up permanent residence. His first communication with Newman was, unexpectedly, not concerned with education at all. Follow-

[33] The name "Godless Colleges" was commonly used by opponents of the Queen's Colleges, owing to their exclusion of religion from the lecture rooms. See F. McGrath, *Newman's University*, Ch. ii; A. D. Culler, *The Imperial Intellect* (New Haven, 1955), Ch. vi.

[34] A flourishing medical faculty had been established by Newman in Dublin and Acton probably felt a new one in England would threaten it.

ing the solicitations of his stepfather,[35] he decided to stand as a Whig candidate for Carlow in the forthcoming parliamentary election and asked Newman to write to Dr. O'Brien, the Vicar-General of Waterford, on his behalf. Newman replied cordially: "I do not know Dr. O'Brien well, but I know him quite well enough to write to him about you, and will do so gladly. It would rejoice me indeed if we had a person like yourself in Parliament."[36] He then added regretfully: "Electioneering duties will, I fear, interrupt literary occupations." But as eighteen months were to pass before Acton had to concern himself with electioneering duties he soon found himself involved in another activity: the founding of the first Catholic Public School.

Convert parents were dissatisfied with the existing Catholic schools and were eager to have a school conducted along the lines of the Public Schools. Acton immediately took an interest in the project and was one of the first to contribute to a fund for the establishment of a new school.[37] Throughout the early months of 1858 he was in frequent consultation with Serjeant Bellasis,[38] a friend of Newman and one of the main promoters of the scheme. It was decided to approach Newman with regard to undertaking such a school in connection with the Oratory at Birmingham.[39] Early in February Acton and Bellasis together visited the Oratory to discuss the matter with the Oratorians.[40]

Newman was willing to give serious consideration to their proposals. His Dublin experiences taught him the great need of improved preparatory training for students who contemplated proceeding to higher studies. As Acton wrote years later: "If the University [Dublin] languished, it was partly due to the lack of preparatory studies. Newman resolved to begin at the be-

[35] F. E. Lally, *As Lord Acton Says* (Newport, Rhode Island, 1942), p. 43.

[36] Newman to Acton, 25 November 1857, Orat. P.C. Of Dr. O'Brien Newman wrote: "He is an amiable, calm, well-judging man. All Irishmen are for their own country, and if I were an Irishman, I should be sorely tempted to hate England; but I shall be surprised if Dr. O'Brien goes beyond this (loving Ireland)."

[37] Acton to Bellasis, 3 January 1858, Orat. O[ratory] S[chool] B[eginning].

[38] Edward Bellasis (1800–1873), educated at Christ's Hospital, Serjeant-at-law 1844, converted to Catholicism 1850.

[39] Bellasis to Newman, 30 January 1858, Orat. P.C.

[40] Bellasis to Newman, 6 February 1858, Orat. O.S.B.; Newman to Bellasis, 9 February 1858, Orat. P.C.

ginning."[41] Before committing himself and his Community, however, Newman wished that Cardinal Wiseman be consulted on the project. Acton and Bellasis arranged an interview with the Cardinal and found him on the whole favorably disposed toward the enterprise.[42] So high was the Cardinal's opinion of Acton that the latter could report to his friend Robert Simpson: "I hear he says that his only security in the affair of the school is my being one of the promoters."[43]

The familiar problems generally accompanying such ventures had to be met. Financial difficulties had to be overcome, and possible opposition from various quarters anticipated. Acton played his part in meeting the former and offered his own special contribution to the latter. It was feared that Frederick Faber, head of the London Oratory, might oppose the scheme on the grounds that the conducting of a school was contrary to the spirit of an Oratory. Acton wrote to Newman informing him that Father Faber had remarked in conversation with him, "I promise you that I will not oppose it, and that I will do what I can to promote the scheme."[44] Acton went on to explain that if any movement of opposition came from that quarter he could publish Faber's words. Newman replied bluntly: "I should not be surprised if F. Faber patronized our school: but I should trust him as little if he did as if he did not."[45]

The anticipated opposition, however, did not arise, and the school opened in May, 1859. It prospered from the beginning and more than lived up to expectations. Staffed by converts who had gone through the Public Schools and had the advantages of a university training it was able to provide an education distinctly superior to anything hitherto available to the Catholic student. Newman himself, it would appear, took little part in the day to day affairs of the school. "He reduces himself," wrote Acton, "to a nonentity in the school, by keeping aloof both from boys and masters."[46] As was expected it evoked a certain amount of criticism from the supporters of the older Catholic Schools. In Acton's words:

[41] CUL Add. Mss. 4988, 227.
[42] Bellasis to Newman, 6 March 1858, Orat. P.C.
[43] *Acton to Simpson*, [March 1858], Downside Mss.
[44] *Acton to Newman*, 9 January 1859, Orat. O.S.B.
[45] Cited in *Acton to Simpson*, [January 1859], Downside Mss.
[46] Acton to Simpson, 5 January 1862, Downside Mss.

It looked out on Oscott across a stretch of blackened midlands, and the admirers of the Seminary system deprecated the competition of the Winchester model. They saw an implied censure of their methods; a complaint of their results.[47]

But the next generation was to witness the older schools such as Downside and Ampleforth adapting themselves more and more to the Public School system and thus tacitly acknowledging the wisdom of Newman's pioneer step.

The Oratory School was barely a year and a half old when an internal crisis arose that threatened its very existence. Father Darnell, the Headmaster, supported by two of the other teachers, wanted the school to conform more to the Public School pattern than Newman deemed wise. He believed that it was necessary (probably to conciliate those who were suspicious of the new venture) to maintain a close link between the school and the Oratory and not to stress its secular character.[48] The whole question of the authority of the Oratory and of Newman himself came to a head at the end of 1861. Mrs. Wootten, a devoted friend of Newman, under whose influence she had become a Catholic, had been appointed by him as Matron of the school. She evidently set out to rule the school, but Darnell along with other members of the staff did not take kindly to the idea. Darnell demanded that she be removed. She appealed to Newman, who decided that he would stand by his original appointment. Rather than dismiss Mrs. Wootten he suffered Darnell, along with two other Masters, to depart.[49]

Acton was kept fully informed on the dispute through Darnell and H. N. Oxenham, one of the ex-Masters,[50] both of whom resided with him for the latter part of January.[51] Although he was very much concerned about the future of the school he refrained from approaching Newman on the subject. "I would do anything to save the school," he wrote to Simpson on first learning of the disagreement, "but I cannot put in my oar be-

[47] CUL Add. Mss. 4988, 227.

[48] Acton to Simpson [January 1862], Downside Mss.

[49] Ward, *Newman*, i, p. 456. Ward gives a misleading account of the dispute by implying that it was solely concerned with "the very special position accorded by Newman to Mrs. Wooten."

[50] Henry Nutcombe Oxenham (1829–1888), Member of Balliol College, Oxford; a convert to Catholicism in 1857.

[51] Acton to Simpson [13 January 1862]; [21 January 1862] Downside Mss.

tween Newman and his liegemen."[52] But he was disappointed by Newman's reticence. He felt that he had contributed through his activity more than anyone else to the foundation of the school and now Newman would not say a word to him about the serious difficulties confronting it. However, he believed that by keeping Darnell and Oxenham "prisoners" in his home he would prevent them from doing anything rash or making a demonstration, and thus he would be of much greater service to Newman than he had been at the time of the foundation of the school.[53]

Newman, on his part, decided to continue the school with a new staff. Father Ambrose St. John was named Headmaster, and Thomas Arnold, the convert son of Arnold of Rugby, was brought from Dublin as second Master. The school reassembled at the end of January as usual and it did not appear to have suffered in any way from the radical changes. Newman himself began to take a greater part in the ordinary affairs of the school, and his work with the boys—especially coaching them for plays— became a real source of consolation to him during the dreary days preceding the *Apologia*.[54]

The success of the Oratory School at Edgbaston encouraged Acton to press actively for the foundation of a Catholic University in England. With a supply of properly qualified candidates now guaranteed he believed the time was ripe for a new attempt to meet an urgent need. He often discussed the question with Newman and even went so far as to offer land at Bridgnorth for a building site and his large house at Morville for accommodations.[55] Newman was not opposed to such a scheme but his Dublin experiences made him wary of embarking on any new ventures. Acton then sought to induce Sir Peter Le Page Renouf,[56] a close friend of Newman and a distinguished orientalist, to take the lead in promoting a new University. "The best

[52] Acton to Simpson, 1 January 1862, Downside Mss.

[53] Acton to Döllinger, 28 January 1862, Woodruff Mss.

[54] Ward, *Newman*, i, p. 457; See "The Oratory School," *Tablet*, 18 April 1959, p. 371 and 2 May 1959, pp. 428–30.

[55] *Lord Acton's Correspondence*, edited by J. N. Figgis and R. V. Laurence (London, 1917), pp. 162–65; Acton to Simpson, 11 November [1862], Downside Mss.

[56] P. Le Page Renouf (1822–97) was educated at Pembroke College, Oxford, and entered the Catholic Church in 1842.

men would be ready to join you," he pressed Renouf; "you would have the whole support of Newman's influence, and I can really see no quarter in which any susceptibilities would be wounded or any opposition excited."[57] But he could elicit no enthusiasm from Renouf. Writing to Acton from Dublin (he was about to resign from the staff of the Catholic University of Ireland) Renouf explained why he could not warm to Acton's plan:

The demand for university education on the part of English Catholic youth and the necessity of a supply being taken for granted, I have still very grave doubts as to the wisdom or even possibility of meeting the want by the foundation of an English Catholic university. In presence of such powerful growths as Oxford and Cambridge, and the ground occupied by the London University, a new university must ever remain a sickly plant. And it seems to me that the old universities would always have it in their power to put an end to the new one whenever they pleased by granting to Catholics advantages equivalent, and therefore on the whole superior, to what a purely Catholic university could afford. If they allowed, for instance, a Catholic college to be founded, or even Catholic halls to exist on equal terms with Anglican, the students being allowed to graduate in all degrees but theology—I do not see what Catholic students or their parents could desiderate or what more they would get in a purely Catholic university.[58]

Newman shared Renouf's doubts about the advisability of attempting a new University, although, like Renouf,[59] he was ready to assist any undertaking other Catholics might initiate. He felt there were too many difficulties in the way: the heavy expense, the great risk of failure, the long period of infancy and consequent weakness necessarily involved, and always the possibility that Catholic parents would have no confidence in it.[60] And finally, his conviction grew that the bishops, confronted with the strong will and narrow intransigence of Manning, would never permit a University in a real sense.[61]

Surprisingly, one of the few Catholics who was of the same mind as Acton on the University question was Manning. As early as 1863 he advocated beginning a Catholic University but gained little support.[62] When in the next decade, as Archbishop

[57] *Lord Acton's Correspondence*, p. 164.
[58] *Ibid.*, pp. 165–66.
[59] *Ibid.*, p. 166.
[60] Newman to Monsell, 6 September 1863, Orat. P.C.
[61] Newman to E. Bowles, 8 June 1872, Orat. P.C.
[62] Newman to Monsell, 6 September 1863, Orat. P.C.

of Westminster, he had his way and established a College at Kensington, Newman's fears were more than justified. The whole enterprise proved, to quote Wilfrid Ward, who attended the College, "a ludicrous failure."[63]

Throughout 1863 and 1864 various other proposals were put forward to solve the problem of University education for Catholics. Probably the strangest one was for the founding of an English University in Rome. "I think," wrote Newman on hearing of it, "the projectors of it must be mad."[64] The proposal that had the widest support was one in favor of a Catholic College or Hall at Oxford. With the relaxation of religious tests it was felt that the University authorities would not oppose some such scheme. Until Manning exerted great pressure it would appear that Cardinal Wiseman and most of the Bishops were not opposed to this solution. Thus in September, 1863 Newman is found writing to his intimate friend, William Monsell:[65]

I saw the Bp[Ullathorne of Birmingham] a day or two ago, and my *impression* is that neither he, nor the Cardinal, nor the Bps in general are opposed to the notion of an Oxford College tho' they think the greatest caution is necessary to hinder such an institution becoming a precedent for Mixed Education.[66]

However, Newman feared (and he was proved right in the event) that Manning and Cullen, who have "more determination than all our Bishops put together,"[67] would influence first the other Bishops and then the Congregation of Propaganda to give a decision against Catholics going to Oxford at all.[68]

And yet Newman personally did not believe that a Catholic College or Hall was the best *practical* solution. He accepted it in principle but felt that it presented "social difficulties."[69] What he favored was an arrangement whereby Catholic students would be permitted to attend the existing Colleges and be provided

[63] Ward, *Newman*, ii, p. 198.

[64] Newman to Monsell, 6 February 1864, Orat. P.C.

[65] William Monsell, Baron Emly (1812–1894), educated at Winchester and Oriel, Liberal M.P. for Limerick (1847–74), raised to peerage in 1874. He was Newman's closest friend among laymen.

[66] Newman to Monsell, 6 September 1863, Orat. P.C.

[67] Newman to Monsell, 8 October 1863, Orat. P.C.

[68] Newman to Monsell, 6 September 1863, Orat. P.C. Although a hierarchy was established in 1850 the Catholic Church in England still retained its missionary status until 1908. This in effect meant that it did not come under the general law of the Church but continued under the special direction of the Congregation of Propaganda. See *The English Catholics 1850–1950*, p. 117.

[69] Newman to Monsell, 6 September 1863, Orat. P.C.

with a Catholic mission to serve as a spiritual center. Writing to Miss E. Bowles in 1872, he reviewed his position and authorized her to tell anyone she pleased: "That I never have by word or act advocated the scheme of a Catholic College at Oxford though many have attributed such a scheme to me."[70] He believed that the Bishops should "let Catholics go to Protestant Colleges (without their formal sanction)" and "provide a strong Mission worked by theologians, i.e., a strong Jesuit mission to protect the Catholic youth from the infidelity of the place."[71]

In 1864 Newman himself, at the request of his Bishop, agreed to undertake a mission at Oxford, but Manning and W. G. Ward, ably assisted by Monsignor Talbot[72] at the Vatican, waged an unremitting campaign against any arrangement that countenanced Catholic students' going to Oxford. The upshot of the crusade of these three Oxford men was that the Bishops at their meeting in December, 1864 drew up a letter, opposing the opening of Catholic Halls at Oxford or Cambridge and strongly dissuading parents from sending their sons to either University. Propaganda confirmed their decision in a rescript dated February 5, 1865. This was sufficient for Newman to cancel his plans for an Oxford mission: if Catholic students were, in effect, forbidden to attend the University he saw no reason for going.[73] In 1867 he made one final effort to open a mission. Although Acton complained that he "was never zealous for that cause,"[74] he contributed twenty-five pounds toward the scheme.[75] But it, too, was successfully frustrated by the opposition.

Unfortunately for the many Catholic young men who, in the meantime, were deprived of a University education, it was not until 1896, three years after Manning's death, that the Bishops finally sanctioned a plan whereby Catholic students could attend Oxford and Cambridge under substantially the same arrangement as the one favored by Newman over thirty years earlier.

[70] Newman to E. Bowles, 8 June 1872, Orat. P.C.
[71] Newman to E. Bowles, 8 June 1872, Orat. P.C.
[72] George Talbot, fifth son of Lord Talbot of Malahide, educated at Eton and St. Mary's Hall, Oxford, received into the Catholic Church in 1842, Chamberlain to Pius IX and special adviser on English ecclesiastical affairs.
[73] Ward, *Newman*, ii, pp. 67–68; see also an article by H. O. Evennett, "Catholics and the Universities," in *The English Catholics 1850–1950*, pp. 291–321.
[74] Acton to [Wetherell], 30 January 1867, Downside Mss. (Copy).
[75] Newman to Acton, 13 March 1867, Orat. P.C.; Acton to Newman, 26 March [1867], Orat. P.C.

II. Catholic Reviews

Acton had bigger things in mind than merely assisting in the foundation of a school or representing a small Irish constituency in Parliament. His German apprenticeship had introduced him to the most advanced thought of the age and he believed he had much to teach his co-religionists. They had to be brought *au courant* of modern developments in the intellectual world.

The more educated of the Catholic community had been made aware, largely through the writings of Cardinal Wiseman and the Oxford converts, of the Catholic revival in Germany and France under the influence of such men as Schlegel, Stolberg, Chateaubriand, de Maistre, Lamennais, Lacordaire, and Montalembert. But the level of learning represented by the work of these men was no longer adequate. It suffered from the defects of their qualities, relying excessively on rhetoric and enthusiasm. With the advance of more critical methods, particularly in Germany, it lost much of its original charm and force of persuasion.

A new group of Catholic scholars developed who grew increasingly conscious of the deficiencies in traditional methods. They were better acquainted with current modes of thought than their predecessors and were more ready to make use of modern critical techniques in their investigations. Like the earlier liberal Catholics they looked to a strong Papacy as the best guarantee of freedom, i.e., they were both liberal and ultramontane.[1] It was in Germany that the challenge to Christianity

[1] See Acton's essay, "Ultramontanism," *Home and Foreign Review*, July, 1863 (vol. iii). For an excellent outline of the origins and characteristics of liberal Catholicism—particularly of those aspects having a special bearing on Acton's career—see Wilfred Ward's chapter entitled "Liberal Catholicism" in his *Newman*, i, pp. 458–77.

24

was greatest and it was there that the new critical school had its greatest strength.

In a striking passage written in 1862, Acton marked out the point of separation between the old and new school:

> Learning has passed beyond the range of these men's vision [he wrote of the older liberal Catholics]. Their greatest strength was in the weakness of their adversaries, and their own faults were eclipsed by the monstrous errors against which they fought. But scientific methods have now been so perfected, and have come to be applied in so cautious and so fair a spirit, that the apologists of the last generation have collapsed before them. Investigations have become so impersonal, so colourless, so free from the prepossessions which distort truth, from predetermined aims and foregone conclusions, that their results can only be met by investigations in which the same methods are yet more completely and conscientiously applied. The sounder scholar is invincible by the brilliant rhetorician, and the eloquence and ingenuity of De Maistre and Schlegel would be of no avail against researches pursued with perfect mastery of science and singleness of purpose. The apologist's armour would be vulnerable at the point where his religion and his science were forced into artificial union. Again, as science widens and deepens, it escapes from the grasp of dilettantism. . . The training of a skilled labourer has become indispensible for the scholar, and science yields its results to none but those who have mastered its methods.[2]

Acton wished to introduce into the intellectual pursuits of English Catholics the same critical spirit he believed he saw in operation in Munich circles. He felt his work could be best accomplished through the pages of a Catholic review. "A writer," he had written to Brownson in 1854, "may influence and instruct both his contemporaries and posterity. By means of a review he can exercise a much more constant and prolonged influence on his own time than by sending forth a single book."[3] With memories of influential German Catholic reviews fresh in mind he surveyed the English periodical field for a possible platform. Three reviews drew his attention: the *Dublin Review*, the *Atlantis*, and the *Rambler*.

The *Dublin Review* was founded in 1836 by Cardinal Wiseman and Daniel O'Connell. From the first it was edited and printed in London. After 1845 there were few contributions from the

[2] "Cardinal Wiseman and the Home and Foreign Review," *Rambler*, October, 1862; reprinted in [Acton, The] *History of Freedom [and other Essays]*, edited by J. N. Figgis and R. V. Laurence (London, 1909), pp. 452–53.
[3] H. F. Brownson, *Brownson's Middle Life*, p. 476.

versatile pen of Wiseman and though it remained his pet child
it gradually grew into a dull, uninteresting journal, sharply
characterized by Newman as "a dreary publication . . . which
wakes up to growl or to lecture, and then goes to sleep again."[4]
H. R. Bagshawe held the post of editor from October, 1857
until W. G. Ward assumed editorship in 1863. At no time was it a
critical Review; it was a party organ, first Wiseman's, then
Manning's.

The *Atlantis* was launched in January, 1858 by Newman in
conjunction with Professor W. K. Sullivan of Cork. It was designed as "A Half-Yearly Register of Literature and Science
Conducted by Members of the Catholic University of Ireland."[5]
Theology as such was to be excluded from its pages though a
purely historical treatment of subjects bearing on theology was
not. It was a solid, scholarly journal and alone among Catholic
publications it remained above party jealousies. From the first
Newman encouraged Acton to contribute to it.[6] Had Acton
chosen to take a serious interest in it he could have made a real
contribution to it, and his writings, appearing in a review which
eschewed current controversies, would have been received as
the writings of a serious scholar. But making the acquaintance of
the brilliant and outspoken Richard Simpson, he discovered a
kindred spirit and decided to throw in his fortunes with him in
conducting the *Rambler*.

The *Rambler* was commenced by John Moore Capes[7] in
January, 1848. It was designed as a weekly magazine of home and
foreign literature, science and art. Within a year it was enlarged
and issued monthly. Newman, from the very beginning of the
new enterprise, was Capes' principal adviser. Although he refused to become a permanent theological censor for the Review
he was constantly consulted by Capes on editorial problems as
well as theological difficulties. Apart from a few poems, however,
he wrote nothing for its pages.

It was the avowed policy of the *Rambler* to discuss openly and

---

[4] (Abbot) Gasquet, [*Lord*] *Acton* [*And His Circle*] (London, 1906), p. xxiv.

[5] *Atlantis*, Introduction, January, 1858.

[6] Newman to Acton, 26 March 1858, Orat. P.C. Newman to Sullivan, 28 June
1858, Orat. P.C.

[7] John Moore Capes (1812–1889) graduated from Balliol College, Oxford;
entered the Catholic Church in 1845. Wilfrid Ward in his biography of Newman
confuses him with his brother, Frederick Capes (1816–1888), who also wrote for
the *Rambler*.

freely the problems facing the English Catholic community. But from its inception it met with hostility. It was conducted wholly by recent converts who showed no great consideration for the peculiar sensitivities of the Old Catholics. Many of the latter resented the constant belittling of their general intellectual standards by converts fresh from Oxford. Cardinal Wiseman, who took a severely restricted view of the layman's role in religious affairs, particularly disliked the *Rambler*'s frequent "meddling" in education. But when Richard Simpson arrived on the scene as a permanent contributor Wiseman's dislike flowered into a marked antipathy.

Richard Simpson, a brilliant convert, "possessed with an incorrigible irreverence and sense of the comic,"[8] as an Anglican found it impossible to avoid disputes with his bishop,[9] and as a Catholic he continued his favorite pastime, bishop-baiting. Newman, a friend of Simpson's since Oxford days, once indicated his line vis-à-vis ecclesiastical authorities:

> He will always be clever, amusing, brilliant, and *suggestive*. He will always be flicking his whips at Bishops, cutting them in tender places, throwing stones at Sacred Congregations, and, as he rides along the high road, discharging peashooters at Cardinals who happen by bad luck to look out of the window.[10]

Yet in spite of (or on account of) his irreverence he emerges as one of the most patently sincere and thoroughly likeable characters among mid-Victorian Catholics.

Simpson had been among the earliest contributors to the *Rambler*, but it was not until 1854 that he agreed to write regularly for the Review.[11] He had a quick incisive mind and his intellectual interests embraced a wide field. Speculative theology held a particular fascination for him; but his readiness to write on the most involved theological subject at a moment's notice was a source of worry to his friends and involved him in frequent disputes with ecclesiastical authorities. In September, 1856 the ailing Capes finally induced him to become his sub-editor. When continued illness compelled Capes to give up his journalistic career in the autumn of 1857, Simpson was persuaded to take

---

[8] Acton, CUL Add. Mss. 4988, 197.
[9] W. Ward, *W. G. Ward and the Catholic Revival* (London, 1893), p. 243.
[10] Ward, *Newman*, i, p. 529.
[11] Gasquet, *Acton*, p. xxj.

over the editorship. Acton, having returned from Rome, grew interested and bought out Capes' shares in the proprietorship.

Acton's arrival marked the beginning of a new era for the *Rambler*. Hitherto it had been almost exclusively the organ of converts and was regarded as such by most Catholics. The typical convert, though a University graduate, only dimly apprehended the new modes of thought that were revolutionizing continental scholarship. Thus while the *Rambler* in the past had aimed at keeping its readers abreast of modern intellectual developments, it was restricted by the provincialism of its writers largely to the English scene. Acton was determined to change all that. He was filled to the brim with notions of the superiority of German scholarship over the most advanced English product and he resolved to introduce a new element into the *Rambler*. In many ways he was as far removed from most of the Oxford converts as they were from the Old Catholics. This was important for the future of the *Rambler*. Henceforward the opposition group to the Review included not only the many Old Catholics who regarded it as an organ of the upstart converts but also converts who (without cause) believed it was very much under the influence of German rationalism.

One of the most remarkable features of the new partnership was Simpson's ready surrender of leadership to Acton. Although fourteen years his senior in age and with a considerable journalistic experience behind him, Simpson almost immediately accepted Acton as the chief formulator of policy and recognized him as an intellectual guide in history and politics. This in no way was a reflection of weakness in Simpson, but rather emphasizes the truly extraordinary endowments of his new associate.

Now that Acton had his platform the question remained: What particular line should he take in educating English Catholics? He had made up his mind some years past that history was to be his "occupation through life";[12] but he felt that there was another field, closely related to history, which demanded the urgent attention of a Catholic scholar. "It seems to me," he had written to Orestes Brownson in 1854,

that there is no science nobler than the one which has no name in literature, than the science of Burke and Maistre, and Donoso Cortés. I believe that a system of laws for those that govern and for those that are governed, a system of political philosophy, if there is no better expression, that such

    [12] H. F. Brownson, *Brownson's Middle Life*, p. 474.

a system remains to be drawn up by a philosopher who should know all the truths that those great writers have discovered, and who should reconcile all the scattered fragments with each other by theories derived from the certain doctrines of the church; such a system as Montalembert speaks of in his life of Donoso Cortés as being a medium between the theories of Gioberti and those of Bonald.[13]

Since he failed to persuade Brownson to undertake a formulation of a Catholic philosophy of politics he decided he would attempt such a work in the pages of the *Rambler*. Thus in his letter to Simpson on February 16, 1858—a letter which is in reality his manifesto and was fitly chosen by Gasquet as the cornerstone of his monument to Acton—he wrote:

> I would have a complete body of principles for the conduct of English Catholics in political affairs, and if I live and do well, I will gradually unfold them. The Catholics want political education.[14]

The scope of the proposed series of essays to effect this education is impressive and suggests the astonishing grasp of political principle already possessed by Acton: Burke's Catholic view of political principles and of history; a true view of emancipation; foreign and English Constitutions contrasted; Liberalism and Liberality; the political influence of the Church in history; Protestantism as a political principle. These were but some of the topics on which he hoped to enlighten his readers.

Acton was supremely confident that he was well-equipped to offer instructions in politics. In the previous years he had travelled through most of Europe and had seen much of America. He had "many friends in almost all countries"[15] and had "thought and read a good deal upon political subjects."[16] All that remained now was to communicate to the English Catholics for their own improvement and the benefit of England some of the good things he had gathered.

His "body of principles" was not simply to be borrowed from the writings of modern political writers; he, in fact, was "very far from agreeing with any of the more famous Catholic writers, or with any of the political parties in England."[17] His system was to be a synthesis derived from Catholicism on the one hand, and

---

[13] *Ibid.*, p. 475.
[14] Gasquet, *Acton*, p. 4.
[15] Gasquet, *Acton*, p. 5.
[16] *Ibid.*, p. 3.
[17] Gasquet, *Acton*, p. 3.

the British Constitution on the other. In no sense was it to be patterned on the political system of any modern Catholic state. His experiences of Catholic countries disabused him of any such notions. As he was to write shortly in the *Rambler:*

The State which is Catholic *par excellence* is a by-word for misgovernment, because the orthodoxy and piety of its administrators are deemed a substitute for a better system. The demand for a really Catholic system of government falls with the greatest weight of reproach on the Catholic States.[18]

Rather, it was England which had in the "midst of its apostasy, and in spite of so much guilt towards religion" preserved "the Catholic forms in its Church establishment more than any other Protestant nation, and the Catholic spirit in her political institutions more than any Catholic nation."[19] Burke should be the great Catholic teacher, the law and the prophets.[20]

As Acton saw it the political responsibilities of English Catholics extended far beyond their own community. The duty had fallen upon them to maintain the Christian character of the constitution. "In England," reads an entry in his Roman Journal of 1857,

the Catholics could not be an element of stability and constitutional security so long as they were in so unfortunate a position that they must set relief above every other consideration. Now I think we are in a position to exhibit the true political effects of Catholic principles, and can render to the constitution the benefits we receive from it. We must maintain the high parts of the constitution and its Christian character in spite of their abandoning it themselves. We cannot do evil that good may come. We are the only permanently conservative element in the state, and in this, and in the religious character, the heirs of the establishment.[21]

Acton was aware of the necessity of restraint if his campaign was to be a fruitful one. Thus he wrote to Simpson:

I should like, especially at first, until my line and tendency is better known, to avoid disputes. My ideas, however, are so little popular just now that disputes will arise soon enough, and it will be important to conduct them with forbearance and dignity.[22]

[18] "Political Thoughts on the Church," *Rambler*, January, 1859; reprinted in *History of Freedom*, p. 210.

[19] *Ibid.*, p. 211.

[20] Gasquet, *Acton*, pp. 4, 60.

[21] CUL Add. Mss. 5751, 290.

[22] Gasquet, *Acton*, p. 6.

It cannot be claimed that Acton kept his wise resolutions for very long. Rather, in his very first "dispute," instead of exercising "forbearance" he impetuously set out to show English theologians what an inferior lot they really were.[23]

His overweening attitude toward those whom he wished to influence is reflected in his response to a suggestion for a council to discuss *Rambler* policy.

As to the proposed council or councils, [he wrote to Simpson in February 1858] it seems to me that it is a harmless but then not very useful plan. For my part I should like to hear occasionally what they would have to say, not so much for the sake of their advice to be followed as of their errors to be made a note of and incidentally combated. . . I cannot look for sympathy with my ideas in any considerable number of men. . . There is so much that is utterly new and unexpected even to our wisest friends to be said, argued and illustrated in the process of politically educating the Catholic body in England, that any increase of numbers at first is sure to dilute our sayings and diminish our strength.[24]

It was not only in political wisdom that he judged his "wisest friends" wanting:

I hold this to be the case too in other than political questions. As to anybody acquainted with German learning and modes of thought the philosophy and theology borrowed from France do not inspire much respect.[25]

That his contempt was not reserved entirely for the scholarship of English Catholics is evidenced by his reference to Buckle's *History of Civilisation*, the first volume of which had just appeared:

I got through Buckle last night. Setting aside the theory, the learning of the book is utterly superficial and obsolete. He is altogether a mere humbug and a very bad arguer. He has taken great pains to say things that have been said much better before in books that he has not read.[26]

Acton, however, did not remain sufficiently detached from current dissensions to give himself the time or the tranquility necessary for the work he set out to accomplish. Hardly had he been initiated into the world of journalism when he restlessly

[23] See below, p. 37.
[24] Gasquet, *Acton*, pp. 8–9; for a completion of Gasquet's defective transcription see [A. Watkin and the Editor], "Gasquet and the Acton-Simpson Correspondence," C[ambridge] H[istorical] J[ournal], vol. x, no. 1, 1950.
[25] Gasquet, *Acton*, p. 9.
[26] Gasquet, *Acton*, p. 13.

looked about for new worlds to conquer. He considered the *Rambler*, the *Dublin Review* and the *Atlantis* the three principle Catholic organs. If one group controlled all three it would "ensure harmony of view and tone,"[27] a not undesirable state of affairs in Acton's mind. The possibility of carrying out the coup arose through the decline of the *Dublin Review*. Writing to Simpson on July 6, Acton explained:

Allies[28] writes that the Dublin is giving up unless somebody takes possession of it, and proposes to me to do so. . . Can both subsist together under similar management? . . . The two Reviews might play skilfully into each other's hands, and represent in different ways the same opinion. I would stick to history in one and to politics in the other. Pray consider carefully whether we can take advantage of this shipwreck in any way, and if not whether the continuance of the D[ublin] in my hands or its total extinction (with the danger indeed of it falling among thieves) will suit our common interests best.[29]

At the same time Acton was in correspondence with Newman, though writing in a far more guarded fashion. "Will you allow me," he wrote, "to put the matter before you rather for your decision than for your advice, and to assure you that I have no wish or will in the case but your own?"[30] Newman, on the one hand, expressed his satisfaction at the *Dublin Review*'s coming into Acton's hands and considered confining the *Atlantis* to scientific subjects "to make the chance of any mutual interference still less."[31] But, on the other hand, he was somewhat perplexed at Acton's intention of conducting two Reviews: "As to the effect of your taking the Dublin on the Rambler, so far I should anticipate, that you would not have time, thought, and zeal sufficient for both, and that, if the Dublin gained, the Rambler would lose."[32] His apprehensions on this score increased, for on August 2, he wrote to him again:

I am glad to hear you are progressing. Did I say anything on the scheme of one Editor being for both periodicals? I am afraid it would

[27] Acton to Newman, 5 July 1858, Orat. P.C.
[28] T. W. Allies (1813–1903), educated at Eton and Wadham College, Oxford, converted to Catholicism in 1850, appointed Professor of Modern History in the Catholic University of Ireland in 1855, secretary of the Catholic Poor School Committee (1853–90).
[29] Acton to Simpson, 6 July [1858], Downside Mss.
[30] Acton to Newman, 5 July 1858, Orat. P.C.
[31] Newman to Acton, 10 July 1858, Woodruff Mss.
[32] Newman to Acton, 10 July 1858, Woodruff Mss.

not work. A Review or Magazine is an absorbing work—it demands, if not a man's whole time, yet his whole interest & his continual thought. I think, even though one man were physically up to the work, one or other publication would suffer. And then again, a periodical has a sort of identity, and part of its interest with the public consists in its individuality. When it was known that only one idea was represented in two works, one or other would cease to attract attention. . . Now there is a sort of impropriety, which we naturally recognise, in two organisations having precisely the same work.[33]

Acton, impervious to Newman's cautions, went on with his plans for taking over the *Dublin Review*. He judged that "the present occasion" was a likely one "to break down Newman's rule about not writing for reviews."[34] To Newman he wrote:

The only thing which would compensate for the diminished number of literary papers in the Atlantis would be your consent to give the Dublin Review or the Rambler some of the crumbs that fall from your table. At any rate nothing would so much increase our chance of succeeding. . . I shall rejoice at the present confused and melancholy state of our periodical literature if it results in inducing you to break your resolution of not contributing to any of the Reviews.[35]

And again two weeks later:

I cannot make up my mind to begin without the hope of your aid at first. An occasional half hour during the next four months would enable you to give us a paper which, however short, would settle the question of success at first, and a good start is a great thing.[36]

Newman, though anxious to help Acton in whatever way he could, for various reasons did not fancy writing for current reviews:

I wish I could promise, but I have quite the *will* to send you some kind of article, but you cannot conceive how much time I lose in finding subjects. At length when I get one, I spend perhaps a good deal of time on it, and after all cannot please myself, and throw it up.[37]

A few months later to Acton's continued importuning to throw himself into periodical writing he replied:

I often feel that I am used up—at least for such purposes. A person should be younger in age, in mind, in thought, in experience, and in

[33] Newman to Acton, 2 August 1858, Woodruff Mss.
[34] Acton to Simpson, 11 July [1858], Downside Mss.
[35] Acton to Newman, 12 July 1858, Orat. P.C.
[36] Acton to Newman, 28 July [1858], Orat. P.C.
[37] Newman to Acton, 27 July 1858, Woodruff Mss.

views, than I am, to write with freshness and energy. And then, things seem to have gone past me, and I don't know whom I am likely to influence. And moreover, I wanted now at length, the University being off my hands, to go back to my old studies, and to do something, if life is given me, more solid than I have done hitherto. And lastly, as to the moment, I intended to lie fallow this next year, for I am very tired.[38]

Shadows appeared to darken Acton's bright hopes for the *Dublin Review*. Cardinal Wiseman and Dr. Russell,[39] two of the main backers of the *Dublin*, wished the *Rambler* to merge with it rather than to continue two distinct Reviews.[40] Burns, the publisher of the *Rambler*, wanted Allies as assistant editor of any new periodical, having personally promised him such a post.[41] This latter point particularly annoyed Acton since his plan turned on Simpson as assistant editor.[42] The situation was even further complicated by H. R. Bagshawe's request to remain on as editor.[43]

That the Cardinal and his associates were unwilling to give to Acton undivided control of the *Dublin Review* is clear. Wiseman, personally, would have preferred almost any other arrangement to handing over his own organ "into the Rambler peoples' hands"[44] and was only led to contemplate it at all by the straitened circumstances of the *Dublin Review*. Nevertheless, had Acton made it clear that Simpson was to play no part in conducting the new Review and accepted Allies as his sub-editor Wiseman most probably would have given in. Yet, such an arrangement would not be satisfactory from Acton's point of view. He required an associate in whom he had complete confidence. As Newman advised him: "If you are Editor you must have a Sub-editor with whom you are absolutely familiar and at your ease, and intimately one in opinion."[45] Simpson was the only possible choice open to Acton.

On August 25, 1858 Acton wrote to Simpson informing him that the Cardinal had broken off the negotiations about the

[38] Newman to Acton, 16 December 1858, Woodruff Mss.
[39] Dr. C. W. Russell, President of Maynooth College.
[40] Acton to Newman, 28 July 1858, Orat. P.C.
[41] Acton to Simpson [25 July 1858] Downside Mss.
[42] Acton to Newman, 28 July [1858], Orat. P.C.
[43] Acton to Newman, 29 July 1858, Orat. P.C.
[44] Wiseman to Bagshawe, 27 October 1858, Westminster Archives.
[45] Newman to Acton, 27 July 1858, Woodruff Mss.

Dublin Review.[46] But undaunted he added: "I have little doubt we shall have another chance soon"; and fired a parting shot at the opposition: "I am not sure there has not been treachery somewhere." Two months later the question of taking over the *Dublin* arose again, but negotiations came to naught. "I have lost," wrote Acton to Simpson at the end of November, "all expectations and I confess all desire, of having the *Dublin Review.* I will talk to Newman about quartering the *Atlantis*."[47]

Newman met with hesitation Acton's entreaties to broaden the scope of the *Atlantis* and make of it a quarterly review, "written by your professors, and by all other competent Catholics who would be ready to join."[48] He was impressed but remained cautious. "I don't think the time has quite arrived for such a periodical as you propose," he wrote to Acton, and directed some excellent personal advice to the impatient journalist:

I think you ought to feel your way more. You would come too with far more weight to the management of a Review, if you first showed, which no one could do better than you, that you had given such time to patient study and thought, that you had a right to take part in current events. A year or two is nothing in your life, or Simpson's whatever it may be in mine.[49]

Acton accepted generously (although he soon forgot) Newman's counsel:

I have no difficulty in agreeing with that part of your letter which I can construe into advice for myself. I shall never obtain in the Rambler any sort of real influence, and the hurry and haste of writing monthly articles harasses and disgusts me. The things that I have accumulated in the course of my studies can find no place in it, and whatever I write in a review of such a popular character seems pedantic.[50]

However, he persisted in encouraging an expansion of the *Atlantis* and Newman reluctantly consented.[51] In the meanwhile other developments were in progress which jeopardized the very

[46] Acton to Simpson, 25 August 1858, Downside Mss.
[47] Gasquet, *Acton*, p. 43.
[48] Acton to Newman, 10 December 1858, Orat. P.C.
[49] Newman to Acton, 16 December 1858, Woodruff Mss.
[50] Acton to Newman, 20 December 1858, Orat. P.C.
[51] Acton to Simpson, 1 January 1859, Downside Mss.; Acton to Newman 17 and 25 January 1859, Orat. P.C.; Newman to Acton, 13 and 21 January 1859, Woodruff Mss.

existence of the *Rambler* and pushed plans for a new *Atlantis* into the background.

In the course of an article on Bossuet in the *Rambler* of June, 1858 the subject of his affinity to the Jansenists was introduced. One passage well-designed to startle the ordinary reader ran as follows:

> The Jansenist controversy served once more to display the curious cast of Bossuet's mind, and brought him again into direct contest with Rome. That he himself held the Port-Royalist doctrine on the subject of divine grace is incontestable. He considered himself, rightly or wrongly, a thorough Augustinian.[52]

There is no evidence that the passage drew any comment at the time. But in the *Rambler* for August the relation of Augustine to Jansenism was introduced in a more provocative fashion in a literary notice of A. Chéruel's *Marie Stuart et Cathérine de Medicis*. The passage read:

> Because St. Thomas died a martyr, we are not tempted to deny that he wavered at Clarendon; nor because St. Augustine was the greatest doctor of the West, need we conceal the fact that he was also the father of Jansenism.[53]

In the September number the following explanatory editorial note appeared in the correspondence section of the Review:

> A correspondent has, with great kindness, warned us that umbrage has been taken at a sentence referring to St. Augustine in our last Number, and has told us that inferences have been drawn from it injurious to our reputation for orthodoxy. In order to remove all ground for such suspicions, we protest that we never intended to identify any errors which the Church has proscribed with the teaching of 'the greatest doctor of the West,' when properly understood; and that we most sincerely hold and profess whatever the Holy See has propounded, and condemn what it has condemned on the questions of grace, free-will and justification. With respect to the terms we used, we venture to remind our readers that we might call Plato the father of scepticism, without identifying sceptical errors with the real teaching of the father of philosophy.[54]

Acton, who had written the passage in the first place, was not pleased by the editorial note. He wrote to Simpson from his home in Aldenham demurring to the explanation:

[52] *Rambler*, June 1858, p. 388.
[53] *Rambler*, August 1858, p. 135.
[54] *Rambler*, September 1858, p. 216.

Döllinger, who is here, is fattening with laughter at the ignorance of our divines betrayed in the Augustinian dispute. . . I could not subscribe to what you have written under "Correspondence," and propose to show why I do most deliberately hold that errors condemned by the Church are to be found in the works of the Doctor Gratiae.[55]

He then prevailed upon his old professor to deliver a lesson to the ignorant divines in the form of a letter to the *Rambler*.

Döllinger's letter appeared—translated by Acton[56]—in the December issue under the title "The Paternity of Jansenism."[57] A short note prefixed to it by the Editor could only irritate anyone who had criticized the *Rambler* in the past. To quote one passage.

It is our right, as well as our duty towards ourselves and those who think with us, to prove that the denunciations made against us spring rather from the timidity of ignorance, the dogmatism of party views, or a ceremonious reverence to great names, than from such a knowledge of the subject in dispute as could give those who accuse us any right to sit in judgment on our opinions. We may at the same time suggest the possibility, that what is true in the present case has been more or less true in former instances where we have suffered from similar misinterpretations of our meaning or from prejudiced condemnations of our views. —Ed. R.[58]

The tone of Döllinger's heavily documented letter scarcely softened the severity of the prefix, and it ended with a pointed vindication of the original expression:

So much at least is evident from what I have said, that the writer of the passage on the paternity of Jansenism, if, as I doubt not, he understood it with the above restrictions, finds himself in very good, I may say, in most select company. I know none better in the Church.[59]

Acton was delighted with Döllinger's performance and wrote to Simpson: "I am in spirits about Döllinger's letter because I never had one moment's misgiving about the propriety of the phrase I used."[60] He recklessly wanted his full measure of revenge and sent off a copy of the letter "to all the bishops, and to all the colleges, and to all the divines" he could think of.[61]

[55] Acton to Simpson [September, 1858], Downside Mss.
[56] Acton to Simpson [13 November 1858], Downside Mss.
[57] *Rambler*, December 1858, pp. 361–373.
[58] *Ibid.*, p. 361.
[59] *Ibid.*, p. 373.
[60] Acton to Simpson [December 1858], Downside Mss.
[61] Acton to Simpson [14 December 1858], Downside Mss.

Forgotten was the caution not to throw German scholarship in the face of his English readers to convict them of "neglect and ignorance."[62]

Cardinal Wiseman was disturbed by Döllinger's interference. "Have you seen Döllinger's letter in the *Rambler*?" he wrote nervously to Dr. Russell of Maynooth. "It is giving great pain, and perhaps scandal."[63] At the same time he wrote to Simpson: "I am sorry to say that the letter in defence of St. Augustine's 'paternity of Jansenism' is exciting considerable uneasiness, likely to lead to the principles and opinions contained in it being referred to authority superior to mine."[64] However, it does not appear that he actually referred the matter to Rome. He took counsel with Dr. Newsham, the President of Ushaw, who judged that the statement "might be explained in a true sense, and had best be left alone."[65]

Acton kept Newman fully abreast of developments. Although Newman had earlier declined his persistent invitations to join a gathering at Aldenham to mark Döllinger's visit—"I should never have thought of the party at all without the prospect of your being one of us" pleaded Acton[66]—he brought Döllinger to the Oratory on two occasions.[67] And on learning from Simpson that Wiseman contemplated denouncing Döllinger to Rome he again called on Newman. His news upset Newman, as may be seen from Acton's report to Simpson:

I had a 3 hours' talk with the venerable Noggs who came out at last with his real sentiments to an extent which startled me, with respect both to things and persons, as HE [His Eminence], Ward, Dalgairns, etc., etc., natural inclination of men in power to tyrannise, ignorance and presumption of our would be theologians, in short what you and I would comfortably say over a glass of whiskey. I did not think he could ever cast aside his diplomacy and buttonment [sic] so entirely, and was quite surprised at the intense interest he betrayed in the Rambler. He was quite miserable when I told him the news and moaned for a long

[62] See above, p. 16.
[63] Wiseman to Russell, 20 December 1858, Westminster Archives.
[64] Wiseman to Simpson, 22 December 1858, Downside Mss.
[65] [Wilfrid] Ward, [*The Life and Times of Cardinal*] *Wiseman* (London, 1897), vol. ii, p. 244, n. 1.
[66] Acton to Newman, 29 July 1858, Orat. P.C.
[67] Acton to Newman [25 August 1858]. Orat. P.C.; Ward, *Newman*, i, p. 443; see also Newman to Acton, 27 July and 2 August 1858, Woodruff Mss.

time, rocking himself backwards and forward over the fire, like an old woman with the toothache. He thinks the move provoked both by the hope of breaking down the R.[ambler] and by jealousy of Döllinger.[68]

Nevertheless, apart from being pained at the indignity to which he feared Döllinger was to be subjected, Newman was disposed to make light of the incident. "Perhaps the denunciation won't be made," he wrote to Acton on the day following his visit. "If it is," he added, "he is able to hold his own. And they will be shy of meddling with him at Rome." Still he was far from satisfied with the *Rambler:*

No one, however, can deny, that it is the bad repute of the *Rambler* which causes it, if it is done. I certainly have long thought that the *Rambler* was in a false position. If I recollect rightly, it commenced as a literary work. At one time it called itself, *Journal of the Fine Arts,* &c. It generally had a tale in series. It was properly a magazine. I think it was a mistake to treat of Theology proper at all; and a double mistake to treat it in magazine fashion. And a third mistake for laymen to do so.

He offered some sound advice to its promoters:

Let it go back to its own literary line. Let it be instructive, clever and amusing. Let it cultivate a general temper of good humour and courtesy. Let it praise as many persons as it can, and gain friends in neutral quarters, and become the organ of others by the interest it has made them take in its proceedings. Then it will be able to plant a good blow at a fitting time with great effect, it may come down keen and sharp and not only on Protestants, and without committing itself to definite statements of its own, it may support authority by attacking views which authority will be the first to be jealous of if the *Rambler* is not the first to attack them. Power to be powerful, and strength to be strong, must be exerted only now and then. It then would be strong and effective, and affect public opinion without offending piety or good sense.

I don't think all this is a mere dream—but to be realised it requires the grace of patience.[69]

Acton agreed with Newman on the necessity of disclaiming a theological character for the *Rambler.* Yet he feared that even if this were done it would still continue to give offence as the people it wished to conciliate were sensitive and intolerant toward the objective treatment of history and politics as well as theology. In brief, they were afraid of free and sincere inquiry.[70]

[68] Acton to Simpson, 1 January [1859], Downside Mss.
[69] Ward, *Newman,* i, pp. 483–85.
[70] Acton to Newman, 4 January 1859, Orat. P.C.

In the *Rambler* for February, 1859, Acton ignored Newman's plea for courtesy and patience. In a slashing article on "The Catholic Press" he gave free rein to his indignation and castigated the intellectual leadership given to English Catholics.[71] He saw the vast accession of strength sent to them by the Oxford Movement being turned to little account. Apart from "certain very elaborate essays in the *Atlantis*" there was hardly anything "serious or durable in the productions of the Catholic literature of the day."[72] There was an abundance of entertaining books— "history made edifying, science religious, and religion exceedingly attractive." But a popular literature by itself was injurious: "it encourages people to forget that something else is wanted, and promotes a superficial self-contented way of looking at all things, of despising difficulties, and overlooking the force of objections."[73] There was a pressing need for an increased literary effort "to break down that Protestant tradition which pervades all the literature, serious as well as popular, and enchains all the intellect, of the country."[74] Without a solid literature Catholics were generally compelled "to meet objections by simple negation and contradiction, and by arguing against each particular error on the assumption that the contrary is true."

Acton then turned to the Catholic Reviews. As he saw it, Reviews should be playing the leading role in raising the character of Catholic literature. But in spite of the presence of great literary ability in the Catholic body and the advantage of an educated public large enough to support a first-rate Journal, the only Catholic Quarterly, the *Dublin Review*, was in serious decline. The reason for its decline was clear:

It has not kept pace with the intellectual movement of the country. It has neglected to draw the attention of its readers to the things which it is most important for them to know, and to inform them of the real secret of the enemy's strength.[75]

The result was pernicious:

It has encouraged the insane delusion that scientific infidelity is not,

---

[71] Reprinted in [Acton] *Essays on Church and State*, edited by D. Woodruff (London, 1952), pp. 260–78.

[72] *Ibid.*, p. 262.

[73] *Essays on Church and State*, p. 262.

[74] *Ibid.*, p. 263.

[75] *Essays on Church and State*, p. 266.

like heresy, an antagonist that it behoves Catholics to encounter; that misbelievers and disbelievers must be allowed to fight it out between them, and the dead left to bury their dead; that no danger threatens the Church from that party, and that Catholics have no special duty towards it.[76]

Catholics, not feeling the value and the dignity of the pursuit of knowledge, often regarded knowledge with contempt and indifference, and this in turn engendered aversion and dread:

The confidence with which the men of science have asserted that religion is opposed to it, has promoted an awe of falsehood and a distrust of the power of truth. The phantom of the eighteenth century pursues many Catholics, and makes them look with suspicion upon the policy which has proved itself the best safe-guard of religion.[77]

But the pretence of an antagonism between science and religion was on neither side sincere:

Solicitude for religion is merely a pretext for opposition to the free course of scientific research, which threatens, not the authority of the Church, but the precarious influence of individuals. The growth of knowledge cannot in the long run be detrimental to religion; but it renders impossible the usurpation of authority by teachers who defend their own false opinions under pretence of defending the faith which they dishonour by their artifices. . . . They impute to others the evil they themselves have caused, and do not see that the progress of error and unbelief is their own work. Partly afraid of truth, and partly ashamed of it, they want to shelter their own ignorance by preserving that of others. But religion is not served by denying facts, or by denouncing those who proclaim them. . . Truth is not the exclusive possession of the ignorant; the sun does not shine only for the blind. Authority can only condemn error; its vitality is not destroyed until it is refuted.[78]

The fostering of a true spirit of impartial inquiry should be the great work of a Catholic Quarterly. But the only existing one, falling so far short of the standards it ought to maintain, made the position of a Review which attempted to operate on true principles "unnatural and difficult to maintain."[79]

The obloquy incurred by the *Rambler* for maintaining the principle of independent inquiry, within the bounds, and for the

[76] *Ibid.*, pp. 266–67.
[77] *Ibid.*, p. 271.
[78] *Essays on Church and State*, p. 272.
[79] *Ibid.*, p. 276.

promotion of the Catholic faith, showed how urgently such advocacy was demanded:

Speaking for no party ourselves we naturally excite the dislike of all partisans. Doubtless we shall incense many soothing prejudices and contradict many cherished opinions, and shall continue objects of aversion to all who are more attached to persons than to principles, to habits than to ideas. Whoever defies an idol must be prepared for the clamour of its worshippers; nobody who assails folly and error is surprised at being answered by a falsehood or an insult.[80]

Whatever the justice of Acton's able article on the Catholic Press it was anything but conciliatory. And in its hostile and self-righteous tone it was poorly calculated to arouse anything but anger in the opponents to the *Rambler*. Coupled with the Jansenist episode it might easily be interpreted by a nervous hierarchy as a declaration of war.

To the surprise of many, the articles which finally decided the bishops to take action against the *Rambler* were moderately written ones offering much needed criticism of certain episcopal utterances on the Royal Commission on Education of 1858. They were written by S. N. Stokes, a Catholic School Inspector, and appeared in the January and February issues. They were interpreted as an unwarranted intrusion into episcopal prerogatives.[81]

On February 13, 1859 Cardinal Wiseman met with Archbishop Errington, Bishop Grant of Southwark (Simpson's Bishop) and Bishop Ullathorne. It was decided to present Simpson with an ultimatum to retire immediately from the editorship, under pain of all the bishops' issuing pastorals against the *Rambler*.[82] On the recommendation of Ullathorne the whole affair was placed in the hands of Newman. "We agreed," Ullathorne wrote to Newman, "first, I should ask you, if you thought well, to write to Mr. Simpson and Sir John Acton."[83]

Within a few days Newman was able to report back to his Bishop: "Mr. Simpson most frankly put the whole question of the 'Rambler' into my hands, and expressed his wish to abide by my decision."[84]

[80] *Essays on Church and State*, p. 277.
[81] See Gasquet, *Acton*, Introd. p. xlix, ff.
[82] Simpson to Acton, 20 February 1859, Woodruff Mss.
[83] Ward, *Wiseman*, ii, p. 245.
[84] *Ibid.*, p. 246.

Simpson, on his part, although intensely annoyed at what he believed was the injustice of the bishops, had absolute confidence in Newman. "Newman's kindness is memorable and worthy of all gratitude,"[85] he wrote to Acton, who was sojourning in Munich since early in February. Simpson found Acton agreeable to whatever he and Newman "decided upon doing in order to meet the troubles which beset the Rambler."[86] Acton intimated, however, that only Newman's editorship could save the situation and added Döllinger's opinion that the disappearance of the *Rambler* would be an irreparable loss.

Newman was perplexed. He had persuaded Simpson to surrender the *Rambler* into his hands, but what was he to do with it? Acton was the obvious choice for editor but Wiseman demanded his exclusion as well as Simpson's.[87] Finally, with the utmost reluctance, Newman decided that he would edit the Review himself. He wrote to Simpson explaining his decision:

My initial, and sine qua non reason for listening to the proposition of my being Editor of a Magazine, is my wish to stop the differences between you and the Bishops, to keep good men, such as yourself from becoming unpopular with the whole Catholic body, to hinder the wreck of a publication, which has done and may still do much good. I have not even a dream, or the dream of a dream, of undertaking 'something' or anything, except in order to effect these ends.[88]

To his own Bishop he wrote:

I please myself with the thought that you will hear with satisfaction that I am, for the present, editor of the *Rambler*; but it is the only sort of pleasure which I can feel in an arrangement which is in itself to me a most bitter penance.[89]

Newman brought out his first number in May. It was a disappointment to those who had hoped for a major change. There was no dissociation with the *Rambler* of the past. Instead the Editor, under "Contemporary Events," discussed the judgment of the bishops on the Royal Commission and sought to reconcile their views with those expressed in the controverted articles by Stokes. In a memorandum of 1882, he explained his reluctance

85 Simpson to Acton, 20 February 1859, Woodruff Mss.
86 Gasquet, *Acton*, p. 62.
87 Ward, *Newman*, i, p. 492.
88 Newman to Simpson, 16 March 1859, Orat. P.C.
89 Ward, *Newman*, i, p. 492.

to follow a path which might seem to imply a repudiation of the old *Rambler*:

> In the 'Advertisement' (to the new series of the *Rambler*) not a word was said of any change of matter, drift, objects, tone, &c., of the *Rambler*, though my purpose was in fact to change what had in so many ways displeased me.
>
> But I had no wish to damage the fair name of men who I believed were at bottom sincere Catholics, and I thought it unfair, ungenerous, impertinent, and cowardly to make in their behalf acts of confession and contrition, and to make a display of change of editorship, and (as if) so virtuous a change.[90]

On May 22 Bishop Ullathorne called at the Oratory and expressed his dissatisfaction with the new *Rambler*. There was a general impression, he complained, "that the old spirit was not clean gone out of the *Rambler*."[91] Following a long unsatisfactory discussion, Newman finally acquiesced in his Bishop's wish that he retire from editorship after the next issue.

In the *Rambler* for July, 1859, the second and last edited by Newman, appeared the controversial composition "On Consulting the Faithful in Matters of Doctrine." Newman wrote it in explanation and defense of a passage in his May discussion of the Royal Commission on Education. The article was delated to Rome as heretical by Bishop Brown of Newport. Newman wrote to Wiseman offering a full explanation if he or Rome so desired it, and hearing no more about it concluded that the matter was closed. But owing to the unfortunate mismanagement of the whole matter by Wiseman, Manning and Talbot his orthodoxy was suspect at Rome until the affair was finally cleared up in 1867. In the meantime public confidence in Newman had been seriously shaken and was not to be restored for several years.[92]

Why, it may be asked, was Newman requested to resign when it must have been clear to the bishops that the *Rambler* would revert into the hands of Acton and Simpson? Newman himself suggests the most probable answer. "Perhaps," he wrote, "the Cardinal, &c., were seized with a panic lest they had got out of the frying-pan into the fire."[93] In other words, the bishops

---

[90] Ward, *Newman*, i, p. 494.

[91] *Ibid.*, p. 496.

[92] Ward, *Newman*, i, p. 504. Newman's controversial essay has recently been edited with a useful introduction by John Coulson (London, 1961).

[93] Ward, *Newman*, i, p. 501.

feared Newman more than Acton and Simpson. With Newman as editor (so the bishops might reason) the prestige of the *Rambler* would rise enormously but its troublesome speculations would continue. "I am told," wrote Talbot from Rome of the *Rambler* under Newman, "that it is a more dangerous publication since its change of hands than it was before, and that it contains positive heresy."[94]

The bishops were immersed in the urgent practical problems of administering a Church that had rapidly increased in membership over a few decades, and they had little time left for serious reflection on the various intellectual currents that were disturbing educated Christians in general. It seemed unreal to them to spread alarm over the relationship between faith and reason, science and theology, inspiration and history, freedom and authority, when the majority of Catholics were not even dimly aware of such problems, if indeed they were problems. In their inability to see beyond the immediate present they failed to grasp the inadequacy of their approach. In a period of depression, Newman summed it up as follows:

> Catholics in England, from their very blindness, cannot see that they are blind. To aim then at improving the condition, the status, of the Catholic body, by a careful survey of their argumentative basis, of their position relatively to the philosophy and the character of the day, by giving them juster views, by enlarging & refining their minds, in one word, by education, is (in their view) more than a superfluity or a hobby, it is an insult. It implies that they are deficient in material points. . . I should wish to attempt to meet the great infidel &c. questions of the day, but both Propaganda & the Episcopate, doing nothing themselves, look with extreme jealousy on anyone who attempts it.[95]

The question still remained: what was to become of the *Rambler*? If it was to continue at all either Simpson or Acton would have to take over its editorship. But for Simpson to resume his old office would have been tantamount to an open defiance of the bishops. If, however, Acton were to edit it there was some hope that the hierarchy would be mollified, since its promoters would at least have indicated that they were disturbed by episcopal disfavor. But there was a serious difficulty in the way of this latter arrangement. Acton had just been elected as liberal member for Carlow and it was not easy to see

[94] Talbot to J. L. Patterson, 22 October 1859, Westminster Archives.
[95] *Autobiographical Writings*, p. 259.

how he could combine the demanding office of editor with a parliamentary career.[96]

On June 22 Newman wrote to him anxiously:

> I really want to see you about the *Rambler*, and have been impatient. You don't say whether you can be Editor. Now that you are in Parliament & your friends in power, I have given the thought up as impossible, but I shall be rejoiced to find I am wrong.[97]

Acton replied on the following day: "I hardly see how the Rambler can survive unless I undertake the Editing of it. There is very little encouragement to do so, but if you advise me I am ready to try."[98]

Although Newman was most anxious that the *Rambler* should continue he remained sceptical that Acton could find time to edit it. And if Simpson were sub-editor things would be as bad as before. "I fear very much your having him for sub-editor," he wrote to Acton on July 5, "he will certainly compromise the work."[99] And to Simpson he wrote frankly: "I don't think you should be sub-editor for the success of the *Rambler*."[100] A month later, after Acton had made up his mind to go ahead, Newman was still troubled and wrote uneasily to him:

> The enormous difficulty is the Editor or Sub-editor. You *cannot* fill the office yourself. I think it would damage the circulation, if you have Simpson. Even if you are not theological, my *fear* is that he will, whatever be his subject, be introducing (like Cobbett in his English Grammar) theological instances & illustrations.[101]

[96] The farcical character of the election campaign and its aftermath is told in James J. Auchmuty's "Acton's Election as an Irish Member of Parliament," *English Historical Review*, September, 1946. This account, however, suffers from the grave defect of being based almost entirely on the reports of highly partisan newspapers. That Acton was not happy about his mode of election may be judged from a reference to it two years later. "Nothing would induce me to stand for Carlow again after certain proceedings which came to my knowledge long after my election," he wrote to Newman on 4 June [1861] (Orat. P.C.).

[97] Newman to Acton, 22 June 1859, Orat. P.C. Archbishop Mathew, in *Acton: The Formative Years* (London, 1946), p. 121, chose a passage from this letter in which Newman speaks of being "as sick of penmanship as a pastrycook of tarts" to indicate that Newman was wearying of his arduous correspondence and wished delicately to break it off for the present, the implication being that his relations with Acton were wearing thin. If the letter is taken in its context it will be readily seen that it cannot bear this interpretation.

[98] Acton to Newman [23 June 1859], Orat. P.C.

[99] Ward, *Newman*, i, p. 635.

[100] *Ibid.*, p. 635.

[101] Newman to Acton, 9 August 1859, Woodruff Mss.

Acton evidently felt that he could not carry on without Simpson's active assistance and made a special effort to convince him of the need for restraint. By the end of August he could report to Newman that he had so impressed Simpson with the necessity of writing with care and caution that on asking him to write an article for the September issue he replied that "it is very difficult for him to get up an article in a few days in conformity with the new Rambler's spirit, and that he felt as if he was beginning to write for the first time."[102] That Simpson's chastened mood was but a temporary thing, however, is evidenced by Acton's plea two weeks later not to engage in an attack on episcopal censorship.[103]

Newman was able to render a valuable service to the *Rambler* by persuading Thomas Wetherell to join its staff as an assistant editor.[104] Wetherell was a convert and had helped Newman during his brief editorship of the *Rambler*. He was highly gifted intellectually and fully appreciated the value of the work Acton and Simpson were attempting to accomplish. But what was even more important he possessed the moderation which Simpson lacked. From the first he got on well with Acton. Some years later Acton was to write of him to Gladstone "that in uprightness, in judgment, in literary taste, in care and exactness, he satisfies my ideal of what an Editor should be."[105]

Before the first *Rambler* under his own editorship appeared Acton again went abroad. He intended to remain away only one month but the serious illness of his mother led to an absence of three months. His letters to Simpson during this period were filled with hope and enthusiasm for the future. He hoped to organize a Lingard Historical Society on his return.[106] Still, the anxiety continued lest Simpson be indiscreet in his writings. "Be sure," Acton cautioned him, "not to give Newman an opportunity of saying that the *Rambler* is apt to run riot if I am not at hand to urge timid counsels."[107]

Newman at this period did fear that the *Rambler* would run riot. On the back of proofs of an article written by himself he

[102] Acton to Newman 15 August [1859], Orat. P.C.
[103] Acton to Simpson [28 August 1859], Downside Mss.
[104] Newman to Acton, 17 July 1859, Woodruff Mss.; Acton to Newman, 15 August [1859], Orat. P.C.
[105] Acton to Gladstone, 1 January 1867, British Museum, Add. Mss. 44093.
[106] Gasquet, *Acton*, p. 87.
[107] *Ibid.*, p. 108.

found, by chance, an article by Simpson on "Toleration." In the course of his article Simpson had criticized Gregory XVI's condemnation of Lamennais in his encyclical *Mirari vos*. Newman took strong exception to what he judged a very inadequate treatment of a highly contentious issue. "If," he wrote to Simpson, "the new article on Toleration appears in the *Rambler* without a *bona fide* revision, I must ask you to be so good as not to publish mine on St. Chrysostom."[108] Simpson in consternation replied: "I frankly confess I do not know what I am to write about. I withdraw the article with pleasure, partly because it is a real satisfaction to do what you ask me to do."[109]

Another incident occurred at this time that brought Newman further anxieties lest his connections with the *Rambler* should bring upon him new troubles. A rumor that the *Dublin Review* was to be discontinued was denied by Mr. Bagshawe, its editor, in letters to the *Weekly Register* and the *Tablet*. He referred to Newman as though he were editor of the *Rambler*. His error is understandable since Newman's resignation was never made public. Newman, the following week, disclaimed any part "in conducting or superintending that able periodical."[110] Six months later this disclaimer was to become the occasion of Acton's first disagreement with Newman.

Newman's deep respect for the lightest wish of his bishop— "I desired to please him personally, as I considered him set over me by the Divine Hand."[111]—explains the extreme subtlety of his relations with the *Rambler* after his own failure to make it acceptable to the bishops. His deep-rooted conviction that it was doing an important work led him to go as far as his principles would permit in helping its promoters. Still, the effort to please a hierarchy with whom he was out of sympathy while, at the same time, remaining true to his own principles, placed a severe strain on him. He has left us in his Personal Journal an intimate record of his state of mind during this period and it is clear how much his apparent failures have depressed him. In an entry dated January 8, 1860, he listed some of the things that disturbed him most:

(1) Let not the contempt which comes on *me*, injure the future of my

108 Ward, *Newman*, i, p. 506.
109 Simpson to Newman [25 October 1859], Orat. P.C.
110 Ward, *Newman*, i, p. 507.
111 *Apologia*, p. 51.

Oratory—about this I am anxious, though I ought to put it, & do put it simply, into Thy hands, O Lord.

(2) And again, O teach me (for it is a subject which tries me very much just now, which I have prayed about, & have said masses about), teach me how to employ myself most profitably, most to Thy glory, in such years as remain to me; for my apparent illsuccess discourages me much. O my God, I seem to have wasted these years that I have been a Catholic. What I wrote as a Protestant has had far greater power, force, meaning, success, than my Catholic works—& this troubles me a great deal—[112]

Five days after writing the above Newman had a new cause for distress. Bishop Ullathorne returned from Rome with news that the authorities there were displeased with his article "On Consulting the Laity" and that the Pope had expressed his concern.[113] To one of Newman's sensitiveness the thought that he gave pain to the Pope brought intense sorrow.

Acton visited him in February, 1860 and found him downcast. "I never saw Newman so much out of spirits," he reported to Simpson, "so distributively angry. He likes the last *Rambler*. Other things greatly trouble him, some of which he would not tell me and some he wished me not to repeat. Personally he was as usual extremely kind."[114]

Acton, on his part, had trouble with Simpson. He wrote to him again after his visit to Newman defending him against Simpson's charge that he was treating them unfairly:

He [Newman] agrees with us in principle, and the question is whether we disagree with him in policy. I do not think it is a personal question, and you seem to me to do him an injustice in speaking of his treatment of us almost as F. Capes speaks, with whom I should be sorry to think that you agreed in all other personal judgments. As things are it is impossible for me to ask him to write or to take any ostensible part in the Rambler, and we must weigh his opinions in our own scales. . . The alternative is to fight it out as Capes thinks you ought to have done last spring when I was abroad. Now Newman attempted to fight in defence of the laity, and the consequence was that he was silenced and insulted, and as I understood Capes, that the circulation did not materially improve.

---

[112] *Autobiographical Writings*, p. 253.
[113] *Autobiographical Writings*, p. 253.
[114] Gasquet, *Acton*, p. 116. Gasquet dates this letter [? January 1860]. It would seem that it was more probably written early in February. Newman refers some months later to a February meeting with Acton (Ward, *Newman*, i, p. 636). The "great papal meeting" mentioned in paragraph two of the letter was actually held on 14 February 1860. (See below, p. 62).

Now since we have taken the Rambler back again, we have made no particular new enemies and have gained some friends. Can we not go on and prosper in this way ?[115]

It was now Acton's turn to be visited with trials. His mother died on March 14, 1860. On learning the sad news Newman wrote him a note of sympathy expressing the homely truth: "A mother can be lost but once. And the trial is unlike any trial before or after it."[116] Soon after Acton left England "to spend a peaceful fortnight at Munich."[117]

A despondent Acton returned from Germany to resume work that had lost its savor. Parliamentary life had grown distasteful and the future of the *Rambler* was unpromising. Writing to Newman shortly after his return he outlined some of his burdens: Newman's denial that he "had any connection whatever" with the *Rambler* had resulted in a forty percent fall in circulation; Wetherell resigned over an article on the Roman Question;[118] without any editorial help except what he could get from Simpson, he worked his legs off in "attending very imperfectly to many different things," and as a result he could "neither prepare speeches for parliament, nor do the Rambler well." "I greatly fear," he continued,

that without your countenance and aid there is very little chance of my going on with success. A great private trouble has come upon me very soon after my mother's death, and I am longing for the recess in order to find some distraction and relief in a journey to Spain.[119]

Newman wrote to him expressing deep concern about the future of the *Rambler* but declined a request to be theological censor or even to give his name to it unless it had a responsible editor and

[115] Acton to Simpson [11 February 1860], Downside Mss.
[116] Newman to Acton, 19 March 1860, Orat. P.C.
[117] Acton to Simpson [23 March 1860], Downside Mss.
[118] See below, p. 116.
[119] Acton to Newman [? June 1860], Orat. P.C. The exact nature of the "great private trouble" is not clear. It was most probably related to his plans for marriage. He told his dying mother (to her great delight) of his hopes of marrying his cousin, the Countess Marie, daughter of Count Arco-Valley, a Bavarian noble (CUL Add. Mss. 4862). In January 1860 he wrote to Newman: "I am going to be married after Easter." (Orat. P.C.). A year later he wrote to Newman: "If you will call to mind an announcement I once prematurely made to you, you will understand me when I say that a private sorrow weighs on my health and energies." (4 June 1861, Orat. P.C.). The marriage to Marie did take place in 1865.

the countenance of such theologians as Father de Buck, Father Gratry, Abbe Maret and Dr. Döllinger.[120] He felt that in view of his responsibilities to the Oratory and the circumstances of his being a convert he could not do otherwise. Acton replied in what was probably the sharpest letter he ever wrote to Newman.[121] He challenged Newman's November announcement that he had "no further connection with the Rambler" as being contrary to their personal arrangement and to such an extent that he felt "an unauthorized person had stated a direct untruth." Newman in his reply, reminded Acton of the exact words used in the November statement and explained why he felt "imperatively bound" to make it; he pointedly added:

I do not think you could have been as you say 'perfectly justified in contradicting' this 'statement publicly'; or that 'you had received no communication from me on this *subject.*' There is nothing in it about '*no connection whatever*'; and I am quite unconscious that I ever was wanting in avowing to the proprietors of the *Rambler* that I would have as little to do with superintending as with editing it, after a Bishop interfered.[122]

But he had sympathy for Acton's difficult position:

No one feels more than I do that it is not fair that, in your position, you should have the *Rambler* on your hands; no one too can be more grateful to you for it than I am, as an English Catholic. The great problem is, the editor; what the *Rambler* says about the University [the Catholic University of Ireland] as wanting a Rector applies, *mutatis mutandis*, to itself.[123]

---

[120] Ward, *Newman*, i, p. 636.
[121] Ward, *Newman*, i, pp. 508-11.
[122] *Ibid.*, p. 511.
[123] Ward, *Newman*, i, p. 512. Wilfrid Ward's account of this dispute does not appear to be accurate. He writes (*Newman*, i, p. 508): "Acton was abroad at the time when Newman's letter to the *Tablet* appeared. On his return to England in February [He was in England in December. See Gasquet, *Acton*, p. 113] he saw Newman at the Oratory and remonstrated with him for appearing to cast off his former colleagues . . . But the sore rankled, and Acton still wrote to him despondently and with a remnant of resentful feeling months after the occurrence." However, on the occasion of the February visit the question of the November disclaimer does not appear to have arisen at all. As has been seen Acton referred to Newman as being "as usual extremely kind" and defended Newman against Simpson. The interpretation that best fits Newman's letter of 1 July 1860 (printed in Ward, *Newman*, i, p. 511) is the one that assumes Acton first raised the question with Newman in his June correspondence.

Now occurred what Newman called "the first *overt* offence of the new *Rambler*."[124]

There appeared in the July issue a letter by H. N. Oxenham, under the initials *X Y Z*, criticising the seminary training of the clergy.[125] It amounted to a condemnation of the whole seminary system as laid down by the Council of Trent. Newman was thoroughly annoyed by the letter. He believed that "the Topic should not have been admitted. It was 'clerical education.' As they wish the Bishops to keep their hands off *lay education*, so should they abstain from clerical."[126] With severe irony he replied to *X Y Z* under the initials *H. O.* and rebuked the writer for treating a clerical subject in a lay magazine and presuming to go against the clear instructions of Trent.[127]

Acton was irritated by Newman's letter. Writing to Simpson he referred to it as "A cleverish and amusing but most unjust and abominably malicious performance."[128] He could not understand why Newman should take so seriously the instructions of an ecumenical council.

To the distaste of Newman the controversy dragged on and was the major topic discussed in the correspondence section of the *Rambler* for almost a year. He submitted a further letter, written by Father Bittleston, an Oratorian, in support of his own views. Acton, however, disagreed with its contents and reluctantly consented to its publication only because it carried Newman's recommendation.[129] Newman insisted on a return of the letter remarking: "I would not and could not for the world consent to allow any letter to appear in the Rambler, of which you say that you are so astonished at it, that without my note you would not have thought of admitting it."[130] A memorandum of Newman's shows how much he felt Acton's disregard for his position on the seminary dispute:

[124] Newman's marginal note on an undated letter from Acton. Newman dated the letter "August 14 or 21, 1860."

[125] "Catholic Education," pp. 248–53.

[126] Continuation of marginal note mentioned in n. 124.

[127] "Seminaries of the Church," September 1860, pp. 398–401.

[128] Acton to Simpson [? August 1860], Downside Mss. Gasquet dates this letter [? April 1860] (*Acton*, p. 128). It is clear, however, from the articles mentioned in it, that it was written shortly before the printing of the September number of the *Rambler*.

[129] *Lord Acton's Correspondence*, p. 35.

[130] Newman to Acton, 11 July 1861, Woodruff Mss.

I felt it very hard that the magazine so ignored the letter of H.O. that Sir John wd not even receive into it a confirmation of it by another hand. He had not only admitted a controversy on ecclesiastical education, (as I thought wrongly) but would not admit without a protest both sides of the controversy, at least (what was worse) my side, *supposing* I took the most serious ground that could be taken, viz. that of the disposition of the Council of Trent.[131]

But as in the controversy over the paternity of Jansenism, Acton and Simpson were convinced that their position was the only sensible one. They planned to end the controversy with "three persons taking in a general way the same reformatory view"[132] and did not wish to spoil the effect by giving too much prominence to what they judged the foolish views of their opponents.

The line taken by the *Rambler* in the controversy on clerical education convinced Newman that he could not prudently take an active part in the Review and he contributed no more to its pages. Yet he remained keenly interested in its progress and was most anxious that it should prosper.

Simpson's article on Edmund Campion in the *Rambler* for May, 1861 engaged him in a protracted correspondence with Acton on the propriety of a writer's introducing controversial questions of the day into grave history and making unnecessary hits at canonized saints like Pius V. [133] Although Newman insisted that he did not differ from him "in any principle, but in fact,"[134] it was apparent that Acton had a growing consciousness of a serious divergence from him on the question of the respect due ecclesiastical authority. "I always feel," he wrote to Newman, "that I am deliberately and systematically further removed from the prevailing sentiment of good and serious Catholics than Simpson is with all his imprudence."[135]

Acton believed passionately that "the encouragement of the true scientific spirit and disinterested love of truth" was the only weapon against the infidelity of the day. He attributed the unpopularity of the *Rambler* to its adoption of this principle.[136] In

[131] Newman's note on his copy of a letter to Acton dated 9 June 1861, Orat. R[ambler] C[ollection].
[132] Acton to Simpson [15 January 1861], Downside Mss.
[133] Ward, *Newman*, i, pp. 527–34.
[134] *Ibid.*, p. 527.
[135] *Ibid.*, p. 532.
[136] Ward, *Newman*, i, p. 531.

doing this, however, he was guilty of oversimplification and was unfair to its critics. He failed to recognize the many failures of the *Rambler* to live up to the high principles it professed to follow. And it was not all the fault of Simpson. Not even the most devoted Actonian would maintain that Acton's pursuit of truth was devoid of all prejudice and preconceptions; yet, owing to some peculiar lack of self-knowledge he seemed to believe that it was. By assuming a highly moralistic role in which he looked down on the rest of men as from an eminence, he was easily able to point out defects in their pursuits, but he made it much less likely that his reforming message would be given a fair hearing and he prepared the way for his own inevitable isolation. It would be unjust to accuse him of being moved by any desire of self-aggrandizement. He sincerely deplored the low state of Catholic scholarship and political thinking and felt keenly the urgent need of a new critical approach to meet the challenge of an age of rationalism. He was far more anxious that the challenge be met effectively than that he should acquire any personal prestige. He was ready to take second place or withdraw completely if it would help further what he believed was essential work. His appalling arrogance, his habit of viewing all opposition in terms of a conspiracy to be met by a counter-conspiracy, his failure to appreciate the concrete difficulties of the hierarchy, all these things cannot be gainsaid, but there was much that was admirable in his uncompromising stand and refusal to relax a single principle at the cost of his personal popularity. It was his misfortune to have entered upon what might justly be termed his apostolate at a most unpropitious period, and through the medium of a journal already viewed with suspicion by most Catholics, lay and clerical. Throughout his journalistic career he felt he had the sympathy of Newman and frequently urged him to assert his leadership. But Newman, stung too often in the past by throwing himself headlong into various projects, was far more cautious and reached decisions with much greater deliberation than the young, impetuous Acton deemed necessary.

While Acton's efforts at home were meeting with little success, events were in progress elsewhere which rendered precarious the continued existence of the *Rambler* as an organ of Catholic opinion enjoying even a negative toleration by the hierarchy. In June, 1861 Monsignor Talbot wrote to Wiseman about Rome's concern at the *Rambler's* policy.[137]

---

[137] Talbot to Wiseman, 10 June 1861, Westminster Archives.

The attention of the Holy See has been drawn to the Rambler, which has become one of the most offensive publications, or Catholic periodicals in Europe. The tone it manifests is simply detestable, and it is a pity that it should be looked upon as the organ of the English Catholics, and especially the converts. There are two Articles in the last number which are a direct attack upon the policy of the Holy See. Simpson in one Article[138] attributes the Apostasy of England to the conduct of the Popes, and speaks in the most supercilius [sic] manner of Pius V. who is a Saint, and one of the greatest Pontiffs, and likewise criticizes the conduct of several others, in a most unbecoming manner. Sir John Acton in another Article[139] attacks the Temporal Power of the Holy See, seems to ignore the Allocutions and Encyclicals of the Pope on the subject, and sets up Dr Döllinger & Passaglia[140] against 700 Bishops, who he says have no weight because they speak *officially*. . . I hope the Rambler will be suppressed. It does no good, & a vast deal of harm.

Talbot's reference to the temporal power draws attention to the great question which so agitated the Catholic world at this time, and exercised a profound influence on the subsequent careers of both Acton and Newman. The Roman Question more than any other single issue determined the course of Catholicism in the second half of the pontificate of Pio Nono. It is now necessary to break the narrative and enter upon a somewhat detailed discussion of Acton's and Newman's position on the question which assumed so exaggerated an importance in the Catholic world of the 1860's.

[138] "Edmund Campion," *Rambler*, May, 1861.

[139] Talbot's reference must have been to the *Current Events* of the *Rambler* (see below, p. 74).

[140] Carlo Passaglia (1812–1887), Italian theologian.

III. The Temporal Power of the Pope

To the modern observer who believes the Papacy to have gained an improved status since it was despoiled of the lion's share of its temporalities, the reaction of most Catholics of the mid-nineteenth century to the Italian revolution appears, perhaps, to border on the absurd. Yet it would be presumptuous to conclude that the supporters of the Papal claims were simpletons and their opponents monopolized the wisdom of the age. The present impasse between Rome and Moscow affords a certain parallel, *mutatis mutandis*, to the division which existed in the 1850's and 1860's between the supporters of the Papacy and of rationalistic liberalism. Unfortunately for most Catholics a person's attitude toward temporal power tended to become the touchstone which determined whether he were "sound" or "suspect" on the broader issues. At a time when the Papal Curia was supported by the entire episcopate in affirming the practical necessity of retaining the Papal States it took a highly individualistic Catholic to go against the current.

While the opposition between Catholicism and the revolutionary doctrines involving the supremacy of the State afforded the main reason for the strong support given to the Papal claims, an added reason, and probably the effective one, lay in the personal character of Pius IX. Although neither a scholar nor a statesman he exerted a greater influence on the Catholic world than any Pope since the Reformation. Imbued with a sense of the dignity of his position and absolutely devoted to duty, he immediately impressed those with whom he came in contact as a man devoid of all self-seeking and desirous only of the good of the Church. Even Gladstone, who assailed his "pretentious" claims, wrote to the Duchess of Sutherland after an interview with him: "Nothing can be more pleasant than the impression made by his demeanour and language."[1] Elected Pope in 1846, as a disciple of Gioberti he naively attempted to be a liberal Pope, and was acclaimed by Europe as the Patriot-Pope. Even Mazzini hailed him as the saviour of Italy.[2] When he fled to Gaeta two years later, disillusioned but wiser in the ways of the world, he carried with him the sympathy of Europe. But the Pio Nono who entered the Vatican on April 12, 1850 was soon to be charged with heading a "loathsome tyranny" which was a "scandal to the age."[3] It was not wonderful that Catholics decided that the scandal was rather the attacks made on Pio Nono.

In England the "No Popery" storm accompanying the establishment of the Catholic Hierarchy in 1850 had focused attention on Rome and in the subsequent years scandalous tales from the land of the Pope were relished by literate and illiterate alike. The *Saturday Review* summed up well the position of the Pope in English eyes in 1858:

The Pope is, to one considerable class of Englishmen, a sort of incarnation of all evil. To another, he is the head of a body which fascinates the imagination. But to the great mass of the people, he is an obscure and mythical personage, invested with obsolete spiritual pretensions, and the temporal head of what is generally supposed to be a very ill-governed Italian principality.[4]

A "very ill-governed Italian principality," such certainly was the territory under Papal rule in 1858. By the summer of 1860 the principality was reduced to the city of Rome itself and the provinces of Frosinone and Velletri. Should the lost territories be restored to the Papacy? What was to be the future of Rome itself? These were the questions that agitated the Catholic world in the 1860's while other more important ones were left neglected.

English Catholics, all outspoken Ultramontanes in contrast to the early decades of the century, ranged themselves almost without exception with the supporters of a complete restoration of the lost Papal territories. The *Dublin Review* expressed the prevailing sentiment:

[1] John Morley, *The Life of Gladstone* (London, 1903), vol. i, p. 850.
[2] E. E. Y. Hales, *Pio Nono* (2nd ed. London, 1956), p. 66.
[3] "The Patrimony of St. Peter," *Edinburgh Review*, July, 1860, p. 131.
[4] "Rome and the Last Four Popes," 3 April 1858, p. 348.

The See of Peter cannot abate one jot or tittle of its creed to please any age, nor can his successor yield one rood of the dominions delivered into his hands for providential purposes.[5]

The line taken by Manning was, as might be expected, more extreme than that of Rome itself. The following is a passage from his lecture *The Temporal Sovereignty of the Pope.*

The first proposition is this: that the temporal power of the Pope is ordained of God. The second: that the temporal power of the Pope has been the root, and the sustaining principle of Christian Europe. And, thirdly: that the dissolution of the temporal power of the Pope would bring with it the dissolution of Christian Europe. And from these three propositions I shall draw three plain conclusions. The first is this: that he who resists the temporal power of the Pope, resists the ordinance of God. Secondly: that he who lends a hand or a tongue to the dissolution of that power, helps, so far as his hand or his tongue can, to the dissolution of Christian Europe. And thirdly: that he that does so will purchase judgment to himself. Which propositions, I think, fall within the limit of the words of St Paul, speaking by the inspiration of God. [Romans xiii, 1,2.].[6]

All English Catholics did not see the problem of the temporal power through the eyes of the *Dublin Review* or Archbishop Manning. Newman thought out the question for himself. Alone among leading Catholics, either in England or on the Continent, he refused to identify himself with those who advocated the restoration of the Pope's temporal domains.

A few weeks after Napoleon III, with the aid of Piedmontese troops, went to war with Austria and opened a critical phase in the history of the Papal territories, the first number of the *Rambler* edited by Newman appeared. It carried two remarkable letters offering comments on the Italian situation. Newman wrote both of them. In their sure grasp of the political realities lying behind the troubles confronting the Papal States they present a stark contrast to most of the contemporary Catholic writings on the subject.

In the first letter Newman represented Italy as being in a state of moral and political decadence. And although he laid the main responsibility on the Austrians, the Papal government was condemned by implication: "The governments may not be worse than the people; but they must be as bad." Newman then pointedly asked:

[5] "The Italian Revolution—its Cause and Character," May, 1860, pp. 174–75.
[6] H. E. Manning, *The Temporal Power of the Pope* (London, 1880), p. 2.

What could France have done worse? Would there have been more deadness in priests and people, more relaxation and disorder in convents in this year 1859,—if France, and not Austria, had held Lombardy all these years by possession, Tuscany and the Duchies by relationship or special treaty, Naples by sympathy and good offices, and Rome by the ties of ancient alliance.[7]

In his second letter, "The Prospect of War" (dated April 2), he offered comments on the Papal territories that were hardly designed to harmonize with the popular Catholic opinion. He saw victory for France in the forthcoming war as holding out the only hope for improvement: "You will perceive that I am supposing the success of France when I speak of 'good,' for what good can come from the success of Austria, I am simply incapable of imagining." He then went on to make some searching observations which no amount of political or moral theorizing could disguise:

a war between Catholic powers is certainly a great scandal; but many will think that the presence of Austrian and French troops in the Pontifical States is a more grievous scandal still. Is it not portentous that the Holy Father, the Vicar of Christ, should be sustained on his throne against the rising of his own people by foreign bayonets? Is it not a thing to make a Catholic blush, to think that the mildest and kindest of men should be made to seem to the world like some Pygmalion, with no home in the affections of his people, no power of exciting their loyalty and veneration, no refuge but in their simple dread of the strong arm of Frank and German barbarians? And here is another thing to be considered—What is so contradictory as a ruler who cannot rule? St Peter had, indeed, not temporal kingdom, nor St Dionysius, nor St Sixtus; but according to the divine will, and for the good of the Church, such power was bestowed upon their successors. The Popes might have it, or they might not have it; but it is neither one thing nor the other to accept it and not be able to use it, to have the name and not the power. If it is the divine will that they should have a temporal sword, it is equally so that they should 'not bear it in vain'. It is an intolerable contradiction that they should reign and not rule. And further still, let it be recollected that one of the principal reasons in the line of expediency put forward, and reasonably put forward, for the Pope having a territory of his own, is, that he may be independent of Catholic powers; and the history of the Avignon Popes is reasonably quoted in favour of this expediency; but how is he independent of them if they garrison his country?[8]

---

[7] "Temporal Prosperity A Note of the Church" (signed: O. H.), *Rambler*, May, 1859 (Vol. i, N. S.).
[8] "The Prospect of War" (signed J. O.), *Rambler*, May, 1859.

He viewed not with unmixed dread the prospect of the impending war:

It will be worth a good deal, then, if the French open a way for replacing the lives of ecclesiastics at Rome on a better tenure than they have at present, and its temporal affairs on a better footing. It will be best, indeed, if this can be done by diplomacy under the threat of war, but without actual war; if there is a war, and this is its result, the guilt of the war must lie some where or other; but the war, with all its miseries, at least will have a compensation, which the Russian war, our pet plaything, had not.[9]

In the *Rambler* for July, the last edited by him, Newman devoted thirty pages to a broad coverage of the Franco-Austrian war. Though personal reflections were kept to a minimum his own dissatisfaction with the state of things in Italy occasionally broke through. Reviewing English sentiments he wrote:

As to the state of feeling of the Italian populations at the existing crisis, but one opinion prevails among the English public, which we have no means of saying is not founded on fact. There is in certain classes of the nation great discontent and restlessness, based on the feeling that Italy is behind the world in social and municipal respects. If they are educated, and employ their minds, they are either infidels, or at least speak with great disrespect of the ecclesiastical *régime*. They wish for revolution, if not for its own sake, at least as a necessary preliminary to reform and advance.[10]

It is difficult to determine to what extent Newman's residence in Italy during 1846–47 influenced his views on the Roman question.[11] The existing records of his Italian sojourn rarely touch on political matters. It is clear that he carried away a high personal regard for Pius IX, a regard he ever retained, and equally that he did not think highly of the men around the Pope. As he wrote to Acton in 1859: "For myself, certainly, I have found myself in a different atmosphere, when I have left the Curia for the Pope himself."[12] But while not impressed with the state of religion in Italy he did not believe that much could be accomplished by surrendering to the revolution. The fruits of conti-

---

[9] *Ibid.*

[10] "Current Events," *Rambler*, July, 1859, p. 279.

[11] A note of Acton's states that soon after Newman's return from Rome "he delivered lectures to his brethren, in defence of the temporal power." (CUL Add. Mss. 4989, 78). No further reference to this could be found.

[12] Ward, *Newman*, i, p. 635.

nental liberalism he saw manifested in the Italy of 1847 convinced him that liberalism run wild could be as dangerous in the political sphere as in the theological. Nevertheless, he was far too much of a realist to imagine that its threat could be met by maintaining the status quo.

Newman refused to accept the almost universal opinion current in England that Napoleon III was an untrustworthy schemer seeking only his personal aggrandizement. Although he did permit a harsh attack on Bonapartism, written by Wetherell, to appear in the July number of the *Rambler*,[13] he replied to it in the September issue in a letter entitled "Napoleonism not Impious."[14] "What I protest against, then," he wrote,

is not your correspondent's extravagant language, as I consider it, nor his running against facts, but his thinking it allowable to slander a remarkable man, merely because he does not understand him. I was far too cautious in my former letter,[15] and am in this, to take Louis Napoleon's part; but it is another thing altogether to indulge in invectives, nay slanderous invectives, against him. Public men have characters, as other men; and their characters are as dear to them. We should do as we would be done by. We may fairly criticise what they have done; we cannot fairly impute what they have not done as yet, and what they disown.

On receiving the above letter Acton, who had just assumed editorship of the *Rambler*, commented to Simpson:

More infatuated letters from Newman about Napoleon. He knows no good of him, and will not believe any harm. It is absurd to say what he says in the last sentence of his printed letter.[16]

The September issue of the *Rambler* also carried an article by Baron d'Eckstein[17] (translated by Simpson) severely treating the Napoleons.[18] To Acton's request for his judgment on the article Newman replied:

In answer to your question, I should say I thought the article on the Buonapartes clever & interesting—but I never can quite enter into the French style, which considers an epigram or an antithesis an argument, or rather a selfevident principle. I thought the writer asserted and brought out a view rather than proved it, and, though it *might* be more, yet it

---

13 "Thoughts on the Causes of the Present War," *Rambler*, July, 1859.
14 Signed: J. O.
15 See above, n. 8.
16 Acton to Simpson [26 August 1859], Downside Mss.
17 F. F. d'Eckstein (1790–1861), a Danish philosophical writer.
18 "The Political Systems of the Bonapartes." See Gasquet, *Acton*, p. 74.

was not shown to be more than one out of many views which might be taken of the subjects of it. I say this in no affection to uncle or nephew, for neither of them seems to me to have that nobility of mind which becomes, or rather which the imagination associates with, the possession of kingly power. They have the illbreeding which is imputed to low birth, at least, so it seems to me.[19]

On the notorious inscrutability of Louis Napoleon's designs Newman once wrote to a friend:

As to the French Emperor, is he not a waiter on Fortune, shaping his course by circumstances? . . . To say then that he is inscrutable, is merely to say that the future is hid from us, and, if we do not know what he will do, it is only perhaps because he does not know it himself.[20]

And upon Napoleon's downfall in 1870 he commented:

I can't help pitying exceedingly Louis Napoleon—he has done a great deal for France, and a great deal for the Church, a great deal for England —but Englishmen, Catholics and Frenchmen are all ungrateful to him. That his basis is hollow, and personal government is a shame and worse, is true—but what claim had he but his uncle's name, what rule of government but his uncle's traditions, what warrant but success like his uncle's? He did what he could—he has risen up to a great height, and his fall is tragical, more tragical than his uncle's.[21]

Yet, although Acton was probably close to the mark when he sensed infatuation in Newman's opinion of Napoleon III—an infatuation stemming from a romantic view of French history and of Napoleon I in particular—Acton himself, as shall be seen, in his hatred of Louis Napoleon and attachment to Austria strayed further from political realities than did Newman.

On January 19, 1860 Pope Pius addressed the Catholic world in an encyclical, *Nullis Certe*.[22] He protested against the obvious designs of the Italian movement and the apparent acquiescence of Napoleon III in the revolution. His words prompted expressions of sympathy from Catholics throughout Europe. In England Catholics planned a great public meeting at the Town Hall in Birmingham. It took place on February 14. Although both Newman and Acton were invited, neither in fact, was present. Newman, instead, wrote a letter to the President of the gathering, Lord Feilding, in which he expressed sympathy for the Pope,

[19] Newman to Acton, 24 October 1859, Woodruff Mss.
[20] Newman to Monsell, 29 November 1860, Orat. P.C.
[21] Ward, *Newman*, ii, p. 554.
[22] E. E. Y. Hales, *Pio Nono*, p. 204.

but carefully refrained from making any mention of his temporal power. The letter, which Acton called "remarkably diplomatic,"[23] is an interesting production:

Although [wrote Newman] I cannot promise myself the pleasure of attending the public meeting, over which you are to preside to-morrow, on the subject of the Pope's present afflictions, I yield to no one in the feelings to which it proposes to give utterance, and I trust my hand-writing may be allowed to speak for me instead of my presence with the Right Rev. Prelate and the Catholics assembled on the occasion. If ever there was a Pontiff who had a claim on our veneration by his virtues, on our affection by his personal bearing, and our devotion by his sufferings, whose nature it is to show kindness, and whose portion it is to reap dis-appointment, it is his present Holiness. If ever a Pope deserved to live in the heart of his own subjects, and to inspire at home the homage which he commands abroad, it is Pius the Ninth. From the hour that he ascended the throne he has aimed at the welfare of his States, temporal as well as spiritual, and up to this day he has gained in return little else than calumny and ingratitude. How great is his trial! but it is the lot of Popes, as of other men, to receive in their generation the least thanks, where they deserve the most. However, these reflections will doubtless be far better expressed in the eloquent speeches which will form the chief business of the evening, and I shall best consult for the object they have in view by bringing this letter to an end, and subscribing myself, dear Lord Feilding, very sincerely yours. . . .[24]

Newman's appended note to a copy of the above letter explains much:

I did not go to this meeting presided over by the Bishop, because, though its ostensible object, *which my letter availed itself of*, was to ex-press sympathy with him in his misfortunes, the *real* object was to be a demonstration in favour of the necessity of his *Temporal Power*.

To Acton he made the dry comments:

So you could not come to the Meeting. The Bp "consulted the faith-ful" for two hours and a half. There was great enthusiasm, except (I hear) among those who had prepared speeches & could not do justice to them. Your animosity to Louis Napoleon would have had a great gratification.[25]

Although most Catholics were filled with alarm at the pros-pects of the Papacy, Newman appeared almost to welcome the

---

[23] Gasquet, *Acton*, p. 122.
[24] A printed copy of the letter with a note appended is found in Newman's "Scrapbook," at the Oratory.
[25] 20 February 1860, Woodruff Mss.

Italian conflagration. To quote a letter to Sir Rowland Blennerhasset,[26] written a few days after the Birmingham gathering:

> Italy requires a thorough castigation & clearing out. And, when
> matters are finally settled, he [the Pope] will be stronger and firmer than
> he has been for a long while. Nothing is more wonderful in the past
> history of the Holy See than the transformation of its circumstances and
> its power of beginning, as it were, a new life in them.[27]

A note of Acton's records the following incident:

> Newman . . . argued in defence of the Italian war, and when the
> flood, rising, threatened the papal throne, he preserved a discreet and
> embarrassed silence, refusing to commit himself, even in private. An
> impatient M.P. went down to Edgbaston, and began, trying to draw
> him: These are terrible times, Father Newman. Look at what is doing
> in Italy. Yes, indeed! and look at China too, and New Zealand.[28]

And a further note relates:

> On St Philip's day [26 May] 1860, when Garibaldi was attacking
> Palermo, he [Newman] asked the congregation to pray for the Oratory
> there, in peril from an enterprising warrior. When a visitor suggested
> that he might seem to favour Garibaldi, he said, with a moment's irrita-
> tion: So I do, and I hope he will not stop until he gets to Naples, and
> to Rome too. This was reported.[29]

The report that Newman favored Garibaldi eventually reached
Rome and it was even believed (without foundation) that he had
contributed to a fund for Garibaldi.[30] The following entry is his
Personal Journal no doubt refers to the incident:

> At present the Temporal Power is the all important point at Rome—
> I, thinking that they would be obliged to rely more on reason, a truer
> defence, than on the sword, if they had it not, am lukewarm on the
> point; and this lukewarmness [h]as been exaggerated into a supposed
> complicity with Garibaldi![31]

Sir Rowland Blennerhasset, writing to Acton years later, seems
to have expressed rather accurately the motives underlying
Newman's lukewarmness:

[26] Sir Rowland Blennerhasset (1839–1909), a close friend of Newman, Acton
and Döllinger; liberal M.P. for Irish Constituencies 1865–85, married Charlotte
Julia Leyden in 1870.

[27] Newman to Blennerhasset, 20 February 1860, Blennerhasset Papers, CUL
Add. Mss. 7486, Item 52, Envelope 19.

[28] CUL Add. Mss. 4989, 77.

[29] *Ibid.*, 82.

[30] Newman to E. Bowles, 8 January 1872, Orat. P.C.

[31] *Autobiographical Writings*, pp. 259–60.

The Temporal Power had according to him a distinct tendency to strengthen the spirit of the world in the Church. The T.P. was not a thing either to be attacked absolutely or to be defended absolutely. It was perhaps, according to him, productive in our own time of more harm than good; at all events it was not to be defended in the wild way Manning defended it.[32]

Newman believed that a basis for a solution to the Roman Question could be found in the neutralization of Rome. As he saw it "temporal dependence was not inconsistent with spiritual independence *in se*." After all, he reminded Monsell, had not Pius VII, the *subject* Pope stood out against Napoleon, whilst Clement XIV "at the voice and by the intrigues of Catholic sovereigns" suppressed the Jesuits against his will. If Pius IX could "hold his own in spirituals tho' supported by French or Austrian bayonets," it was not "in the *nature of things*, or from the *reason of the case*, impossible that he should be able to do so, when, (not a subject, but) not a sovereign, i.e. in a neutral city."[33] A memorandum written in 1882 recalled the same idea: "I had no thought of making him a *subject* to any secular power. I thought he might have Rome and a slice of territory to the sea, or at least an honorary sovereignty."[34]

Acton, in the first year of his association with the *Rambler* took a much more conservative line than Newman on the Roman Question. He found it difficult to believe that a change favored by the bitterest enemies of the Church could really be for its ultimate benefit. It was not until the end of 1860 that he came to admit that a restoration of lost territories to Papal control might not be demanded in justice.

Acton's visit to Rome in 1857 first made him alive to the complex issues involved in the government of the Papal State. He was well received there and through Döllinger made contact with some of the most important Curial officials. The Journal he kept during his visit is rich in interesting observations on Roman affairs.[35]

Thus we read that Pius IX "gave the impression of great kindness and suavity, well acquainted with religious questions,

[32] Blennerhasset to Acton, 16 October 1890, CUL Add. Mss. 4989, 121 (extract in Acton's hand).

[33] Newman to Monsell, 17 March 1861, Orat. P.C.

[34] Ward, *Newman*, i, p. 521.

[35] CUL Add. Mss. 5751. Some of the observations in this Journal are obviously the fruit of conversations with Döllinger.

but not so with the state of other countries." His efforts to be a liberal pope failed so completely that "he has in reality abdicated all political power and authority, and leaves all that completely in Antonelli's hands." His judgment (or is it Döllinger's?) on Pius IX as a theologian is severe:

The Pope unfortunately has no knowledge whatever of theological matters, and this is very inconvenient in a personal point of view . . . now nobody feels that the Pope will think less of him because he knows nothing at all. Generally however it does little harm, as all things are so fixed and regulated by congregations &c.[36]

He was not impressed with Roman Scholars: "The Dominicans have no great men and no other order but the Jesuits has." But even the learning of Passaglia (one of the leading Jesuit scholars) was "commonplace."[37]

In his account of an interview with the Pope the prejudices imbibed during his Munich apprenticeship break through:

Friday—June 12th 1857. Saw the Pope at 9.o'clock this evening. Introduced by Talbot & [Cardinal] Pacca. He spoke very loud immediately on seeing me, that he was glad to see me, that he had been much pleased to see the mother of the Cardinal at Rome,[38] and remembered that I was with her. He asked if I was now returning to England, and what the Cath. expected from the new Parl. I said we had very little—da sperare, he interrupted. I said yes, but little also to fear—He said oh yes, Palmerston had made himself quite necessary in the present crisis, and appeared useful. I said he was less dangerous at home than abroad. Yes, he said, because he is quite an infidel, and cares not about Catholics but seems restless to disturb Catholic countries abroad. I observed that he disliked Catholics too, and that was part of his reasons for interference, especially in the Roman states. I added that the husband of my mother was a minister—oh yes, you are the son of the Lady Gr[anville] who was in Moscow. Well we have less to fear from Lord G.[ranville] but Gladstone I believe was better, and a Puseyite near Cath.[olicism]. I said that ambition made him useless, as it was a very bad thing. Oh he said, secundo me, le passioni inubbriacono li [sic] uomini come il vino, and when it masters them, makes them incapable of good. Then I said G.[ladstone] was also unsafe in foreign affairs, and he said yes, he had been carried away and deceived in Nap.[Naples].[39]

---

[36] *Ibid.*
[37] *Ibid.*
[38] Charles J. E. Cardinal Acton (1803–1847), an uncle of John Acton.
[39] The reference is probably to Gladstone's visit to Naples in 1850 and its aftermath (See Morley, *Gladstone*, pp. 389–404).

A conversation with Talbot was noted and particularly Talbot's high approval of the Austrians:

Monsignor Talbot on the day of my audience with the Pope, spoke with me for nearly an hour, sensibly but not remarkably. Nothing like disaffection has been shown since they started, tho' this is the worst part of the states. The people is everywhere well disposed. The nobles are worthless, have no courage or determination, and do no good, here or in Rome . . . The French in Rome are a very unsatisfactory set. The officers are all infidels, and only give less scandal because they have very little money. There is no trusting them, as any change at Paris wd. make them very dangerous. Soyon well meaning, Montréal the best they have had. The Austrians everyway better. Subordinate, respectful. They have greatly pleased the Pope. At Ancona many who were going home stayed another year to see the Pope. All behaved perfectly and can well be trusted; the pope conspicuously prefers them to the other—wish we had them in Rome.

He had several interesting observations to record on some of the basic weaknesses of the papal temporal government:

The pontifical states can never be well governed according to modern ideas because it has not yet gone through that which has influenced other states. Many things are not done by the government because it has not acquired the power of doing it. The people besides have no great *Trieb* like the English for municipal self-government. No great ends have caused all the powers of the state to be united for any common purpose. Besides men can do only one thing well—not both spiritual and temporal power. It can never be governed like the modern states, and one or the other must suffer. The spiritual government has never been injured by the temporal power. If it came ever to be considered as an impediment then the last hours of the papal states would have sounded. The Church was 700 years without a territory, and might be so again for 7,000 years. As things now are it cannot be, but such a state of things might be possible.

The above passage is pure Döllinger. Some years later Acton would challenge the thesis that spiritual advantage could ever justify defective temporal rule.[40]

Noticeably absent from Acton's Roman Journal were any serious reflections on the spiritual condition of the inhabitants of Papal territories. His interests seemed to have been held primarily by the political and intellectual character of Papal rule. Although it might be unfair to expect a twenty-three-year-old youth to be very much concerned with the spirituality of the

[40] See below, p. 80.

Italian world, yet the omission is of some significance since throughout his whole life he tended to regard the Church more as a political and educational organization than as a society primarily concerned with the salvation of sinners.

It would seem fair to conclude that Acton returned to England not greatly impressed with what he found at Rome, but not seriously disturbed. He saw much that was unsatisfactory but nothing that caused undue anxiety.

Acton's election to Parliament coincided with the opening of the Italian war. Though representing a formally Whig constituency he had little sympathy for the foreign policy of the Palmerston administration, a policy of neutrality almost certain to redound to the advantage of France and Sardinia against Austria. He considered himself as one who had "neither a party nor a leader."[41] His intense dislike for Napoleon III and his strong leanings toward Austria colored his approach to the question of temporal power and led him to advocate a much more conservative policy than that supported by Newman.

His article on the "Roman Question" in the *Rambler* for January, 1860 could be interpreted as an apologia for temporal power. He lamented the fact that all Catholics did not follow the unanimous opposition of the Episcopate to the attacks on the Papal States. The protests all came from Ultramontane quarters. It was to be regretted that "Ultramontane" was not recognized as synonymous with "Catholic." He considered the Italian war as but "one act in the execution of a design of which the end is the extermination of the Catholic Church." Austria was the first object of attack because she was the only country to have resisted the revolution: "The states which assisted the revolutionary movement against the Church combined against the state which was combating the revolution by the aid of the Church."

Acton, in his defense of Rome, readily admitted that there were defects in the government of the Papal States but insisted that the revolution was not aimed at correcting abuses but rather at destroying divine institutions. He saw an "irreconcilable disagreement, between the political notions of the modern world and that which is essentially the system of the Catholic Church." This disagreement manifested itself

particularly in their contradictory views of liberty, and of the functions of the civil power. The Catholic notion, defining liberty not as the power

[41] CUL Add. Mss. 4862, 11.

of doing what we like, but the right of being able to do what we ought, denies that general interests can supersede individual rights.

The modern state, based on the theory that authority was derived from the people and the general will was binding on all, destroyed Christian liberty whether the power was diffused or concentrated. Acton saw an inherent antagonism between the political system of an unbelieving age and that of the Catholic Church. There could be no question of the Pope coming to terms with such a system. He attributed the failure of the clerical rulers of the Papal States to provide good government to their efforts to compromise with the revolution:

with the revolution came centralisation, and the concentration into feeble hands of useless power . . . The people are not fit for the old system, the government is unfit to administer the new, which the people demand, and which is pressed upon it by the whole weight of the public opinion of Europe.

Is temporal sovereignty necessary to the Holy See? Acton went on to answer:

It is not absolutely essential to the nature and ends of the Church; it has its sources in causes which are external to her, in the temporal condition of the world, not the spiritual aims of the Church; and as the world becomes impregnated with her ideas, the necessity of the temporal power would probably disappear.

He dismissed summarily the consideration that the Church would be stronger in its own sphere if freed from the reproach of a defective temporal government:

It is hard to believe that both its friends and its enemies should have miscalculated to so great an extent; that a change which the Bishops of the Church have universally condemned, which no Catholic of note has anywhere admitted as a possibility, and which at the same time her bitterest enemies so eagerly labour to enforce, should in reality promise a great benefit to her.

It is significant that Wetherell on reading the above article felt constrained to offer his resignation. He believed that Acton had gone too far in his support of temporal power. However, on talking things over with Acton their differences were resolved and he resumed the assistant editorship.[42]

[42] Acton to Newman [? June 1860], Orat. P.C.; Gasquet, *Acton*, p. 115, n. 1. Wilfrid Ward (*Newman*, i, p. 508) inaccurately attributes Wetherell's resignation to ill-health.

In the "Foreign Affairs" of the March issue Acton turned to a consideration of the famous pamphlet, *Le Pape et le Congrès*, the officially inspired document which proclaimed to an angered Catholic world Napoleon's acceptance of the Romagna revolution as a *fait accompli*. He condemned roundly its conclusion that it was to the Pope's advantage to forsake his claim to the Papal States with the exception of Rome. He saw in the reasons adduced for the Pope's retention of Rome only "the artifice of preparing the future destruction of the Papal authority over Rome itself."

Newman was angered by the politics of the *Rambler* and protested against the inconsistency of its English anti-Toryism and foreign Toryism.[43] A note of Acton's reads: "When he [Newman] complained of inconsistency in the *Rambler*, Tory abroad and Whig at home, he meant its attitude on the Roman question."[44]

Acton's visit to Munich in the autumn of 1860 introduced a period of transition in his view of the Italian movement. He found Döllinger preoccupied with the future of the Papacy and reported to Simpson on the peculiar interests of the Munich spectators:

We must certainly be prepared to see the pope leave Rome and take refuge in Spain or Germany. If in Germany (at Würzburg, where there is a splendid palace of the old prince bishops and a faculty of theology, particularly Roman), the reaction upon German Protestantism will be immense. I had the luck to hear a long conversation on this point the other night between Döllinger and the ablest of the Bavarian Protestants. Their mutual confidence was astonishing to a beholder. Döllinger said that one thing at least was certain that the Romanism of the Church was destroyed for good, and the other was convinced that the presence of the Holy See in Germany, on the borderland of the two religions, must lead to the reunion of the German Protestants with the Church. But there are a great many more consequences connected with the fall of the Temporal Power, which when the time comes we must try to point out . . . In speaking of the loss of the Roman states I could not speak of the chance of a restoration, for a restoration of the old regime, and of the position of the pope as a ruler of millions, is I am persuaded, out of the question.[45]

Shortly after his return from Munich a new session of Parliament opened and the Italian question came up for discussion.

[43] Gasquet, *Acton*, p. 162; Ward, *Newman*, i, p. 637.
[44] CUL Add. Mss. 4989, 87.
[45] Acton to Simpson, 6 December [1860], Downside Mss.

Lord John Russell's policy, outlined in his speech of February 5th and 6th came in for heavy fire in the pages of the *Rambler*. Acton was strangely confident of the judgment of history on English policy:

A future historian will have better opportunities than a chronicler of contemporary events of describing the policy of the English cabinet in the Italian revolution. He will be able to prove that two ideas contended for the mastery among men united by no common principle, and divided by conflicting notions of religion and honour. One is a disinterested desire to see representative government, or at least representative action, triumphant in Italy; a desire honestly entertained, but coupled with a fatal eagerness to realise it even by the most treacherous and disloyal means. On the other hand he will be able to prove, what no man can detect in any thing published by ministers, the existence of a secret wish to put an end to the trouble and annoyance given in almost all parts of the empire by a religion which is difficult to deal with even on principles of religious liberty, and of a hope that this will be accomplished, that at least the hierarchical organisation, which renders Catholicism so formidable to statesmen, will be destroyed, by precipitating the Papacy into a ruin which no human institution could survive without a miracle. And perhaps it will be shown that the wish to see the divine character of the Church tested by such a trial was felt not only by those who hated her, but still more by those who feared her, because they had felt her influence, and who sought the solution of a religious problem as well as of a political difficulty.[46]

Early in March some of the Catholic members provoked a debate on the government's Italian policy. Acton prepared to speak but finally decided against it. He explained his reluctance to enter the debate to Simpson:

As to my speech about Italy, I will not waste powder, make enemies and get into so much trouble without an object and occasion. A man who never speaks cannot speak with effect on an unpopular question, and I do not know whether I could do any good at all.[47]

A draft of Acton's undelivered speech is found in his Cambridge notes.[48] It is not an impressive effort. He appeared torn between his anti-French, anti-revolutionary sentiments and the growing realization that some radical change was demanded in Italy. Whereas in his earlier writings he had refused to countenance

[46] "Current Events," *Rambler*, March, 1861, pp. 426–27.
[47] Gasquet, *Acton*, p. 172.
[48] CUL Add. Mss. 4862, 5 ff.

any suggestion that the Papacy might be better off if deprived of its extensive temporalities he now admitted that

the Roman state exists only for the Church. If it does not fulfill this end, and only if it ceases to be requisite for this end, it will come to an end. At present it undoubtedly does not. So far from being a source of independence it is one of dependence. The pope would be free without a territory, he is not free now, by reason of his territory. Besides, so large a territory cannot be wanted. Rome and a small state would be enough for good, and not enough for trouble and danger.[49]

He had finally arrived at Newman's 1859 position. But he remained an unrepentant Franco-phobe. His notes carry a curious tirade against English foreign policy:

A French orator said 20 years ago when a cordial alliance was understood to subsist between France and England: The English alliance is a lie. At present it appears that nobody amongst us has the courage to say the same, and what is in the hearts of all men, none have the courage to speak. Perhaps it will be well that truth should be uttered even by incompetent lips; perhaps it will be safer coming from me who has neither a party nor a leader, and whose plainness of speech commits nobody.

We have all seen the progress of things in France. We all remember the great services which marked the commencement of the present ruler, and the still greater promises he made. There was a time when he stood before the world as the saviour of society, as the protector of order in Europe, by the bonds in which he held a people incapable of governing itself; when he found friends among all the friends of order, and declared that his care would ever be to preserve the alliance of the two great conservative powers, England and Rome. And that alliance served him well. And the fidelity with which it was observed bordered in both cases upon infatuation. Then in alliance with him we struck a great blow at the preponderance of Russian despotism in Europe. We have not been the first to strike down the more dangerous preponderance of the despotism of France whose power and whose ambition, bold enough to be no longer perfidious, threatens our power not in the distant East only but at home, not our dependencies only but ourselves—and that not with armies only, but with a fleet more perfect than our own, in all material respects. Who is to be our ally in a conflict with him?

It is no credit to the wisdom of those who direct the destinies of this country that the natural affinity of their governments should have brought France and Russia at once together neutralising the effect of recent hostilities, before the discordance of every principle of policy and every consideration of honour has forced us to break with this unnatural alliance.

[49] CUL Add. Mss. 4862, p. 6.

If you did not know him then, when he revived the slave trade in Africa, and persecuted at home the admirers of English freedom, he stands revealed before us now . . .[50]

In the great war with France 3 per cent of the millions which it cost were enough to enable the coalitions of the military powers to renew those efforts which in spite of the revolutionary energy of the French people and of the military genius of their leader, twice carried them in triumph to Paris.

As many pence given to sustain the armies of Austria, whose poverty dogs the heroism of her soldiers and dooms them to waste their lives in fruitless contests, would save more than an equal no. of pounds hereafter.

The young parliamentarian clearly anticipated an attack on England when Napoleon III felt the time was ripe. Political wisdom demanded support of Austria. "Nothing can be less inscrutable or more easy to calculate than his policy," he had written of Napoleon III a few months previously, "nothing more certain than that some day a war with England will suit his interests, and that when that time comes he will not hesitate to declare it."[51]

Although Acton chose to remain silent himself he did not refrain from severely criticizing the Catholic members who did speak out in Parliament. In his review of the debate in the *Rambler* he took them to task for their abandonment of political principle.[52] He deplored that English Catholics were not

in possession of a political system, nor even of a comprehensive political principle. We are not so united in a common doctrine respecting authority, liberty, and right, that we should be ready to pursue it to its consequences, and to accept its results. We stand, not upon a political principle, but upon a religious interest, which we are unwilling to avow, and which we seek to disguise by whatever arts seem most specious, most popular, most suited to the audience, or to the occasion. We have therefore not even the pretence of agreement, nor the reality of consistency, nor the appearance of sincerity.[53]

In April Döllinger had delivered a series of lectures on the Temporal Power to crowded audiences in the Royal Odeon at Munich. He proceeded to paint such a black picture of papal misgovernment in past centuries that it appeared to many he was offering a justification for the revolution. (These lectures drew from the *Dublin Review* the caustic comment: "Döllinger

---

[50] The dots belong to the text.
[51] "National Defence," *Rambler*, September, 1860, p. 300.
[52] "Current Events, Home Affairs," *Rambler*, May, 1861, pp. 126–32.
[53] "Current Events, Home Affairs," *Rambler*, May, 1861, pp. 126–27.

is the Lingard of Germany—Lingard in his most unfavourable aspect—hard, dry and critical."[54]) The May number of the *Rambler* reflected the great influence of Döllinger's discourses. The "Foreign Affairs" on the Italian scene carried some startling (to the Catholic reader) observations. Acton frankly admitted the impossibility of maintaining the temporal power, and while expressing abhorrence for the principles of the revolution referred to its Italian phase as "Felix Culpa." "The sacrifice of power, like the sacrifice of property, could not be the spontaneous act of the Church," but since it was accomplished by the revolution it should be seriously considered whether it was not for the good of religion. Acton went on to lament that "the masters of religious thought maintained an impressive silence . . . Those who know Rome best are the least disposed to regret the temporal power." England was no exception to the rule that "where the greatest sanctity and the greatest wisdom are united, there is a belief that the revolution which has overthrown the temporal power has been directly a blessing to the Church."[55] It seemed only proper to the writer that an end to the discreet silence should first have been made by the German Ultramontanes:

It may be simply from the confidence which the superiority of German science confers, that they hold conscience supreme over policy, that they do not sacrifice truth to expediency, and that they observe no regard for persons or opinions, and no conditions in dispensing it.

Döllinger was held up as the realistic champion who clearly showed in his April lectures that the temporal power,

never of real substantial necessity to the Church, ceased to be a benefit when Consalvi accepted the inheritance of the French and that it has become an obstacle instead of a security to the liberty of the Holy See since the revolutionary movement has prevailed.

Since the Pope on principle could never come to terms with the revolution a temporary exile was demanded. The writer concluded with sober words which would not have been appreciated by most Catholic readers:

A very serious responsibility has been incurred by Catholics in allowing the expression of their reverence and attachment to the Holy See to silence so completely the sense of the dangers and evils of the Roman government, and of the urgency of a great reform. It may have helped,

[54] "Döllinger and the Temporal Power of the Pope," *Dublin Review*, May, 1861, p. 200.
[55] The allusion was to Newman. See Gasquet, *Acton*, p. 191; also below, p. 76.

in conjunction with the hostile fanaticism of the revolutionists, to delude the advisers of the Pope into the belief that in their policy of passive resistance they were defending what was regarded by the Catholics of every country as the common cause of the Church, and it may have led thousands into the belief that the triumph of the Italian revolution is a victory over an essential bulwark of their faith.

The *Rambler's* summary of Döllinger's discourses was based on a "defective and incorrect" report and did not accurately represent his position.[56] It was not until Döllinger's *Kirche und Kirchen: Papstthum und Kirchenstaat* was published in the autumn of 1861 that Acton realized that Döllinger after all supported the conventional Catholic view, viz., that the lost territories should be restored to the Pope. For the first time Acton found himself at odds with his Professor on an important issue.

Newman, however, was in agreement with Acton's comments. Indeed, his influence was probably decisive in deciding Acton's own position. At least Acton believed it was, for one of his notes reads: "Newman's influence made the Rambler anti-Roman. My defense of the Temporal Power."[57] And although there is no evidence that Newman ever actually encouraged the *Rambler* to take an anti-Roman line it is clear that he concurred with it in its new assessment of the Italian situation. Thus on May 2, 1861 Acton reported to Simpson:

I saw Newman, who was full of your praises. He said exactly what I have said on the Roman question, as to the general change of feeling in the new direction, the weight of authority all on one side, the time for speech and the time for silence, the futility of the bishops, the blessings of the revolution, etc. He ought to be ashamed not to pronounce himself.[58]

And on June 7, Newman himself wrote to Acton:

Your remarks on the Pope's temporal power in the last no. of the Rambler were not only interesting and instructive, but such, I think, as no one ought to find fault with.[59]

Why was Newman so reluctant to speak out? His long reply to Acton's importunings gives the answer:

[56] "Döllinger on the Temporal Power," *Rambler*, November, 1861, p. 1, (vol. vi, N.S.). The opposition his lectures aroused probably led Döllinger to take a more cautious line in his published work.
[57] CUL Add. Mss. 4988, 212.
[58] Gasquet, *Acton*, p. 188.
[59] Newman to Acton, 7 June 1861, Woodruff Mss.

And now as to myself, since you evidently wish me to say that I am not an advocate of the Temporal Power. I really do not feel there is any call on me to give my opinion—rather, duty lies the other way. It is difficult to state all my reasons.

1. The Duke of Wellington said that a great power cannot have a little war—and I say that a great subject cannot have a little book. Such a theme would require a whole treatise in order to bring out what I thought and why I thought it.

2. I simply have no right to speak. I am not called to do so by position, or any external relation. Why should I speak more than another? If I had deeply studied the subject, that might be a reason, *est cuique in sua arte credendum*. But what is the fact? Why, that my life has been cut up so that I have followed out nothing, and have got just a smattering of many things, and am an authority in none. I might have pursued history, or theology, or metaphysics; but I am at the end of my life, and have no claim to give an opinion in any one of them. You can't think how this weighs upon me. Every one has his *prima facie* view of things, and I have mine. I have a right to have it, no right to obtrude it on others. This would not justify me to pretend to hold what I do not see my way to hold, but it does oblige me not to profess what I do not see my way to prove.

3. Accordingly I think I fulfill my duty in keeping silence. You may be sure that people wish me to speak on the other side, and to maintain the Temporal Power. That I have not done; and the omission itself is going a great way. People take words in the last *Rambler*[60] to allude to me; and the very fact that I do not repudiate the sentiment ascribed to me there is in some measure avowing that sentiment myself. You may be sure that there are people watching me very narrowly, and who would rejoice if I brought out in any tangible form what they believe I hold in my heart.

4. I cannot but feel bound to consult for my *body* here. An imprudent act might get them into great trouble. To tell you something *in confidence*, already has Propaganda been on the point of inflicting a most serious injury on us, by altering, without telling us, our Rule, at the suggestion of others. It might destroy us by a stroke of the pen. The Pope out of kindness appointed me Head fourteen years ago. If I died, Propaganda would have a precedent, if it chose, of dispensing with our Rule, and choosing a second head for the body (please not to mention this) and in a number of other ways it might be our ruin.

5. But lastly, who saved us, in our late danger? It was the Pope himself, and the Pope only. I am bound in gratitude to him.[61]

Acton could derive little satisfaction from Newman's sensitive cautions. If Newman felt he had no right to speak out, what

[60] See above, n. 55.
[61] *Lord Acton's Correspondence*, pp. 32–33.

right had he? And to add to his frustration parliamentary life had become almost unbearable. There seemed no hope "of obtaining any influence" for his principles. He contemplated abandoning his political career. "I am sure I can do better in another sphere," he wrote to Newman.[62]

Newman was moved and wrote sympathetically to him:

I assure you I have felt much for you, and at the end of last Session, when I saw you looking so fagged and ill, I understood how much you had gone through in various ways.

But now to go on to something more practical. You talk of giving up public life—this is so grave a question and one which requires so much knowledge, which I have not, of the world, that I can't pretend to answer it—but this I will say—that I am sure you should not be two things at once, if you are to be either satisfactory . . . And so you, I fully think, must give up political life, or literary. What is it that is impeding your parliamentary action in behalf of Catholics? Is it not your writings or supposed writings? This is a large subject, but I need not say more—if I am right, I need not say more—and if I am wrong, you will be able to say so at once.

As to your writings—I have [been] trying to call them to mind; and, as far as I can do so, I must say there are none of them which I should not have thought it a feather in my cap to have written. I don't agree with you always in politics certainly—and of course, if I tried, doubtless I could find other points of difference—but I am speaking of them as a whole . . .[63]

But there were new troubles looming on the horizon. The anti-Roman line of recent *Rambler*'s had given grave offense in Rome and Cardinal Antonelli wanted something done about it. Acton's journalistic career was in the balance.

[62] Acton to Newman, 4 June [1861], Orat. P.C.
[63] Newman to Acton, 7 June 1861, Woodruff Mss.

IV. The Twilight of Liberal Catholic Reviews

As the revolutionary tide in Italy swept on unabated the attitude of the English government was jealously studied by Cardinal Antonelli. He associated the *Rambler* with the policy of the
Liberals, a policy which appeared to favor the revolutionaries
against the Pope. Catholic M.P.'s who supported the government were believed to be under the influence of the *Rambler*.
"Antonelli," Acton wrote to Newman, "told Blennerhasset of
Catholic MP's selling the pope for paper, so I have had a hit at
those who would give up paper for the pope."[1] The intervention
of Antonelli, however, could not be dismissed with a quip.

Manning, who by this time had taken over from an ailing
Wiseman the effective leadership of the Church in England,
informed Acton that a censure of the *Rambler* was impending
from Rome owing to its line on the temporal power and advised
him to disengage himself from the Review in time to escape it.[2]
Newman, on learning this, saw no alternative to the suspension
of the *Rambler* and advised Acton accordingly, while expressing
the thought that he would not be sorry to see his literary under-
takings "taking a less ephemeral shape than the pages of a magazine."[3] Acton was thoroughly annoyed. "This is not a time," he
replied, "in which I can consider whether it would not be more
agreeable to have all my time free for more serious work than
the Rambler . . . I should be sorry to think that you consider it
useless as well as impossible to go on with it."[4] In a further

[1] Acton to Newman [29 June 1861], Orat. P.C.
[2] Ward, *Newman*, i, pp. 522–523.
[3] Ward, *Newman*, i, p. 523.
[4] Acton to Newman, [29 June 1861]. Orat. P.C.

78

exchange of correspondence the whole question of the relations of a Catholic review to ecclesiastical authority and to the public was vigorously discussed. Newman, to whom, from Anglican days, "A Bishop's lightest word *ex cathedra*" was heavy,[5] had a far greater respect for authority than Acton could ever arouse. He insisted against Acton that the *Rambler* did come under ecclesiastical authority since it was "ever nibbling at theological questions."[6] Further, since it delighted in hitting at ecclesiastical authority it could be expected that authority would hit back, and the public would not think it "surprising or a shame."[7]

In spite of an exceedingly trying period Acton's regard for Newman does not appear to have been in any way diminished. When Newman wrote to him in August that he was "put on the sick list and told to wander about,"[8] Acton coaxed him to accompany him to Munich for a holiday:

> It would, I am sure, do you a great deal of good; and there are mountains and lakes and rustic dwellings an hour or two from Munich which are the best place in the world to recruit. A little while out of England would do you greater service than a much longer rustication in this country.[9]

But Newman chose to remain in England.

Although the threatened censure of the *Rambler* was not forthcoming a new crisis arrived during Acton's absence in Munich. Burns refused to publish the Review without a new arrangement which would be a guarantee to the Catholic public.[10] To Simpson's suggestion that complete control be given to Newman he demurred, stating that among other things the great objection to Newman was his unpopularity. Newman felt this acutely. He continued to urge Simpson and Wetherell that the *Rambler*, having lost its position among Catholics, was in a false position and had better be suspended.[11] They, however, chose to continue under a new publisher, William and Norgate.

[5] *Apologia*, p. 77.
[6] Ward, *Newman*, i, p. 527.
[7] *Ibid.*, i, p. 534.
[8] Ward, *Newman*, i, p. 534.
[9] Acton to Newman [August, 1861], Orat. P.C. The first page of this undated letter is not extant.
[10] In a long letter to Newman, dated 30 September [1861], Orat. R.C. Simpson gave a full account of his lengthy correspondence with Burns.
[11] Newman to Simpson, 4 October 1861, Orat. R.C.; Newman to Wetherell, 5 October 1861, Orat. R. C.

The Roman Question continued as the great topic of the day. In the first number under the new publishers two important articles appeared. Acton devoted a long article to a review of Döllinger's new book, *Kirche und Kirchen*,[12] and Simpson severely criticized Manning's extravagant lectures on the temporal power.[13]

Acton, in his article, carefully refrained from betraying his "disagreement with Döllinger on the question of the restoration" of papal territories.[14] Döllinger, though admitting the grave shortcomings in the papal government, went on to argue that the advantages to religion demanded a restoration. His object, as Acton wrote in 1890, was not materially different from that of Antonelli and Merode.[15] Acton would not grant this. The plea of religious advantage could never justify misgovernment or else "the Romans would be worse off than other people because of the Pope.[16] In his opinion the Powers had clearly no right "to restore the Pope for the sake of religion" unless they restored freedom "for the sake of the people."[17] A guarantee of political reform should be a *conditio sine qua non* of restoration.

As 1862 progressed Acton reached the resolution to convert the *Rambler* from a bi-monthly publication to a quarterly doubled in size. Such an arrangement, he felt, would cater better to serious articles, and the extended period between publications would assure improved work and a reduction of the strain involved in more frequent printings.[18] To preclude any opposition from the *Dublin Review*, he wrote to Dr. Russell of Maynooth informing him of the proposed change and assuring him

[12] "Döllinger on The Temporal Power," *Rambler*, November, 1861.

[13] "Dr. Manning on the Papal Sovereignty." Wilfrid Ward (*Newman*, i, p. 536) following a reference to this article states: "It was now certain that the *Rambler* would not be allowed to continue its existence as a Catholic Review, approved or even tolerated by the Episcopate. The alternative before its conductors was either to acquiesce in Newman's verdict and simply suspend publication, or to make some change in name and form which might possibly secure it a fresh start and fair trial. Acton and Simpson chose the latter course." There seems no basis in fact for this interpretation. Three more numbers of the *Rambler* (January, March, May, 1862) did appear and there is no evidence that fear of immediate censure prompted the change-over to the *Home and Foreign*.

[14] Gasquet, *Acton*, p. 241.

[15] *History of Freedom*, p. 414.

[16] Gasquet, *Acton*, p. 229.

[17] *Ibid.*

[18] Acton to Russell, 26 March 1862, Westminster Archives.

that he was most unwilling to do anything which might be interpreted as an aggression against the *Dublin*.[19] Dr. Russell replied to him at once in "a friendly letter, begging him at all events not to take any public step for a little while," and thereupon immediately informed Wiseman and Bagshawe.[20] He urged them to merge the *Dublin Review* with the *Rambler*. "I feel strongly," he wrote to Wiseman, "that it is impossible to carry it on satisfactorily any farther, and I think the most honourable close of its career would be to merge it or let it be merged in the new Quarterly."[21]

Newman, who was consulted by Acton, thought that an amalgamation of an independent Review with one sponsored by a Cardinal was out of the question:

How is it possible then that either the Dublin or its conductors can in any distinct way sanction the Rambler, which is *nullius addictus jurare in verba magistri?* As well might Lord Derby commit himself to the Times or the Eclectic Review (if it still exists) as a Cardinal have relations with a publication which professes to be simply free in questions which are not *de fide*.[22]

Wiseman once again was reluctant to have anything to do with the *Rambler* people. After much indecision he decided to carry on with the *Dublin Review* and in October the irrepressible W. G. Ward took over its editorship from Bagshawe.[23]

As it became apparent that a merger with the *Dublin* was an idle dream the conductors of the *Rambler* went ahead with the original plan to convert it into a quarterly. They were most anxious that Newman's support be continued and Wetherell kept him informed on proceedings.[24] But Newman was cautious. He declined to comment on a draft prospectus submitted to him, preferring to wait until two or three numbers were brought out before deciding whether the review "has been successful in obliterating the associations w*h*[ich] at present attach to its name."[25]

[19] Acton to Russell, 26 March 1862, Westminster Archives.

[20] Russell to Wiseman, 27 March 1862, Westminster Archives.

[21] *Ibid*. Wilfrid Ward wrongly implies that the initiative for the merger came from Acton and that it was prompted by the financial situation of the *Rambler*. He makes no mention of the difficulties of the *Dublin Review*. (See Ward, *Newman*, i, p. 537, n. 1).

[22] Newman to Acton, 5 May 1862, Woodruff Mss.

[23] Ward, *Newman*, i, p. 547.

[24] Acton to Newman, 5 April 1862, Orat. P.C.; Wetherell to Newman, 20 March 1862, Orat. R.C.

[25] Newman to Wetherell, 13 April 1862, R.C.

The final issue of the *Rambler* came out in May. In its prospectus announcing the forthcoming change it was made clear that the new review was to be a continuation of the old:

We trust that the history of the *Rambler* affords a sufficient guarantee for its continued maintenance of those principles to which it owes its distinctive character, its past difficulties, and the success it has finally attained.[26]

It was not even mentioned that the Review was to bear a new name: *The Home and Foreign Review*. Acton explained to Monsell the reason why the link with the old Review was so carefully maintained: He wished to keep a hold on Newman and maintain his connection as a former editor of the *Rambler*.[27]

The decision not to make a new beginning meant that the bishops remained as suspicious of the new journal as of the old. This was of some importance for in May, 1862 Cardinal Barnabò, the Prefect of Propaganda, sent them an instruction to issue a circular warning the faithful against the *Rambler*.[28] Though in the same month the final number of the *Rambler* appeared there was no question in the bishops' minds that the instruction did apply to the forthcoming *Home and Foreign Review*. However, it was not until October that they finally acted and, with one exception, in their pastorals issued a formal protest against the *Rambler* and the *Home and Foreign*.[29]

In the meantime, Newman found that his reputed support for the *Home and Foreign* was the source of new troubles. Reports reached him that the future of the Oratory School was in jeopardy. A letter to Mrs. Wootten from an anxious mother who had three sons at the school, suggests his perplexing position, pulled between loyalty to Acton and Simpson and his obligations to parents and to his fellow Oratorians:

Surely Edgbaston is safe from party intrigues. It cannot be that the School, of so much value to our children and their children's children is to be smashed for certain ideas bordering on German Rationalism, mooted in the Review. And yet strange rumors of *excommunication* and schism are reported, (more than hinted at) and a nasty party is chuckling over the total overthrow of Edgbaston in consequence. Oh, *I* hope and

---

[26] "Enlargement of the 'Rambler,' " *Rambler*, May, 1862, p. 430.
[27] Monsell to Newman, 11 and 19 November 1862, Orat. P.C. See also Newman's note on Monsell's letter of 11 November Orat. R.C.
[28] [Cuthbert] Butler [*The Life and Times of Bishop*] *Ullathorne*, vol. i, p. 322.
[29] Wilfrid Ward, *W. G. Ward and the Catholic Revival*, p. 154.

trust such a calamity will never take place. I cannot tell you all I know, from very high authority: But I, having three boys at Edgbaston am quite in a *nervous state* of suspense.[30]

The October number of the *Home and Foreign* brought Newman a fresh cause for dissatisfaction. It carried an article by Simpson[31] with highly speculative comments on the first chapter of Genesis "lugged in without any occasion."[32] Newman was thoroughly annoyed. He wrote to Thomas Arnold in disgust:

Alas, why will not reviewers leave that chapter alone? It is not contemporary literature. The Review is not a retrospective one. A grave, *ex professo*, comment indeed, a learned, argumentative discussion upon it, this will always be worth reading; but . . . the article in question does not attempt such a process. If I must describe it I should call it a speculation edged with an insinuation, or an insinuation hoisted on a speculation.[33]

At this juncture English Catholics seem to have been completely exasperated with the Review. Monsell reported what must have been the general sentiment to Newman:

I have been much among the English Catholics in the last month, & they are so furious against the Home & Foreign that it is useless to argue with them about it.[34]

Why should an admittedly able Catholic review so arouse the hostility of the Catholic body? The following letter written to Simpson by one who was favorably disposed to the *Home and Foreign* goes a long way towards providing the answer:

You wished me to put on paper the substance of what we were talking about the other day; and I do so because I am sure you will not mistake me or suppose that I am actuated by other than a most friendly spirit towards the H. & F.

In the first place as to the line formerly pursued by the Rambler, I have the strongest feeling that it was faulty in the following ways—As a Catholic periodical touching on theological subjects it sadly lacked what one means by loyalty to the Church. It never seemed to make the Church's cause its cause. I don't mean the cause of Cardinal Wiseman or any special clique in the Church, but in no sense did it identify itself with the Church or attempt her vindication. There must be *some facts*

[30] Mrs. Charlton to Mrs. Wootten, 15 or 22 October 1862, Orat. R.C. (copy).
[31] "Döllinger on Heathenism and Judaism."
[32] Ward, *Newman*, i, p. 543.
[33] Ward, *Newman*, i, p. 543.
[34] Monsell to Newman, 7 November [1862], Orat. P.C.

which make for the Church as well as against her but the R never discovered them. The Rambler was great in criticising the blunders of Catholics, but when did it stand up for the faith?

It presented the strongest contrast to the writings of Döllinger or Bronson [sic]. These authors are fearless and independent enough in asserting what they believe to be the truth but no one can doubt their sincere love for the Church and devotion to her interests. I don't mean to doubt your loyalty as individuals but in the Rambler it escaped notice. Again there was I should say a complete absence of all sense of responsibility. You never seemed to write as men dealing with matters of grave import. You went at subjects requiring the most delicate handling in the most reckless manner. You never seemed to weigh the probable effect of what you were going to write—whether it was likely to advance or impede the cause of truth—so that you gave the impression of being careful perhaps about particular truths, but indifferent to the truth as a whole.

As to the Home & Foreign I think the particular ground on which the Cardinal attacks it very weak, but he condemns it as a continuation of the R. You have then an excellent opportunity of putting yourself on a proper footing. I cannot say how glad I should be could you express your unwillingness to be identified with the Rambler, your regret at certain mistakes that journal made; could you give something like an assurance that a different spirit will be found in the Home & Foreign. I think you will show that a Catholic periodical cannot exist as such in open war with the Episcopate.[35]

But Acton had no intention of discontinuing the *Home and Foreign* or of eating humble pie at the court of the bishops. Although he acknowledged that Rome had "virtually spoken" he decided that it should be carried on in spite of her.[36]

The case of Wetherell presented a new complication. He offered his resignation and only with difficulty was Acton able to persuade him to withdraw it. However, he continued to feel that he was being used as a scapegoat to conceal an offensive alliance between Acton and Simpson.[37] Acton, with the apparent object of pacifying Wetherell and creating the impression in Catholic circles that Simpson had no further say in the Review, persuaded Simpson to give up *nominally* his part-proprietorship. He was thus able to write to Monsell and Newman that Simpson no longer was a proprietor.[38] Monsell hopefully remarked to

[35] J. W. Roberts to Simpson (undated letter in Downside Mss.).
[36] Acton to Simpson [9 December 1862], Downside Mss.
[37] Acton to Simpson [4 November] and 21 December [1862], Downside Mss.
[38] Acton to Newman, 23 December [1862], Orat. R.C.; Monsell to Newman, 11 January [1863], Orat. P.C.

Newman: "I presume that Simpson's disconnection with it will gradually ooze out."[39] Simpson, however, never entirely acquiesced in what he felt was a dishonorable arrangement, and during the remaining life of the Review Acton had considerable difficulty retaining his compliance.[40]

Newman was very much impressed by the high standard achieved by the *Home and Foreign*. He continued to hope that it would establish itself and gain general favor. To F. G. Lee of the *Union Review* who sent him a copy containing aspersions on the *Home and Foreign* he replied with a sharpness which must have left the well-intentioned Mr. Lee breathless:

My dear Sir,

I thank you for the copy of the Union Review &c &c. I cannot but feel sorry for the terms in which, as I cut open the leaves, I saw the Review speak of the Rambler and Home and Foreign. In Article 1, it is a 'semi-infidel periodical'. In Article 2, the persons whom it represents have 'culminated in a slough (i.e. risen to a depth?) of semi-infidelity'. In Article 3, they are "a school of rationalizing speculators."

It is said 'Hit because he is down'. *I* certainly would rather keep hands off from men whom I believe to be good Catholics, and take a deep interest in.

I am reminded of my own words, 'Controversy in this age is a sort of night battle, in wh. friend and foe stand together'.

To call the writings of these men semi-infidel, without clear grounds, is surely something more than ungenerous and cruel. They themselves would feel it to be calumnious. I say, 'without clear grounds' for I am led to speculate whether your three writers conscientiously believe the work to be semi-infidel on their own examination of it, or on authority (as they suppose) of the Bishop of Birmingham.[41] Are they willing then after all to submit to his authority? Are they ready to submit to his judgment upon their own publications, their own position, their own duty?

Excuse this frankness and believe me &c &c.[42]

But shortly after his zealous defense Newman was distressed to read in the January number of the *Home and Foreign* a contro-

---

[39] Monsell to Newman, 20 January 1863, Orat. P.C.

[40] Simpson to Acton, 23 December [1862] and 2 March [1863], Woodruff Mss.: Simpson to Acton [4 March 1864], Downside Mss.

[41] Bishop Ullathorne had followed up his Pastoral letter with a pamphlet against the methods and opinions of the *Rambler* and *Home and Foreign*. See Butler, *Ullathorne*, i, pp. 322 ff.

[42] Newman to Lee, 11 January 1863, Orat. R.C. (Newman's copy).

versial article on Charles Périn by M. Roscher.[43] The article was translated and adapted by Acton with no mention that the original writer was not a Catholic. Newman was aggrieved that Acton had not published frankly that the writer of such an article was a Protestant, or at least had informed the world that he admitted Protestant articles into the Review. He wrote to Monsell:

> Sir John will say, 'words are words; the sentences run the same whoever wrote them'. But this is only half the truth, for the *meaning* is not the same in a Protestant & in a Catholic. When M. Roscher spoke of 'so-called orthodoxy', he had an heretical meaning; and what he has himself, he may, by the tone & spirit of his writing, whatever words he uses, convey to another . . . I am not prepared to say that Catholics may not write in the same Review with Protestants; but surely such a Review cannot be called, and ought not to be called, a Catholic publication. In what sense *is* the Home and Foreign Catholic? Sir J. Acton is still some years on the youthful side of 30; he will recognise his imprudence some time hence.[44]

As 1863 progressed it appeared that a certain *modus vivendi* had been achieved and Newman's hopes increased that the very able *Home and Foreign* would finally gain the recognition it deserved. But in the heated atmosphere of the 1860's when the Papacy was attacked from all sides, "loyalty" to the Papal line was at a premium. The cold, detached tone of the *Home and Foreign*, interrupted intermittently by a severe instruction to the "ignorant" Catholic body, held slight appeal for most Catholics. A time of crisis was not the best time to point out their shortcomings and if it was to be done at all required consummate tact. But tact was a rare quality in Victorian Catholic journalism.

The timid found the frank approach of the *Home and Foreign* writers to problems of the day unsettling. Most Catholics tended to reply to the challenge of the new skepticism by denying that it really constituted a challenge. Ill-equipped to meet the enemy on its own grounds they sought to retreat into old shelters which were inadequate and as often as not suffered from rotten foundations. The *Home and Foreign* writers, very much alive to the shortcomings of old methods in the face of modern advances, were sometimes suspect of leading unsuspicious readers to infidelity because they frankly stated the nature of the challenge

---

[43] "Périn's Political Economy."
[44] Newman to Monsell, 28 January 1863, Orat. R.C.

facing Christianity. Monsell, for instance, wrote to Newman at the end of 1863, that Father Vaughan told him that "he has heard of two cases of apostasy caused by the Rambler & Home & Foreign."[45] Newman replied in a characteristic fashion:

> I don't believe the case of apostasy caused by the Home & Foreign; that is I should require to cross-examine witnesses before I considered they had evidence . . . I can easily *conceive* (tho' I trust and believe not) that a wavering mind would be disgusted and lose heart and faith from the fact that the Bishops &c so strongly opposed it—and to ascertain how the facts lay between these two hypotheses would be the drift of a cross-examination.[46]

But events abroad were rushing to a climax the whole question of the position of the Catholic intellectual relative to ecclesiastical authority. These events more than anything that occurred at home were to prove decisive in determining the ultimate fate of England's first and last Liberal Catholic Review.

The two Catholic congresses held at Malines and Munich in the last quarter of 1863 opened a critical phase in the history of Liberal Catholicism. To the enthusiastic Catholics gathered at Malines who heard Montalembert on August 20 and 21 deliver his famous discourses in favor of freedom and toleration it seemed that a new era had dawned for the Liberal Catholic movement.[47] This impression was heightened when within a month the Malines Congress was followed by a gathering of German Catholic scholars in Munich who boldly championed freedom of inquiry and asserted the inestimable value of scientific scholarship.[48] It was this latter gathering especially that held Acton's attention. Döllinger was the moving spirit behind it. In his Presidential address he set the theme for the whole Congress. He dealt with the shortcomings of the scholastic method and stressed the urgent need of a reassessment of scholastic theology in the light of recent biblical and historical criticism. In his opening address he conveyed something of the contempt with which German scholars viewed Italian theologians, who largely made up the entourage of the Pope. In Döllinger's mind German scholars had the duty to lead the Church to salvation.[49]

[45] Monsell to Newman, 3 December [1863], Orat. P.C.
[46] Newman to Monsell, 27 December 1863, Orat. P.C.
[47] R. Aubert, *Le Pontificat de Pie IX*, pp. 250–53.
[48] *Ibid.*, pp. 205–209.
[49] "The Munich Congress," *Home and Foreign Review*, January, 1864.

Acton saw a new Jerusalem on the horizon. In the *Home and Foreign* for February he presented a glowing report of the Munich Congress.[50] He concluded with an outline of the important results that would issue from it:

By being faithful to this its origins it will have power to infuse a new spirit into the Catholic body, and to create a new and authoritative centre of learning, which shall prevent hereafter the conflict between science and religion. It will enable the Catholic writers of Germany to vindicate the Church from the reproach that faith is inimical to freedom, that we are hampered in our investigations, that we acknowledge a power which may prevent the publicity of truth, or impose untruths on our behalf. Then indeed it will mark the dawn of a new era, and will justify the words of the Bishop of Augsburg, that, in giving the impulse to it, Dr. Döllinger has set the crown on the splendid series of his services to the Church.

Acton was brought down to earth again with a rude shock. Rome had no intentions of surrendering the direction of the Church to a coterie of German scholars. The Munich conference following so closely upon the Malines gathering convinced the Pope that the time had come for him to reassert the authority of Rome. He did so in a brief to the Archbishop of Munich dated December 21, 1863. Acton, in his masterful essay, "Conflicts with Rome,"[51] summarized as follows the substance of the decree in its bearing on his own efforts:

Besides the censure of the doctrines of Frohschammer, and the approbation given to the acts of the Munich Congress, the Brief contains passages of deeper and more general import, not directly touching the action of the German divines, but having an important bearing on the position of this *Review*. The substance of these passages is as follows: In the present condition of society the supreme authority in the Church is more than ever necessary, and must not surrender in the smallest degree the exclusive direction of ecclesiastical knowledge. An entire obedience to the decrees of the Holy See and the Roman congregations cannot be inconsistent with the freedom and progress of science. The disposition to find fault with the scholastic theology, and to dispute the conclusions and the method of its teachers, threatens the authority of the Church, because the Church has not only allowed theology to remain for centuries faithful to their system, but has urgently recommended it as the safest bulwark of the faith, and an efficient weapon against her enemies. Catholic

50 *Ibid.*
51 *Home and Foreign Review*, April, 1864. Reprinted in Acton, *Essays on Freedom and Power*, edited by Gertrude Himmelfarb (London, 1956).

writers are not bound only by those decisions of the infallible Church which regard articles of faith. They must also submit to the theological decisions of the Roman congregations, and to the opinions which are commonly received in the schools. And it is wrong, though not heretical, to reject those decisions or opinions.

In a word, therefore, the Brief affirms that the common opinions and explanations of Catholic divines ought not to yield to the progress of secular science, and that the course of theological knowledge ought to be controlled by the decrees of the Index.[52]

Acton felt that neither he nor his associates could yield their assent to the opinions put forward in the Munich Brief. There was no alternative to ending the Review:

No Catholic can contemplate without alarm the evil that would be caused by a Catholic journal persistently labouring to thwart the published will of the Holy See, and continuously defying its authority. The conductors of this *Review* refuse to take upon themselves the responsibility of such a position.[53]

The decision to stop the *Home and Foreign* was no doubt a disappointing one to Acton. Nevertheless it would be wrong to assign to it the character of a tragedy or to picture Acton emerging broken from futile efforts to help his unappreciative coreligionists. There were other factors present which made the step a less distressing one than is commonly supposed. Mention already has been made of the difficulties with Wetherell and Simpson. Another problem was the perennial one which has brought an end to many excellent reviews: falling circulation. Thus a month before stopping the Review Acton wrote to Simpson:

I would not horrify W.[etherell], if it is not necessary, by reports of our small circulation, for several reasons. When he took an increased allowance he said it was on the supposition that money was beginning to come in; and he would therefore be disturbed to find it so little.[54]

Had the Munich Brief never appeared the position of the *Home and Foreign* would still have been critical and Acton probably abandoned it with a certain relief. "For myself," he wrote to Newman, "I shall rejoice at the freedom and leisure I shall obtain for work of another kind, and in this I believe I shall have your kind wishes and encouragement."[55]

[52] *Essays on Freedom and Power*, pp. 264–65.
[53] *Ibid.*, pp. 270–71.
[54] Acton to Simpson, 7 February 1864, Downside Mss.
[55] Acton to Newman, 15 March 1864, Orat. P.C.

Newman was grieved to learn of Acton's decision. He believed that the Review had been "improving, number after number, both in religious character and literary excellence."[56] Still, he was glad that Acton was finally released from work that was unworthy of his talent. Surely now he would get down to the great historical work he was capable of executing!

Concurrently with the ending of the *Home and Foreign Review* an event took place which was destined profoundly to alter Newman's standing in the Catholic community and give him a position from which he could not be dislodged by all the fire of his opponents, Catholic or Protestant. Charles Kingsley attacked his veracity and drew from Newman his incomparable *Apologia Pro Vita Sua*. Though at first sight there might seem to be little connection between the disappearance of a Liberal Catholic Review and the writing of a personal apologia, closer study reveals that the two events were not unrelated and that Acton can claim at least a small part of the credit for Newman's triumph.

To understand why Newman wrote the *Apologia* one must revert to his Anglican days. He did not write it to answer the furious tirade of a Kingsley. He wrote it to show England that he, John Henry Newman, ever acted in an honorable way in the years leading up to his reception into the Catholic Church. Thus, while actually engaged in its composition he wrote to Dean Church: "It has always been on my mind that perhaps some day I should be called on to defend my honesty while in the Church of England."[57] And to James Hope Scott: "I have never defended myself about various acts of mine, e.g. No. 90,[58] so I am actually publishing a history of my opinions."[59] Newman retraced his Anglican career in his *Apologia* and when he reached 1845 in his narrative his work was done. *His* apologia was ended.

Why, then, did he choose to take upon himself the responsibility of answering the charge of dishonesty levelled against Catholics in general? After all, he had no call to offer a general defense of the Catholic Church. His career as a Catholic had so

[56] Ward, *Newman*, i, pp. 565–66.
[57] Ward, *Newman*, ii, p. 19.
[58] Tract 90, the famous Tract in which Newman sought to give a Catholic interpretation to the 39 Articles.
[59] Ward, *Newman*, ii, p. 14.

far been largely a succession of failures. He was out of sympathy with the hierarchy on almost every major question of the day. His mood, reflected so painfully in his Personal Journal, was hardly such as to prompt him to rush into print with a defense of anyone but himself.

Undoubtedly his sense of loyalty influenced him to defend his fellow Catholics against the cruel imputations of Kingsley. But this is not the whole answer. The episode of the *Home and Foreign* must also be taken into consideration. Although Acton had in a dignified manner stopped the Review he had no illusions about the interpretation Protestants would place on his action. They would see in it one more example of Papal suppression of freedom of expression. "I fear," he wrote to Newman after reaching his decision, "it will be difficult to make Protestants regard the event in a light which shall not be injurious to religion."[60] And on hearing rumors that Newman was contemplating replying to Kingsley's pamphlet, "What Then Does Dr. Newman Mean?," he wrote to him an important letter outlining the sentiments prevailing in Protestant circles:

All admit, so far as I have heard, and I have heard several of Kingsley's relatives and friends, the victory you gained in your first pamphlet, and the failure of the attack upon you in Kingsley's reply. There they say that your dialectics were triumphant, but that you did not take, as you were not bound, or even invited to take, the general defence of the Catholic clergy. This, they conclude, would be very difficult, and they see in your omission another proof of your skill and good judgment. In these minds, therefore, and I must include among them several of the most eminent intellects both in literature and in the state, the effect of the controversy is adverse to the Church almost in proportion as it is favorable to you. They connect with this question several instances that have occurred of late years, and even some things with which the H. & F. Review has been mixed up.[61]

This was forthright language, and must have affected Newman considerably. Acton's remarks would not have been lightly received. The inference was clear: if Newman simply offered the world a personal apologia he might do more harm than good to the Church. The English Protestant world would exclaim: What a rare being is Dr. Newman, an honest Romanist!

Acton then went on to express a fear that there was danger of ill effects "if the discussion is narrowed," or if it avoided a dis-

[60] Acton to Newman, 15 March 1864, Orat. P.C.
[61] Acton to Newman, 10 April 1864, Orat. A[pologia] C[ollection].

cussion of the practice of "proscribing truth and positively encouraging falsehood in the Church." He saw no way out but "a discussion of the question which shall be so complete as to enlighten not only the Protestants but such Catholics as have got a little confused by the policy which is adopted in order to avoid scandal."

Acton's letter found Newman feverishly engaged in writing the first part of the *Apologia*. Coming from one who was so exact in his use of words his reply shows that he attached great importance to Acton's counsels:

> Your letter is a very valuable one to me. I am writing from morning till night, and against time, which is not pleasant—this is the cause that I have not thanked you before, & why I do not write longer now. I get so tired.

> As to the points you mention, you may be sure I shall go as far as ever I can.[62]

"Your letter is a very valuable one . . . you may be sure I shall go as far as ever I can"—here was an assurance that the *Apologia* was not to be a simple justification of John Henry Newman but would embrace a wider field.

Once again, on reading in the *Saturday Review* Longman's advertisement for Newman's forthcoming reply to Kingsley, Acton wrote to Newman anticipating that he would "take the opportunity of speaking not only *pro domo* but *pro ecclesia*."[63]

There can be no doubt that Acton had some influence on the final form of the *Apologia* but it is, of course, impossible to determine its exact extent. It was probably considerable. When Newman, in the final chapter, abandoned the personal note and made of it a general defense of the Catholic system he may well have had in mind Acton's cautions. Certainly his lengthy treatment of the infallibility of the Church in its relations to intellectual freedom was his answer to Protestants who looked upon recent acts of ecclesiastical authority as so many acts of tyranny against independence of mind and who saw in the history of the *Home and Foreign* confirmation of their views.

The concluding chapter of the *Apologia* was of momentous import, for Newman's subsequent career as well as for English Catholicism. The *Apologia* was in its conception a highly egotistical production; the focus was designedly on Newman. He

---

[62] Newman to Acton, 15 April 1864, Orat. P.C.
[63] Acton to Newman [? April 1864], Orat. A.C.

had in the past been attacked and accused of many things and he wished to justify himself. As he noted years later: "Kingsley . . . was accidentally the instrument, in the good Providence of God, by whom I had an opportunity given me, which otherwise I would not have had, of vindicating *my* character and conduct in *my* 'Apologia,' "[64] However, had Newman's *Apologia* been nothing more than a personal vindication he would never have received such a spontaneous outpouring of gratitude from Catholic England. Before its appearance his reputation and influence were at their lowest ebb. But a year after its publication he could write that

in the last year a wonderful deliverance has been wrought in my favour, by the controversy, of which the upshot was my Apologia. It has been marvelously blest, for, while I have regained, or rather gained, the favor of Protestants, I have received the approbation, in formal addresses, of good part of the English clerical body. They have been highly pleased with me, as doing them a service, and I stand, with them, as I never did before.[65]

Newman's decision to write "pro ecclesia" as well as "pro domo" was no less important for English Catholicism. R. H. Hutton, one of the most acute observers of the nineteenth-century religious scene, once remarked that the *Apologia* "has done more to break down the English distrust of Roman Catholics, and to bring about a hearty good fellowship between them and the members of other Churches, than all the rest of the religious literature of our time put together."[66]

There is due to Lord Acton a belated recognition of his contribution to this work.

Despite the large measure of agreement that has been shown to have existed between Acton and Newman throughout the *Rambler* and *Home and Foreign* period—an agreement which hardly justifies Wilfrid Ward's statement that Newman "emphatically dissociated himself from the *Rambler* and the *Home and Foreign Review*"[67]—there was present an indeterminate factor which rendered difficult if not impossible a fundamental intellectual sympathy. When Newman, in writing to Lord

[64] Ward, *Newman*, ii, p. 46 (Italics added).
[65] *Autobiographical Writings*, p. 260.
[66] Richard H. Hutton, *Cardinal Newman* (2nd ed. London, 1891), p. 230.
[67] Ward, *Newman*, i, p. 19.

Blachford in 1872, referred to his great liking for Acton "ever since I knew him near 20 years ago," and added, somewhat wistfully, "but alas, we have never quite hit it off in action," he was pointing out in his own way that he was not quite satisfied with their relations.[68] He nowhere explains why they did not "quite hit it off" and it is not evident that he ever fully understood the reason. It is tempting to attribute it, as does Archbishop Mathew,[69] to a difference in temperament and background. This, of course, explains why they were never intimate but it does not seem to touch the more fundamental difference which Acton had in mind when he wrote to Simpson: "Now Newman has great sympathy with our cause, inasmuch as he is enlightened and liberal and highly cultivated; but I do not believe he really understands our theory, and certainly would not more admit it than de Buck."[70]

Acton's *cause* was to introduce into English Catholicism something of the critical spirit of German academic circles. His *theory* was that intellectual activity in union with scientific learning would provide the necessary answers to the errors of the day in both the political and religious spheres. "The impartiality of scientific research" was his guiding principle.[71]

Now, Newman as much as Acton insisted on the necessity of objective scientific inquiry. His University lectures leave no doubt on this score. But he seemed more conscious of the difficulties inherent in the process and less confident of the definitive character of its findings. In matters of religion however—and here is the crucial point—he believed that unaided reason would not bring men to satisfactory conclusions. He would not deny that truth is the real object of the reason. On the contrary, he would maintain that if reason did not attain to truth either the premise or process was at fault; but, considering human reason as exercised by fallen men, actually and historically, in religious inquiries it tended to simple unbelief. An authoritative Church, divinely guided, was the only ultimate assurance against "the fierce energy of passion and the all-corroding, all-dissolving skepticism of the intellect in religious inquiries."[72] The Catholic Church

---

[68] Newman to Blachford, 6 July 1872, Orat. Copied Letters.
[69] David Mathew, *Acton: The Formative Years*, pp. 114–22.
[70] Gasquet, *Acton*, p. 315.
[71] *Essays on Church and State*, p. 275.
[72] *Apologia*, p. 243.

was a Divine provision "to preserve religion in the world, and to restrain that freedom of thought, which of course in itself is one of the greatest of our natural gifts, and to rescue it from its own suicidal excesses."[73] Leaning so heavily on the Church he was prepared to suffer more from its human representatives.

It may be objected that all this is merely a roundabout way of saying that Newman was more skeptical than Acton. Perhaps, however, it would be nearer the truth to say that Newman better comprehended the difficulties confronting the Christian intellectual. He was the profounder thinker. Acton, as a Catholic, accepted the ordinary Catholic teaching on authority but never inquired deeply into its grounds. He carried his ancestral faith lightly and conducted his researches confident that there could be no conflict between natural and revealed truths. Like that of so many born Christians, his faith covered a multitude of difficulties. But by failing sufficiently to integrate his religious life with his intellectual pursuits he exposed himself to the danger of building up an intellectual system that made no provision for the truths he held on faith. Although this tendency to live on two levels is only barely perceptible in his early career it will be seen to reach more serious proportions in later years.

[73] *Apologia*, p. 245. Newman used the term *Liberalism* to designate the false liberty of thought which presumed to subject even truths of revelation to human judgment. Since in the ordinary sense of the words he was a Liberal Catholic his opposition to Liberalism in the sense of excessive rationalism or anti-dogmatism in matters of religion can be the cause of much confusion.

v. A Period of Transition
(1865-1867)

The Munich Brief and the condemnation of Montalembert's discourses at Malines convinced Newman and Acton that the Holy See was against any attempts by Catholics to effect an accommodation with the liberal spirit of the age. In the words of Newman:

> It seemed to be specially a time in which Christians had a call to be patient, in which they had no other way of helping those who were alarmed, than that of exhorting them to have a little faith and fortitude, and to 'beware,' as the poet says, 'of dangerous steps.'[1]

Newman was more inclined than Acton to admit the possibility of there being wisdom in the counsels of the highest Catholic authority. After all, it was difficult to say precisely what was the nature of the challenge to Christianity. In a period of rapid change it was not easy to keep one's balance. "I am far from denying," he wrote in the *Apologia* "that scientific knowledge is really growing, but it is by fits and starts; hypotheses rise and fall; it is difficult to anticipate which of them will keep their ground, and what the state of knowledge in relation to them will be from year to year."[2] Perhaps restraint was the best policy for the Church. And before 1864 had run its course a new bolt from Rome established beyond the shadow of a doubt that was the policy it intended to follow.

In December the Pope sent to the bishops of the world an encyclical *Quanta Cura* with an accompanying Syllabus of Errors which brought delight to the Church's enemies and confusion to Liberal Catholics. The two documents were

---

[1] *Apologia*, p. 263.
[2] *Ibid.*, pp. 262–63.

received by the non-Catholic world as an unqualified condemnation of modern civilization. The Syllabus of Errors in particular, couched in curt uncompromising statements, seemed to deny everything that Liberal Catholicism stood for.

The Syllabus was a collection of 80 propositions maintained at some time or another by various people or groups during the lifetime of Pius IX and judged by him to be erroneous. The list was extracted from his various allocutions, encyclicals and official letters extending over the previous eighteen years. Although in each case a reference was given to the original document no further effort was made by the anonymous compiler to place the various propositions in context. Read as an independent document in its own right, some of it appeared preposterous to non-Catholics and "stupefied the majority of Catholics."[3] Propositions 77 to 80, "the errors which had reference to the liberalism of the day,"[4] seemed especially severe. Thus, for example, the famous 80th proposition read: "The Roman Pontiff can and should reconcile and harmonise himself with progress, with liberalism, and with recent civilisation." To the ordinary reader the listing of such a proposition as an error was patently absurd, but once it is known that it was extracted from a papal allocution, *Jamdudum Cernimus*, directed against Cavour's demands that the Pope come to terms with the Italian revolution the proposition appears in a different light.[5] Yet, even when read in context the Syllabus was bitter medicine for most Liberal Catholics and brought joy only to the extreme Ultramontanes.

Newman was not very disturbed by either document. Only the animus of their authors and their way of doing things made him uneasy.[6] Their actual substance left him unperturbed. After all the Pope was dealing with an abstract theory of Church and State not so very different from the High Church theory and not with what was prudent or expedient. To quote a letter to Monsell:

I see little which would not be condemned by Archdeacon Denison, or by Keble, or the great body of the Anglican Church thirty years ago

---

[3] R. Aubert, *Le Pontificat de Pie IX*, p. 255.
[4] H. Denzinger, *Enchiridion Symbolorum Definitionum et Declarationum De Rebus Fidei et Morum* (28th ed. Freiburg, 1952), Nos. 1777–80.
[5] E. E. Y. Hales, *Pio Nono*, p. 258.
[6] Newman to Monsell, 5 February 1865, Orat. P.C.

. . . The high Church theory of Church and State may be true, but may be virtually suspended and in fact superseded.[7]

But Acton saw things differently. He found the rigid policy of Rome hard to endure. It appeared to him that Liberal Catholicism was being inexorably stifled. He was pursuing archival researches in Italy when the Encyclical and Syllabus broke upon the world. Shortly after their appearance he was asked to join in an address of loyalty to the Pope from non-Italian Catholics. He accepted on the understanding that events of the day and internal controversies of the Church were to be kept out, and he even drew up the draft address. But when it was objected that the Pope would rather not listen to an address at all than to one that made no mention of the Encyclical he withdrew both the draft and his name. He felt that he was one of those against whose ideas the Encyclical was directed and that he could take no part in a demonstration in its favor.[8]

Acton's researches during this period affected him deeply and resulted in a radical reassessment of his approach to the history of Catholicism. The process was rendered even more acute by the fact that Döllinger's history was also undergoing a transformation. "The ecclesiastical history of his youth," wrote Acton in 1890 of his beloved Professor, "went to pieces against the new criticism of 1863, and the revelation of the unknown which began on a very large scale in 1864."[9] Acton was no longer the young enthusiast with "the springs of emotion running free."[10] A more inflexible person was emerging. The oppressive and conspiratorial incidents in Church history began to hold a peculiar fascination for him, possibly because he saw in his present frustrations a definite link with the past.

In these transitional years his contacts with Newman were limited. Newman, however, maintained a warm interest in his

[7] Newman to Monsell, 5 February 1865, Orat. P.C.
[8] Acton to Döllinger, 5 February 1865, Woodruff Mss.; see also E. L. Woodward, "The Place of Lord Acton in the Liberal Movement of the Nineteenth Century," *Politica*, September, 1939.
[9] "Döllinger's Historical Work," *History of Freedom*, p. 422. Döllinger spent his vacation in 1864 working in the libraries of Vienna and Venice and began to appreciate for the first time (says Acton) the real significance of unpublished manuscript materials (*Ibid.*, pp. 421–22).
[10] H. Butterfield, *Lord Acton* (Historical Association Pamphlet, London, 1948), p. 6.

career and upon Acton's election for Bridgnorth in July, 1865 he wrote to him expressing the hope that he would "hit upon some means of being represented in the newspaper press."[11] And added: "You will be looked after very sharply, and your influence may be very great." But Acton's representation was of short duration as he lost his seat on a recount early the next year. His parliamentary career was at an end.

Meanwhile the Roman Question continued to dictate Vatican policy. Pio Nono believed that Italian liberalism with its pronounced tendencies toward pantheism and naturalism represented in miniature a general movement which if left unchecked would engulf Christianity. He had hurled *Quanta Cura* and the Syllabus of Errors in the teeth of the new order but his act of defiance had done little to bolster up his tottering temporal domains. Personal sympathy for one surrounded by so many trials remained universal throughout the Catholic world, and in the eyes of many Catholics unquestioning acceptance of the political policy followed by Rome was the badge of a true Catholic.

Newman followed developments in Italy carefully and finally decided to break his long silence on the temporal power issue. An occasion was provided by his bishop who requested that all sermons preached in his diocese on October 7, 1866 should include an instruction to the faithful on their obligations to the Holy See. On the appointed day Newman preached in the Oratory Church at Birmingham his sermon "The Pope and the Revolution."[12] While some listeners may have considered it a defense of the temporal power a careful reading of it shows that it was nothing of the kind. Newman took care to point out that the temporal possessions of the Pope were given to him by men, not God, and implied that the Pope becoming a temporal ruler was not all for the good. While branding the "outsiders" who took possession of the Papal States "sacrilegious robbers" he, nevertheless, repeated what he had stated in 1859 in one of his letters to the *Rambler:* "While his subjects are for him, no one can have a word to say against his temporal rule; but who can force a Sovereign on a people which deliberately rejects him?"[13] He carefully refrained from leaving an impression that

---

[11] Newman to Acton, 21 July 1865, Orat. P.C.
[12] *Sermons Preached on Various Occasions*, pp. 280–316.
[13] *Sermons Preached on Various Occasions*, p. 293.

he believed temporal power necessary for the Papacy. Rather he suggested that the present period might well see its end:

We pray when we are uncertain, not when we are certain. If we were quite sure what God intended to do, whether to continue the temporal power of the Pope or to end it, we should not pray.[14]

And again:

Temporal power has been the means of the Church's independence for a very long period; but, as her Bishops have lost it a long while, and are not the less Bishops still, so would it be as regards her Head, if he also lost his.[15]

In the early 1890's Acton, in a work he planned on Döllinger, thought of devoting a section of it to a consideration of Newman's position on the Roman Question.[16] He was puzzled by Newman's attitude. Was it the product of spirituality or liberalism? He was inclined to believe that it was neither but resulted from Newman's personal irritation and indignation at the treatment he had received as a Catholic. His experience (argued Acton) had taught him to distrust authorities "and those who specially represent them." He found himself "hampered, checked, opposed, wherever he turned" and he generalized his personal experiences. His attitude on the Roman Question, Acton concluded, was really the outgrowth of resentment.[17]

This conclusion tells us more about Acton than Newman. Acton in his later phase strove to show Newman up as anti-liberal pure and simple, and his prejudice misled him. In his notes he failed to make any distinction between the Newman of the 1859–1863 period and the Newman of the post-*Apologia* period. The earlier Newman was depressed and discouraged by the weight of resistance to his attempted works and the apparent lack of appreciation in any quarter. But the success of the *Apologia* renewed his spirits and rendered him impervious to further criticisms. One can only see this by reading his autobiographical writings covering the two periods. Acton, of course, never had the opportunity of reading these frank writings and knew well only the 1859–1863 Newman. Whenever he wrote of him late in life, this is the Newman he had in mind. Newman's attitude to the Roman Question followed from his attitude to the Church

---

[14] *Ibid.*, p. 309.
[15] *Ibid.*, p. 313.
[16] Acton to Gladstone, 20 May 1892, British Museum Add. Mss. 44094.
[17] CUL Add. Mss. 4989, 21, 114, 115.

and this position he adopted long before he became a Catholic. In the very sermon under discussion—a sermon which Acton analyzed but only with one eye—one can find a statement of Newman's view of the Church which explains his stand on the Roman Question:

> To say that the Church cannot live except in a particular way, is to make it 'subject to elements of the earth.' The Church is not the creature of times and places, of secular politics, or popular caprice. Our Lord maintained her by means of this world, but these means are necessary to her only while He gives them; when He takes them away, they are no longer necessary. He works by means, but He is not bound to means. He has a thousand ways of maintaining her; He can support her life, not by bread only, but by every word that proceedeth out of His mouth. If He takes away one defence, He will give another instead. We know nothing of the future: our duty is to direct our course according to our day; not to give up of our own act the means which God has given us to maintain His Church withal, but not to lament over their loss, when He has taken them away.[18]

Newman's genius lay in his original approach to all questions. He was little influenced by the prevailing spirit of the day and remained unmoved by considerations which disturbed other intellectuals. It was most characteristic of him that he should take his own independent line on this particular issue. In a letter written shortly after his sermon on "The Pope and the Revolution" he revealed with what perfect equanimity he anticipated a radical change in the position of the Papacy.[19] In the following passage it is not a discouraged or resentful Newman who speaks, but a self-assured thinker who is confident that the policy of the narrow clique in the ascendancy at the present would not always prevail.

> Not till some great convulsions take place, which may go on for years & years, and when I can do neither good nor harm, and religion is felt to be in the midst of trials red-tapism will go out of Rome, and a better spirit come in, and Cardinals & Archbishops will have some of the reality they had, amid many abuses, in the middle ages. At present things are in appearance as effete, though in a different way, (thank God) as they were in the tenth century. We are sinking into a sort of Novatianism, the heresy which the early Popes so strenuously resisted. Instead of aiming at being a world-wide power, we are shrinking into ourselves, narrowing the lines of communion, trembling at freedom of thought, and using the language of dismay and despair at the prospect before us,

---

[18] *Sermons Preached on Various Occasions*, pp. 312–13.
[19] Newman to E. Bowles, 11 November 1866, Orat. P.C.

instead of, with the high spirit of the warrior, going out conquering and to conquer. Can anything be more unworthy of a Christian prelate, than the laments of the Irish Bishops that no hope is left, that there is no earthly power to aid the Holy See, and that it is all along of that wicked Louis Napoleon? One is tempted to adopt the words of the blaspheming Assyrian, as capable of an allowable application to such craven conduct. 'Do thou trust upon the broken staff of a reed, upon Egypt; upon which if a man lean, it will go into his hand and pierce it—so is Pharao'—So is Napoleon, so Francis Joseph, so Isabella, so King Bomba—so are all of them. Haud tali auxilio &c. I believe the Pope's spirit is simply that of martyrdom, and it is utterly different from that implied in these gratuitous shriekings which surround his throne. But the Power of God is abroad upon the earth, and He will settle things in spite of what cliques and parties may decide. I am glad you like my sermon—the one thing I wished to oppose is the coward despairing spirit of the day.

These are severe words. But they are not those of a carping, petulant critic. They are the words of a profoundly Christian thinker whose vision of history transcended the petty maneuvers of temporal principalities. Neither the ultra-liberal policies of the Italian revolutionaries, nor the ultra-conservative policies of the Holy See afforded the Christian any grounds for despair. The Christian's faith was rooted in God, not man. And God could use as His instrument not only the freest thinking Liberal but also the narrowest of Ultramontanes. Why Acton failed to recognize spirituality as the true basis of Newman's stand on the Roman Question will become clearer in the final chapter of this work.

The beginning of 1867 found Acton engaged in plans to re-enter the world of journalism. Wetherell persuaded him to join in the launching of a new secular periodical, the *Chronicle*. Almost all the old *Home and Foreign* writers, including Simpson and Renouf, as well as non-Catholics such as D. C. Lathbury took part. Gladstone was to be its silent inspiration.[20]

As far as its Catholic readers were concerned the paper did not get off to a happy start. An essay by Acton on Fra Paolo Sarpi contained a passage which shocked Catholic readers.[21] It ran as follows:

[20] Acton to Gladstone, 1 January 1867, British Museum, Add. Mss. 44093. Gasquet, *Acton*, p. lxxvij ff.

[21] "Fra Paolo Sarpi," *The Chronicle*, 30 March 1867. Reprinted in *Essays on Church and State*. The editor of the latter failed to note Acton's blunder in naming Pius V for Pius IV.

A circumstance related by Cantù in his *History of the Italians* shows how seriously the habits engendered by the religious conflict had weakened respect for the sacredness of human life and had made consciences familiar with schemes of murder. Certain natives of Lucca went into foreign countries and became Protestants. A law was made by which any citizen of the Republic who should kill one of the refugees was to be rewarded with a free pardon for all former crimes; and if the indemnity was of no use to him, he might transfer it to any friend who happened to need it; so that the murder of a heretic was not only an innocent but a meritorious action—so meritorious that it was held to compensate and redeem the guilt of any quantity of other murders. Cantù says that this enactment was applauded by the Archbishop of Milan and by the Pope, that is to say, by St. Charles Borromeo and St. Pius V.[22]

A letter from the Bishop of Leeds to Manning a few days after the appearance of the *Chronicle* reflects the offense given in Catholic circles:

I have just come from York & I have also seen some of the clergy in Leeds. There is abroad, quite an outcry against [the] Chronicle. One long letter was written to me most strongly about the article on Sarpi & another drew the very conclusion about S.Pius V and S.Charles you point out.[23]

Manning, on his part, carefully noted that the promoters of the *Chronicle* were the very ones "who have urged on the sending of our youth to the Protestant Universities."[24] This clearly implicated Newman, who, at the time, was engaged in a final abortive effort to open an Oratory at Oxford.[25]

When Newman read Acton's Essay he immediately wrote to Wetherell in protest:

I was going to write to you a letter on the 1st no. of the Chronicle generally, when I came on a passage in it, which has distressed me very much, and against which I must even in self defense, (if the words are not strange to you) and do now distinctly, hereby, protest.

It is only a week or two since the Weekly Register spoke of my being in some way connected with the Chronicle, and, knowing how earnestly you wished to avoid dangerous matter, I saw no reason to correct so harmless (as I thought) or rather, to me so complimentary a statement. But if you know what a great effort is at this moment making to reverse the decision of Propaganda in favor of the Oratory going to Oxford, and the various charges I have to meet you would understand how the

[22] *Essays on Church and State*, pp. 258–59.
[23] R. Cornthwaite to Manning, 4 April 1867, Bayswater Archives.
[24] Manning to Ullathorne, 9 April 1867, Bayswater Archives.
[25] See above, p. 23.

passage of the Chronicle to which I refer will affect the question, how it is sure to be put before the Pope, and how absolutely incumbent upon me it is to declare that I have had nothing directly or indirectly to do with it.

I do not enter into any argument about the historical truth or false-hood of Cantù's statement, or about the moral character of the acts for which he vouches, (to say no more, I am overpowered with the number of letters I am just now writing—) but I must without loss of time protest against the passage as it stands in the Chronicle.[26]

On the following day he again wrote to Wetherell and returned to a consideration of the offensive passage, paraphrasing it thus:

the force of the passage in the Chronicle lies in this: that when men who have adopted Protestantism instead of showing fight, instead [of] forming a political party, or stirring up insurrection, or trying to make converts to their religious views, simply went away from their country, to some place where they could worship God in their own way without molesta-tion, a Pope and an Archbishop of Milan sent after them all the most bloodthirsty fellows of the native land of the refugees, the bravi and vagabondi of Mazoni's [sic] Promessi Sposi, to murder them, with the reward of a free pardon for their own crimes, nay, those of their friends. This is assassination in its most terrible form. Will not Protestants take it up? What can they say which will tell more agst. us?[27]

In a further letter he discussed the question of criticizing the actions of Saints:

I think that the failings of saints need not be passed over in a grave history, when they come in the direct line of the narrative or discussion; but to bring them out for the first time (yes, first for English readers) in a periodical, & its first number, and apropos of an article on another subject, & only incidentally, seems to me another matter.[28]

Newman would have been immensely relieved had he known that Acton, writing the passage from memory, named Pius V in error for Pius IV,[29] and that the action of the Pope and

[26] Newman to Wetherell, 2 April 1867, Orat. P.C.
[27] Newman to Wetherell, 3 April 1867, Orat. P.C.
[28] Newman to Wetherell, 9 April 1867, Orat. P.C.
[29] Acton to [?] Wetherell, [13 May 1867], "Gasquet and the Acton-Simpson Correspondence," C.H.J. vol. x, no. 1, 1950, p. 103. Only Gasquet's transcrip-tions are extant for a group of letters written by Acton from Rome in 1867 on matters relating to the Chronicle. Though the addressee is not named it must almost certainly have been Wetherell.

St. Charles, as indeed the whole incident, was grossly misrepresented.[30]

Gasquet, in his original introduction to *Lord Acton and His Circle* discussed Acton's treatment of this topic, but was dissuaded from publishing it by Acton's son, who feared family displeasure.[31] Since Gasquet, in the preparation of Acton's correspondence for publication, went to extraordinary lengths to present him to a rather dubious public as a pillar of orthodoxy and a paragon of Catholic scholarship, his expurgated remarks on Acton's accusation against Pius V and Charles Borromeo are of especial interest:

It is impossible to understand how Acton could have penned such a sentence and still more how he could have failed to detect his error in subsequent years. We now know that in regard to St. Charles and the Pope the writer rested his accusation merely on a statement of Cantù, who, although a Catholic historian should not have been taken as a sufficient authority for so serious a charge. Moreover, as we now know from the letters here printed, the whole passage was written from memory.[32] It will be noticed that he speaks of 'St. Charles Borromeo and St. Pius V.' On this being pointed out to him, he wrote, 'There is no excuse for my blunder about Pius IV. The fact is I had not seen the book (Cantù) for more than a year, and ought not to have written a historical article away from Aldenham. This is said only to explain the thing to yourself (Mr. Wetherell) not in mitigation.' In another letter he says that he merely quoted Cantù and had 'never had an opportunity of verifying it.' Apparently, although he made use of this false accusation on several subsequent occasions, Lord Acton failed to test the truth of it, but, by some strange and wholly inexplicable neglect of critical methods, which he would have been first to condemn in others, accepted the statement on the authority of that multitudinous writer Cantù.[33]

[30] C. G. Cantù to Acton, 27 August [1867], CUL Add. Mss. 4915. See H. Thurston, "Was St. Charles Borromeo a Murderer!", *Tablet*, 29 July 1905. Thurston's article was prompted by the publication of Acton's *Letters to Mary Gladstone* (1904) containing repeated accusations (based on the Lucca incident) against St. Charles.

[31] The three pages in proof, omitted from the Introduction, are in the Downside papers, as are also letters from the second Lord Acton to Gasquet.

[32] When Gasquet withdrew this portion from the Introduction he also omitted the letters in the text referring to the incident.

[33] Gasquet is not quite accurate when he concludes that Acton failed to test the truth of Cantù's statement. In his letter to *The Times* of 24 November 1874, he cites as his reference, "*Archivio Storico Italiano*," vol. X, Opp., p. 177; the accusation against St. Charles is repeated on p. 148 in his *Letters to Mary Gladstone*

Gasquet then went on to eulogize Newman:

That these statements were true, Newman refused to believe: there was, and he was sure must be, some mistake or mis-statement somewhere. And so, *forty years after the lie has had its start and after it has done duty on several occasions*,[34] Father Thurston's researches have shown the world that Newman's Catholic instincts were right, and that there was in reality no historical basis for the accusation.

Gasquet's praise of Newman's Catholic instincts is surely excessive, since Newman, as has been seen, did not challenge the truth of the accusation but protested on other grounds.

Wetherell apparently wrote to Acton expressing concern over the accuracy of his passage from Cantù, for on April 11 Acton wrote assuring him that he had not blundered, and ended with a curious passage:

Remember that I have not any faculty of forseeing what may be offensive, and though I do my best to avoid it, I may very often miscalculate. Therefore it may happen that I send you things that had better not appear, or it [sic] least require modification. Any defence, hereafter, of my article, ought to be in the shape of an answer to those who would use the facts against the Church; therefore, by a careful explanation of the reason and genesis of such opinions.[35]

The apparent temporizing in the above passage is most unlike Acton and is the type of thing he would roundly condemn in another. One might easily conclude that he was a poor innocent reluctantly consenting to a policy of concealment in order to placate Catholics who were afraid of historical truth. However, his offensive writings appear to have been more the product of one who derived real satisfaction from the revelation—and often in the most provocative form—of obscure historical incidents involving erring ecclesiastics than of one who "had not the faculty of forseeing what may be offensive."

with a reference to the edited letters of St. Charles. Thurston charges Acton with a serious misrepresentation of available documents and seems to establish his charge beyond any doubt. Since it would be wholly alien to Acton's character to engage in any sort of deliberate misrepresentation one can only conclude that the faulty version first recorded in the *Chronicle* impressed itself on his mind and remained with him, and although he subsequently noted the original source of Cantù's statements he never really restudied the documents.

[34] The Downside proof sheet is underlined in red pencil.

[35] "Gasquet and the Acton-Simpson Correspondence," *C.H.J.* vol. x, no. 1, 1950, p. 102.

The expressed desire to avoid what was offensive notwithstanding, Acton's next important contribution to the *Chronicle* was his most outspoken writing to date. Pio Nono's announcement of a forthcoming Church Council called forth his impassioned Essay, "The Next General Council."[36] The death struggle between the new Ultramontanism and Liberal Catholicism had arrived. The time for compromise was over.

[36] See below, p. 110.

VI. The Vatican Council

Pius IX first broached the question of summoning an Ecumenical Council to the Cardinals present at a meeting of the Congregation of Rites on December 6, 1864. Two of the twenty-one Cardinals present were definitely opposed to the idea and half a dozen more expressed doubts as to its opportuneness.[1] Political unrest within Italy itself and the outbreak of the Austro-Prussian war prevented a final decision from being reached for several years, and it was not until June 26, 1867 that the Pope announced in Public Consistory that a Council would be called. Over two years were to elapse before it was inaugurated.

Papal Infallibility was one point among many others likely to be discussed and there is no evidence that either the Pope or the Bishops considered it the primary one; but soon after the news went round that a General Council was in the offing interested onlookers fixed upon Infallibility as the central question and in journals of the day other considerations were given scant notice.

In France those who advocated the extremest form of papal authority were the most vocal, and the Pope left no doubt where his sympathies rested. Louis Veuillot, the intrepid defender of the rights of the Pope, preached an irresponsible form of Infallibility, and even the bishops could not restrain him. When one reads Veuillot's almost blasphemous eulogies on Pius IX[2] it can be better understood how Montalembert, one of the greatest

[1] Cuthbert Butler, *The Vatican Council* (London, 1930), vol. i, p. 81.
[2] See Wilfrid Ward, *W. G. Ward and the Catholic Revival*, p. 246; also R. Aubert, *Le Pontificat de Pie IX*, pp. 302–03.

108

champions of Catholicism in the last century, could protest from his deathbed with terrible bitterness against what he believed to be

the permanent triumph of those lay theologians who, beginning by squandering all our liberties, all our principles, all our former ideas before Napoleon III[3] afterwards immolated justice and truth, reason and history, in one great holocaust to the idol they have raised up for themselves at the Vatican.[4]

In Italy in the pages of the *Civiltà Cattolica*, a Jesuit publication specially favored by the Pope, an outspoken Ultramontane campaign was waged. Even in this semi-official organ shocking aberrations appeared, e.g., "When the Pope thinks, it is God who is thinking in him."[5]

Döllinger led a growing opposition to the neo-Ultramontanism in Germany. As Acton wrote: "Since 1863 he becomes dimly aware that Rome backs the theologians who are against him."[6] Döllinger saw in the extreme form of Infallibility advocated by the neo-Ultramontanes a logical culmination of the claims to universal jurisdiction of the medieval papacy. It was the product of "a genuine theological theory, growing for centuries."[7] Acton made another interesting observation:

The Syllabus caused the opposition. Infallibility, with a little precaution, D[öllinger] himself would have had no very clear objection to. But it took, beforehand, an extreme shape. No more decided Inf[allibilists] in some shape than the leading Liberals.[8]

The English scene had its own battles, with Ultramontanes of the Manning cast apparently reigning supreme. But their supremacy did not go unchallenged. In the Catholic Reviews invective too often did duty for argument. The clergy excelled in exchanging anathemas, so much so that one correspondent could open his letter: "You will easily recognize by the mildness of my language that I am a layman."[9]

W. G. Ward, from the moment he became editor of the

---

[3] Veuillot supported Napoleon III until 1860.
[4] Quoted by J. G. Snead-Cox, *The Life of Cardinal Vaughan* (London, 1910), vol. i, pp. 235–36.
[5] Quoted by C. Butler, *Vatican Council*, i, p. 77.
[6] *Lord Acton's Correspondence*, p. 58.
[7] CUL Add. Mss. 5609.
[8] *Ibid.*
[9] Cited by J. G. Snead-Cox, *Life of Vaughan*, i, p. 215.

Dublin Review in 1863, waged an uncompromising war in favor of the Infallibility of the Pope in an extreme form. In his view the only Catholic worthy of the Pope's approbation was one characterized by an

unlimited obedience to the Roman, as distinguished from all other churches; unalterable attachment to Roman traditions and observances; and acceptance of the infallible authority, in dogma and discipline, over every other power on earth, of the Vicar of Jesus Christ—the recognition that his every doctrinal pronouncement is infallibly directed by the Holy Ghost.[10]

The absolute character of the Pope's authority he stated thus:

The only bound to their authority which the Popes of Rome have ever recognized, is that appointed directly and immediately by God Himself; and which the Holy Ghost inspires themselves infallibly to declare.[11]

He was not satisfied with putting this forward as his own personal view but vigorously insisted that no other was possible. Manning unreservedly endorsed Ward and Manning ruled supreme.

Herbert Vaughan, in effect Editor of the *Tablet*, refused to admit into that journal any letters which challenged his own equally extreme views on the Infallibility of the Pope, arguing that since it was sure to be defined it would be immoral to provide arguments which might harden men's hearts against it.[12] One sympathizes with Montalembert's despairing plaint:

How unfathomable are the designs of God in allowing such oracles as Dr. Ward, Mr. Vaughan, and others to be the representatives of Catholic intelligence in the eyes of that immense Anglo-Saxon race which is so evidently intended to cover the whole modern world![13]

Acton was not one to grant a victory by default to the neo-Ultramontanes. Despite the anti-liberal policy of the Holy See since the early 1860's, he had not entirely given up hope that a more liberal policy would somehow prevail. With the public announcement in June, 1867 of a forthcoming General Council Acton rushed into print with an article entitled "The Next

[10] "Pius IX and the 'Civiltà Cattolica,'" *Dublin Review*, October 1866, p. 418.
[11] *Ibid.*, p. 419.
[12] J. G. Snead-Cox, *Life of Vaughan*, i, pp. 201–203.
[13] *Life and Letters of Ambrose Phillips de Lisle*, edited by E. S. Purcell and E. de Lisle (London, 1900), vol. ii, p. 262.

General Council." It was largely concerned with the question of Infallibility, and it revealed the fears he held that a definition of the Pope's Infallibility was designed to smother all opposition to the extremist line and enshrine the opinions of the ignorant masses as the only orthodox expression of Catholicism. His summary of the consequences of such a definition shows clearly with what alarm he viewed it:

It is more profitable to study the consequences than to estimate the chances of success. A decree proclaiming the Pope infallible would be a confession that the authority of General Councils has been an illusion and a virtual usurpation from the first; so that having come to the knowledge of their own superfluousness, and having directed the Church into the way she ought always to have followed, they could only abolish themselves for the future by an act which would be an act of suicide. It would invest, by its retrospective action, not the Pope and his successors only, but all his legitimate predecessors, with the same immunity. The objects of faith would be so vastly increased by the incorporation of the Bullarium, that the limits would become indistinct by distance. The responsibility for the acts of the buried and the repented past would come back at once and for ever, with a crushing weight on the Church. Spectres it has taken ages of sorrowful effort to lay would come forth once more. The Bulls which imposed a belief in the deposing power, the Bulls which prescribed the tortures and kindled the flames of the Inquisition, the Bulls which erected witchcraft into a system and made the extermination of witches a frightful reality, would become as venerable as the decrees of Nicaea, as incontrovertible as the writings of S. Luke. The decisions of every tribunal (by the decretal *Novit*) would be made subject to the revision of the Pope, and the sentences of every Protestant judge (by the Bull *Cum ex apostolatus officio*) would be invalid. The priesthood would be, by Divine right, exempt from all secular allegiance; and the supreme authority over all States would revert to the Holy See—for thus it stands in the Bull *Unam Sanctam*, repeated by Leo X. in the Fifth Council of Lateran. Catholics would be bound, by order of Innocent III., to obey all the laws of Deuteronomy. A successor of Alexander VI. might distribute the New World over again; and the right by which Adrian disposed of Ireland would enable another Pope to barter it for a Concordat with America, or to exchange Great Britain for a French garrison. The assurance by which the Church has obtained her freedom would be revoked; and the survivor of the Irish bishops who signed the Declaration of 1826 would discover that he had deceived his country by false representations. The Church would take the place of a moon, reflecting passively the light which the Pope receives directly from heaven, but liable to be left in total darkness, sometimes for three years together, during the vacancy of the Holy See, and during much longer periods of schism, when she knows not her rightful head. And as the Pope's decisions would be, not a testimony of the existing faith of the Church, but a result of his own enlightenment by the Holy Ghost, his interpretation and application of Scripture would be also infallible, the dogma could not be separated from the proofs, and the arguments of the mediaeval Bulls would become a norm for theology. The chances of union with the Greeks, the means of discussion with the Protestants, would vanish utterly, and Catholicism would forfeit its expanding power; . . . but there is no fear that a General Council will testify falsely to the faith of the Church.[14]

It is difficult to determine to what extent Acton exaggerated his fears in this article. It was characteristic of him to endeavor to reduce his opponents to silence by a *reductio ad absurdum*, and, again, he no doubt took a certain delight in outspoken criticism. Too often in Victorian journalism fairness toward one's opponents seemed to have been considered an admission of weakness. But allowing for all this Acton was genuinely disturbed and his fears waxed stronger as the campaign of the neo-Ultramontanists increased in intensity. What Acton dreaded is succinctly stated in the following passage:

Rome has before now insisted on opinions which set a barrier to conversions and supplied a motive for persecution. The preservation of authority is a higher object than the propagation of faith. The advocates of Roman views are more used to controversy with their fellow Catholics than with Protestants. Their first aspiration is to suppress divisions of opinions within the Church; and this object could not be achieved more effectually than by converting the Vatican into a sort of Catholic Delphi.[15]

This smacks of exaggeration today, but certainly Louis Veuillot's vision of the Vatican lent some credibility to Acton's fears.

Newman, also, was disturbed by the statements of the extremists. In particular he took exception to Ward's pontifications. In his reply to Pusey's *Eirenicon* he took care to dissociate himself from Ward's views:

And as to our friend, do not his energy, acuteness, and theological reading, displayed on the vantage ground of the historic 'Dublin Review' fully account for the sensation he has produced, without supposing that any great number of our body go his lengths in their view of the Pope's infallibility?[16]

---

[14] "The Next General Council," *Chronicle*, 13 July 1867, pp. 369–70.
[15] "The Next General Council," p. 370.
[16] *Difficulties of Anglicans*, ii, p. 23.

Writing to Pusey on November 17, 1865 he remarked:

As to the Infallibility of the Pope, I see nothing against, or dread in it—for I am confident that it *must* be so limited practically that it will leave things as they are. As to Ward's notions, they are preposterous,— nor do I see anything in the Pope's Encyclical to confirm them.[17]

Throughout this period he was associated, in the minds of many, with Acton and Simpson in what Vaughan called "the liberal and national school of thought."[18] His intimate friend T. W. Allies went so far as to write him a warning against the claims of Acton and Simpson to be the only true exponents of his thought. "Few things in this world would grieve me more," added Allies, "than not to feel that there was a deep gulf between you and Acton and Simpson, though particular circumstances lead you to sympathize in one or two points with them."[19] If Allies expected a repudiation of Acton and Simpson he was disappointed for Newman returned a non-committal answer.[20] When Newman accepted a dedication of a translation of one of Döllinger's works,[21] Bishop Ullathorne, in writing to Manning, expressed what was no doubt the general sentiment of the Bishops: "I am sorry that Dr. Newman accepted Oxenham's dedication of Döllinger's history. I don't like this particular association of names."[22]

Newman was further linked with what one might term the Acton School through his encouragement to Renouf to publish a work on the case of Pope Honorius who was condemned as a heretic by the sixth General Council (680). This case was believed to present the most serious historical objection to Papal Infallibility. Upon its publication Newman wrote to Renouf:

I certainly did not know how strong a case could be made out against Pope Honorius. But with all its power, I do not find that it seriously interferes with my own view of Papal Infallibility.[23]

And a few months later:

[17] Ward, *Newman*, ii, p. 101.
[18] H. Vaughan to Manning, 10 April 1867, Bayswater Mss.
[19] Allies to Newman, 10 March 1866, Orat. P.C.
[20] Newman to Allies, 13 March 1866, Orat. P.C.
[21] *The First Age of Christianity and the Church* (London, 1866), translated by H. N. Oxenham.
[22] Ullathorne to Manning, Bayswater Mss.
[23] Ward, *Newman*, ii, p. 236.

I have ever held the Pope's Infallibility, that is, held it as a theological opinion, the most probable amid conflicting historical arguments. But it is a great duty to consult for others as well as for oneself; and I welcomed the prospect of your Pamphlet, not only as expedient at a time when ecclesiastical history is studied less carefully than is its due, but especially because its publication is a virtual protest against that narrow spirit, so uncharitable to the souls of men, which turns theological conclusions into doctrines of obligations.[24]

That it was the "narrow spirit" of the advocates of Papal Infallibility more than the theological doctrine itself that aroused opposition is evidenced by Renouf's words to Newman: "It is quite certain that I should not have dreamed of writing at all upon Pope Honorius if others had been content to hold the view of Papal Infallibility which you hold."[25] Renouf, for his efforts, achieved the notoriety of having his pamphlet placed on the *Index*.

Acton's interest in the Honorius case was startlingly demonstrated in the autumn of 1870. Counting on a diversion by the invading Italian troops he planned to break into the Vatican Archives and obtain a papal document, *Liber Diurnus*, in which new popes from the eighth to the eleventh century had recognized Honorius as a heretic. Unfortunately for the success of his remarkable exploit, he was detained by the Italian troops.[26]

Two months before the opening of the Vatican Council another essay by Acton, "The Pope and the Council," appeared in *The North British Review*.[27] It was a commentary on a German work, *Der Papst und das Concil*, that had just appeared under the pseudonym *Von Janus*. This work, written by Döllinger[28] and translated immediately into English, was one of the most trenchant attacks on Infallibility ever written. Newman, who believed it would do "immense mischief," could not believe that Döllinger wrote it.[29] Acton's only complaint in his review of it was that it let the opposition off too lightly. A reader of Acton's article who had no further knowledge of the personalities or issues involved in the controversy over Infallibility might justly conclude that

[24] Newman to Renouf, 30 November 1868, Orat. P.C.
[25] Renouf to Newman, 30 August 1868, Orat. P.C.
[26] Theodor von Sickel, *Römische Erinnerungen* (Wien, 1947), pp. 46, 135, 170–71.
[27] "The Pope and the Council," October, 1869.
[28] *History of Freedom*, p. 420.
[29] Butler, *Ullathorne*, ii, p. 50.

the bishops of the Church were a sycophantic group led by a self-deluded religious fanatic. In the same Review appeared Acton's article, "The Massacre of St. Bartholomew." Newman, in acknowledging Wetherell's complimentary copy of the Review, singled out the article on St. Bartholomew as especially good. He added:

> I don't want a Review to be religious, or even to profess Catholicity; but did not I know the quarter whence it came, I should think it written by liberal Scotchmen, religious in a way, who looked at the Church as a fiction of past time.[30]

From the first Newman decided against attending the Council, despite invitations from the Pope, Bishop Ullathorne, Bishop Brown of Newport and Bishop Dupanloup.[31] In a letter to Monsell he explained his reluctance:

> I *am too old for it*, in various ways I am too old. Take a single view of it. I think the Roman diet would most seriously compromise my health. I have for many months been living by rule and with medicine, and have had cause to be alarmed, tho' I trust without reason. Then again there are men, & some of them have been Saints, whose vocation does not lie in such ecclesiastical gatherings. St. Gregory Nazianzen & St. Chrysostom, not to say St. Basil, as instances, and I suspect also St. Jerome. I am their disciple. I am too old to learn the ways of other great Saints, as St. Athanasius, St. Augustine, & St. Ambrose, whom I admire, but cannot run with. They are race-horses. I am a broken-kneed poney.[32]

Nevertheless on the eve of the Council Simpson reported to Acton that Newman "is now rather sorry not to go."[33]

Acton, though he enjoyed no official appointment, had no intention of being absent from Rome during the most important ecclesiastical gathering of the century. He went to Rome in September, 1869 with one object in view: to prevent the definition of Infallibility by hook or by crook. Simpson kept him *au courant* on the English and Irish scenes but held out little hope for the support of the Irish episcopate: "Blennerhasset tells me that all the Irish Bishops will probably go wrong, except McHale."[34] Acton's personal connections and his knowledge of

[30] Newman to Wetherell, 7 November 1869, Orat. P.C.

[31] Simpson to Acton, 9 November 1869, Downside Mss.; H. P. Liddon, *Life of E. B. Pusey* (London, 1893), vol. iv, p. 161.

[32] Newman to Monsell, 31 December 1867, Orat. P.C.

[33] Simpson to Acton, 9 November 1869, Downside Mss.

[34] *Ibid.*

languages brought him into familiar association with many of the ecclesiastical dignitaries, particularly those of liberal tendencies. Although he may have gone about Rome "in mortal and daily fear of being assassinated,"[35] it was probably the most inspiriting period of his life.

At this period he would have cut an impressive figure. H. R. Tedder, his librarian during the early 1870's, has left us a good picture of Acton as he remembered him:

> A fine presence, a most courtly manner, a thoroughly amiable and kindly nature gave added grace to rich and varied mental gifts, to extraordinary knowledge of books and men, to a wonderful aptness in quotation and illustration, to a keen interest in all modern phases of thought. To have known Lord Acton was to respect and admire the man and the scholar.[36]

This thirty-five-year-old cosmopolitan scholar, immensely active, in the thick of ecclesiastical and political maneuvers, presented a marked contrast to the prematurely aged Newman, living in cautious seclusion in his Oratory, following at a distance proceedings in which he was no less interested but feared to participate. Yet it was the recluse, depending upon his personal correspondence, who grasped more surely the nature of what was going on at Rome.

Acton's work during the months of the Vatican Council represented his final great effort to save Liberal Catholicism. Throughout the course of the Council he kept Gladstone informed on proceedings. His lengthy letters to the Prime Minister were to form a basis for Gladstone's belated attack on the Vatican decrees in 1874. Despite Acton's importunings for civil intervention Gladstone wisely refused to go any further than to give him *carte blanche* permission to make known his opposition.[37] Acton's long reports to Döllinger on proceedings at Rome provided the basic information for the famous *Letters from Rome* by "Quirinus." These letters appeared regularly in the Augsburg *Allgemeine Zeitung* and gave a detailed account of what went on both inside and outside the Council.[38] On their

[35] J. Fitzsimmons, "The Wavy Line," *Blackfriars*, October, 1952, p. 410.
[36] "Lord Acton as a Book-Collector," *Proceedings of the British Academy 1903–1904*, vol. i, p. 288.
[37] *Lord Acton's Correspondence*, pp. 84–113; D. C. Lathbury, *Correspondence on Church and Religion of William Ewart Gladstone* (London, 1910), vol. ii, p. 49.
[38] Many of Acton's letters were reproduced verbatim by "Quirinus." An English translation of *Letters from Rome* appeared in 1870 (Rivington).

essential accuracy Newman provides the following testimony: "Lady Howard last night said that both Dr. Amherst and Dr. Clifford told her, that *Quirinus* is the most accurate witness of what took place at the Council."[39] But their accuracy of reporting notwithstanding, the *Letters* of Quirinus still remain propaganda on behalf of a cause and must be interpreted accordingly. Acton's personal report on the Vatican Council written for the *North British Review* was a more sober effort, but in this essay his preoccupation with the political aspects of the Council tended to blind him to the far more important theological considerations.[40]

Acton's fears reached the frantic stage when on March 1, 1870 the Pope confirmed the decision to introduce the question of Infallibility to the Council. He anticipated a decree proclaiming unlimited Infallibility. To quote his letter to Gladstone of March 10:

> The proposed decree makes the Infallibility of the Pope embrace everything to which the Infallibility of the Church extends. But in the twenty-one Canons *de Ecclesia* the Church is declared infallible in all matters that are necessary to the preservation of the faith. The Infallibility of the Pope would therefore be unconditional and unlimited, as he alone would have to decide what is necessary for the preservation of the faith.[41]

It was not until May 13, that the great debate on Infallibility finally opened. By the second week in June it was clear to Acton that the Infallibilists were to have their way and he left Rome for his summer home in Tegernsee, Bavaria.

Newman, through his correspondence with Bishops Ullathorne, Clifford and Moriarty was kept fully abreast of developments at Rome. A month after the commencement of the Council he wrote to Bishop Ullathorne an impulsive letter which he later characterized as "one of the most passionate and most confidential letters I ever wrote in my life."[42] In this letter—which

[39] Newman to A. St. John, 17 January 1871, Orat. O[ratory] L[etters].

[40] "The Vatican Council," October, 1870; reprinted in *The History of Freedom*. The German translation of this Essay (*Zur Geschichte des Vaticanischen Concils*, Munich, 1871) was not accurate and annoyed Acton. Thus on March 5, 1871 he wrote to Döllinger: "Sie werden mich aus einer grossen Schwierigkeit retten, wenn in den Besprechungen meiner Schrift die bestimmte Erklärung gegeben wird dass ich für die Uebersetzung nicht verantwortlich bin, und die Änderungen ohne mein Wissen und Willen gemacht würden" (Woodruff Mss.). F. E. Lally in his *As Lord Acton Says*, p. 106, n. 37, wrongly states that Acton himself was the translator.

[41] *Lord Acton's Correspondence*, p. 108.

[42] Butler, *Ullathorne*, ii, pp. 58–59.

became public, and created a sensation—Newman wrote of the definition of Infallibility as a tragedy to be averted:

What have we done to be treated as the faithful were never treated before? When has a definition of doctrine *de fide* been a luxury of devotion, and not a stern painful necessity? Why should an aggressive insolent faction be allowed to 'make the heart of the just to mourn, whom the Lord hath not made sorrowful'?

A careful reading of this bitter letter, in which Newman gave free rein to his indignation, reveals that he had no personal theological difficulty regarding Papal Infallibility, e.g.:

When we are all at rest, and have no doubts, and at least practically, not to say doctrinally, hold the Holy Father to be Infallible . . . As to myself personally, please God, I do not expect any trial at all, but I cannot help suffering with the various souls that are suffering.

It may be supposed that the opponents to the definition would pass over these phrases hidden away in a mass of colorful prose and welcome Newman as a champion in full sympathy with themselves.

Döllinger, at any rate, believed Newman was in agreement with him and wrote to him on March 19, 1870 to speak out: "Let the trumpet give a clear and certain sound."[43] Newman replied that the publication of his private letter to his Bishop presented a more forceful utterance than he could ever have made publicly: "Can anything I say move a single Bishop?"[44]

Newman undoubtedly was right; any further word on his part would have had no influence on the Bishops, who already had their minds made up. Yet, on the publication of his private letter, he had "a faint hope that there might have been some expression of opinion from the laity to back up its contents." He then would "have written strongly."[45] But, Acton excepted, the laity either remained silent or spoke out in favor of a definition. In England all the Catholic organs of opinion were controlled by the neo-Ultramontanes and it was not easy for an opponent to find a platform unless he had recourse to a non-Catholic journal. The lack of a critical Catholic publication was sorely felt in the years immediately preceding the Vatican Council. The *Home and Foreign* had no successor.

On the morning of July 18, 1870, just four months after

---

[43] Döllinger to Newman, Orat. V[atican] C[ouncil] C[ollection].
[44] Newman to Döllinger, 9 April 1870, Orat. V.C.C. (Newman's draft copy).
[45] Newman to Monsell, 21 April 1871, Orat. P.C.

Döllinger's call to Newman to speak out, the dogma of Papal Infallibility was defined in the Constitution *Pastor Aeternus.* The Ultramontanes apparently had achieved all they desired.

Newman, distressed by reports of the high-handed activities of the majority group responsible for the definition, received the news without joy. "Our good God is trying all of us with disappointment and sorrow just now," he wrote to a correspondent.[46] The definition itself presented him with no personal theological difficulty:

> It is too soon to give an opinion about the definition. I want to know what the Bishops of the Minority say on the subject, and what they mean to do. As I have ever believed as much as the definition says, I have difficulty in putting myself into the position of mind of those who have not.[47]

A fear remained that "the tyrant majority" was aiming at enlarging the province of Infallibility.

> But we must hope, [he wrote to Ambrose St. John], for one is obliged to hope it, that the Pope will be driven from Rome, and will not continue the Council, or that there will be another Pope. It is sad he should force us to such wishes. Our friends seem to me rather to have made the fight at Rome something of a game or a prize fight—but I may be wrong.[48]

That the Franco-Prussian war of 1870 was brought about by the promptings of higher powers may be open to question, but with the withdrawal of the French garrison from Rome to defend the home frontier, and the consequent capitulation of the Eternal City to the Italian armies, the Vatican Council was indefinitely suspended.

Only in Germany was there any widespread opposition to receiving the Vatican Decrees. The Archbishop of Munich had the painful duty of calling upon the members of the faculty of Catholic Theology at the University of Munich for a declaration of adherence to the Decrees. Döllinger, the Dean of the Faculty, after some delay replied on March 28, 1871 in a surprisingly intemperate manifesto, rejecting them as involving a spiritual despotism:

> [The Pope's] authority is unlimited, incalculable; it can strike, as Innocent III. says, wherever sin is; it can punish every one; it allows no appeal and is itself Sovereign Caprice; for the Pope carries, according

---

[46] Ward, *Newman*, ii, p. 308.
[47] Ward, *Newman*, ii, p. 308.
[48] Newman to A. St. John, 21 August 1870, Orat. O.L.

to the expression of Boniface VIII., all rights in the Shrine of his breast. As he has now become infallible, he can by the use of the little word, "orbi", (which means that he turns himself round to the whole Church) make every rule, every doctrine, every demand, into a certain and incontestible article of Faith. No right can stand against him, no personal or corporate liberty; or as the Canonists put it—"The Tribunal of God and of the Pope is one and the same." This system bears its Roman origin on its brow, and will never be able to force its way in German lands. As a Christian, as a Theologian, as a Reader of history, as a Citizen, I cannot accept this doctrine; for it is irreconcileable with the spirit of the Gospel, and with the clear declaration of Christ and the Apostles; it wishes directly to set up the kingdom of this world which Christ declined; it covets the Lordship over the Churches which Peter forbad to all and to himself. Not as a Theologian; for the whole, genuine Tradition of the Church stands in irreconcileable opposition to it. Not as a Reader of history can I accept it; for as such, I know, that the persistent striving to realize this theory of world domination, has cost Europe rivers of blood, has distracted and desolated whole countries, has torn to pieces the beautiful, organic constitution of the ancient Church, and has engendered, nourished, and maintained the worst ecclesiastical abuses. Finally, as a Citizen, I must beckon it away from me; because by its claims to the prostration of States and Monarchs and the whole political order of things under the authority of the Pope, and by the privileged position which it demands for the Clergy, it lays the foundation for an endless and destructive schism between Church and State, between Cleric and Layman. For I cannot conceal from myself, that this Dogma, among the consequences of which, the old German empire was destroyed, would, were it to become dominant in the Catholic section of the German nation, immediately also plant, in the new Empire, which has just been established, the germ of an incurable disorder.[49]

On April 2 the Archbishop of Munich again wrote to Döllinger warning him that a rejection of the dogmatic constitutions of an Ecumenical Council involved heresy and automatic excommunication. Döllinger remained adamant. The Archbishop waited for another two weeks before formally excommunicating him for open heresy. The case of Döllinger attracted much attention in England. Among Catholics his excommunication evoked mixed reactions, some of the Manning school taking it as a confirmation of their suspicions that a Liberal Catholic was not a true Catholic, whilst others of liberal sympathies were distressed at the tragedy involved in the excommunication of one who had labored so long and so well for Catholicism. Monsell,

[49] *A Letter Addressed to the Archbishop of Munich* (London, 1871), pp. 22–23.

one of the latter, encouraged Newman to write something on the Döllinger case.[50] Newman, while stating: "I don't agree with Döllinger either as to the truth of the doctrine or the validity of its definition," could see no point in his writing. A free spoken statement such as he would have to write would do more harm than good. "And as for the wishes of the authorities," he wrote to Monsell, "I think they would be best pleased if I held my tongue."[51]

Writing to Newman from Munich some months later Alfred Plummer reported on Döllinger:

> I believe I may say with certainty that he is quite as much pained to think that you are not with him, as you can be to think that he is not with you in this great trial. Forgive me if I may venture to add that I believe he is more surprised at your position than you seem to be at his.

It was Döllinger's conviction, continued Plummer, that

> the meaning which the extreme party give to the Dogma is the one which to most people would seem to be the obvious meaning, [and] is the one which future generations will put on it.[52]

Newman, as will be seen, rejected this and maintained that only the strictest theological interpretation was allowable. For confirmation he could call upon the two semi-official interpretations which received the unqualified approval of the Pope: 1) a tract, *The True and the False Infallibility of the Popes*, by Bishop Fessler, the General Secretary of the Council; 2) the joint "Pastoral Instruction" issued by the Swiss Bishops in June, 1871.[53]

In Newman's opinion the point at issue between the extreme Ultramontanes and their opponents was the extent of the limitations of the Infallibility of the Pope. He held that Infallibility was limited to an evolution of the deposit of faith, the body of truths entrusted to the Church through Divine revelation. This view Father Ryder, with Newman's encouragement, put forward in his attack on Ward in 1867.[54] His fear throughout the Council was of the efforts of the Ultramontanes to extend the province of Infallibility: "Now see what an enormous power it will give

[50] Newman to Monsell, 21 April 1871, Orat. P.C.
[51] *Ibid.*
[52] Plummer to Newman, 14 July 1872, Orat. V.C.C.
[53] Butler, *Vatican Council*, ii, pp. 213–19.
[54] Ward, *Newman*, ii, p. 223 ff.

the Pope, if *he is not restrained even by the Depositum.*"[55] After the Council Döllinger maintained that the extremists had won the day. Newman denied this. The following passage from the Pastoral of the Swiss Bishops seems clearly to support Newman:

It is the revelation given by God, the deposit of faith, which is the domain perfectly traced out and exactly circumscribed, within which the infallible decisions of the Pope are able to extend themselves, and in regard to which the faith of Catholics can be bound to fresh obligations.[56]

Since the Vatican Council the course of action followed by the Popes has gone against Döllinger's forecast. As Dr. Mascall has recently written:

It has been increasingly recognized that the definition as actually promulgated represented nothing like the victory for the maximising party which it was commonly believed to represent at the time.[57]

Two weeks after Döllinger's defiant reply to his Archbishop, Rowland Blennerhasset, a Liberal in full sympathy with the recalcitrant German Catholics, reported to Acton on Newman's position:

On my way through Birmingham I went to call on Dr. Newman. I found him in an extremely odd state of mind. He expressed himself strongly against the Archbishop of Munich for having asked Döllinger for a declaration on the subject of Infallibility and at the same time professed his own belief in the new dogma although unable to reconcile it with well ascertained historical facts.[58]

A recent writer has used this passage to demonstrate Newman's position on Infallibility.[59] However, it hardly appears fair to Newman to take as a definitive expression of his views on a highly controversial issue a rather ambiguous paraphrase of a

[55] Newman to Monsell, 3 September 1869, Orat. P.C.

[56] Cited by Butler, *Vatican Council*, ii, p. 218.

[57] E. L. Mascall, *The Recovery of Unity* (London, 1958), p. 220.

[58] 10 April 1871, CUL Add. Mss. 4989 (original letter).

[59] G. Himmelfarb, *Lord Acton, A Study In Conscience and Politics* (London, 1952), p. 156. Miss Himmelfarb writes the following misleading sentence: "During the Vatican Council much was made of Newman's attack upon the 'aggressive and insolent' faction that had introduced the new decrees, but he was furious when his words became known and later explained that he accepted and believed the dogma of Infallibility although he was 'unable to reconcile it with well-ascertained historical facts' " (Reference is given to the cited letter of Blennerhasset). Miss Himmelfarb obviously has in mind the decrees on Infallibility when she writes of "the new decrees." 1. Since the Pope did not confirm the decision to discuss in the Council the question of Infallibility until 1 March and the ar-

conversation, and especially when the report was written by a person deeply involved. In the absence of other evidence Blennerhasset's statement might appear to carry considerable weight, but Newman made no secret of his views before or after the Council and his private letters and published works abound with references to Infallibility. Further, the charge that he accepted the dogma of Infallibility despite his own conviction to the contrary was made publicly, and answered publicly by Newman himself; it would seem only just to call him as his own witness, something that is not always possible in an historical inquiry.

In the course of a letter to the *Guardian* on September 11, 1872, J. M. Capes wrote as follows:

We all know how Dr. Newman felt the enforcement of the dogma of Papal Infallibility. There were published a few sentences of the expressions of intense distress which were wrung from him, when he foresaw the imposition of a doctrine which would cut up the historical basis of his faith by the very roots. At the same time, as he then avowed, he himself contrived, by some mysterious subleties, to accept the tyrannical and false decrees. But it was evident that it was only by putting a terrible force upon his previous convictions that he could bring himself to submit as he has submitted; and the strain upon his principle of absolute obedience to Rome was plainly such as he had never contemplated when he left the English communion.[60]

In the next number of the *Guardian* appeared the following letter from Newman:

Sir—I cannot allow such language as Mr. Capes used of me in yesterday's *Guardian* to pass unnoticed, nor can I doubt that you will admit my answer to it. I thank him for having put into print, what doubtless has often been said behind my back; I do not thank him for the odious words which he has made the vehicle of it.

rangements necessary for its introduction were not completed until 13 May (Butler, *Vatican Council*, ii, pp. 27, 43–44) Newman's attack, dated 28 January could not have been directed against those "who had introduced the new decrees." Newman hoped at that date the decrees would not be introduced, hence his attack. 2. Rather than being "furious when his words became known" he was, on the whole, glad (Ward, *Newman*, ii, p. 291). 3. The last half of the statement seems to imply that Newman was forced to explain his letter away. But he publicly stood by every word of it (See reply to Capes below, p. 123). 4. His "explanation" to Blennerhasset was not related to his attack on the "aggressive and insolent faction." It was made over a year later.

[60] *The Guardian*, p. 1154. Capes, after a period of indecision, had left the Catholic Church. He returned to it in 1886, three years before his death. See a letter from his daughter, Florence M. Capes, to the *Times*, 23 January 1889.

I will not dirty my ink by repeating them; but the substance mildly stated, is this—that I have all along considered the doctrine of the Pope's Infallibility to be contradicted by the facts of Church history, and that, though convinced of this, I have in consequence of the Vatican Council forced myself to do a thing that I never, never fancied would befall me when I became a Catholic—viz., forced myself by some unintelligible quibbles to fancy myself believing what really after all in my heart I could not and did not believe. And that this operation and its results have given me a certain pain.

I could say much, and quote much from what I have written, in comment upon this nasty view of me. But, not to take up too much of your room, I will, in order to pluck it up "by the very roots" (to use his own expression) quote one out of various passages, in which long before the Vatican Council was dreamed of, at least by me, I enunciated absolutely the doctrine of the Pope's Infallibility. It is my Discourses on University Education, delivered in Dublin in 1852. It runs as follows:—

'Deeply do I feel, ever will I protest, *for I can appeal to the ample testimony of history to bear me out*, that, in questions of right and wrong, there is nothing really strong in the whole world, nothing decisive and operative, but the voice of him, to whom have been committed the keys of the kingdom and the oversight of Christ's flock. That voice is now, as it ever has been, a real authority, *infallible* when it teaches, prosperous when it commands, ever taking the lead wisely and distinctly in its own province, adding certainty to what is probable and persuasion to what is certain. Before he speaks, the most saintly may mistake; and after it has spoken, the most gifted must obey . . . If there ever was a power on earth who had an eye for the times, who has confined himself to the practicable, and has been happy in his anticipations, whose words have been deeds, and whose commands prophecies, such is he in the history of ages who sits on from generation to generation in the Chair of the Apostles as the Vicar of Christ and Doctor of His Church . . . Has he failed in his successes up to this hour? Did he, in our father's day, fail in his struggle with Joseph of Germany and his confederates; with Napoleon—a greater name—and his dependent kings; that, though in another kind of fight, he should fail in ours? What grey hairs are on the head of Judah, whose youth is renewed like the eagle's whose feet are like the feet of harts, and underneath the everlasting arms?—pp. 22–28.'

This passage I suffered Father Cardella in 1867 or 1868 to reprint in a volume which he published at Rome. My reason for selecting it, as I told him, was this—because in an abridged reprint of Discourses in 1859 I had omitted it, as well as other large portions of the volume, as of only temporary interest, and irrelevant to the subject of University education.

I could quote to the same purpose passages from my *Essay on Development*, 1845; *Loss and Gain*, 1847; *Discourses to Mixed Congregations*, 1849; *Position of Catholics*, 1851; *Church of the Fathers*, 1857.

I underwent then no change of mind as regards the truth of the doctrine of the Pope's Infallibility in consequence of the Council. It is true, I was deeply, though not personally, pained both by the fact and by the circumstances of the definition; and, when it was in contemplation, I wrote a most confidential letter, which was surreptitiously gained and published, but of which I have not a word to retract. The feelings of surprise and concern expressed in that letter have nothing to do with a screwing one's conscience to profess what one does not believe, which is Mr. Capes's pleasant account of me. He ought to know better.[61]

Whatever Capes, Blennerhasset or Döllinger may have believed, Acton had no illusions about Newman's position. Nowhere in his notes is there the slightest suggestion that Newman did not believe in Infallibility before its definition. Indeed, the contrary is true, e.g.:

Newman in his Development insists on papal Infallibility . . .[62] It was the dogma of Papal supremacy, of Papal Infallibility that brought Newman over . . . Clearly in favor of Infallibility, yet anxious to prevent the dogma.[63]

Acton's own position remained ambiguous until Gladstone's attack on the Vatican Decrees brought matters to a head. Two months after the definition of Infallibility he published an open letter to an anonymous German Bishop calling upon the minority Bishops to stand out against the Decrees, quoting to great effect their own words against the definition.[64] It appeared for a time that he would certainly follow Döllinger. His name appeared (as 'Lord Acton-Dalberg') on a declaration signed by a group of German priests and laymen rejecting the decrees as illegal.[65] But it was put there without his authorization. He wrote to Döllinger in protest:

[61] The *Guardian*, 18 September 1872, p. 1184. F. L. Cross in his *John Henry Newman* (London, 1933), pp. 148–49, states that observations of Newman "written before July, 1870, can be found which imply that he himself disbelieved in the doctrine which was about to be defined." Mr. Cross makes no mention of where such observations can be found.

[62] CUL Add. Mss. 5463.

[63] CUL Add. Mss. 5666.

[64] *Sendschreiben an einen deutschen Bischof des vaticanischen Concils* (Nördlingen, 1870).

[65] This "Munich Declaration of Whitsuntide, 1871" marks the beginning of the Old Catholic movement. It was first published in the *Rheinischer Merkur* and was reprinted in J. F. von Schulte, *Der Altkatholicismus* (Giessen, 1887), pp. 16–22. G. Himmelfarb in her *Acton*, p. 113, states that Sir Rowland Blennerhasset—whose name also appeared on the declaration—in a letter to the *Times* repudiated "his own and Acton's signature". Sir Rowland, however, only repudiated his own signature. See his letter to the *Times*, 19 June 1871.

Ich war aber nicht in der Versammlung welche die Art der Redaktion entschied: ich bekam die Erklärung nicht zu sehen, obwohl ich einige Mal den Wunsch zu erkennen gab; und ich kann mich nicht erinnern dass mich je jemand gefragt hat ob mein Name darunter stehen sollte.[66]

As the Old Catholic movement developed Acton remained aloof from it. He believed that many of the men associated with it were no better than the Infallibilists they condemned. "Ich muss gestehen," he wrote to Döllinger from Herrnsheim,[67]

dass der moralische Abscheu der mich von den Infallibilisten trennt ganz und genau so mich von einem Theil der Herrn trennt die in Ihrer Nahe sind. Darum will ich mich in der Zukunft von jeder Gemeinschaft mit ihnen fern halten; darum, vor allen Dingen wünschte ich Sie hier zu sehen.[68]

In the months after the Council he saw the minority bishops one by one submitting to the Vatican Decrees until the opposition was left without the support of a single bishop. The case of Archbishop Kenrick of St. Louis, in particular, may have had some influence on his own position. Kenrick was the stoutest opponent of Infallibility during the Council. At the very time when Döllinger was publishing to the world his spirited rejection of the Decrees, Kenrick wrote as follows to Acton:

I reconciled myself intellectually to submission by applying Father Newman's theory of development to the case in point. The Pontifical authority as at present exercised is so different from what it appears to have been in the early Church, that it can only be supposed identical in substance by allowing a process of doctrinal development. This principle removed Newman's great difficulty and convinced him that, notwithstanding the difference, he might and should become a Catholic. I thought that it might justify me in remaining one.[69]

Yet, it is not clear that Acton's difficulty with Infallibility was specifically theological. His opposition, like Newman's, seems

[66] Acton to Döllinger, 19 June 1871, Woodruff Mss. "The fact is that I was not at the meeting where the wording was decided on; I had not seen the declaration, although I repeatedly expressed the wish to do so; and I do not remember anybody ever asking me whether my name was to stand under it."

[67] Herrnsheim was Acton's estate on the Rhine which had come to him on the death of his mother.

[68] Acton to Döllinger, 19 August 1871, Woodruff Mss. "I must confess that the moral aversion which separates me from the Infallibilists separates me entirely, and in the same fashion, from some of the gentlemen who are near you. I therefore wish to keep myself aloof from all communion with them in the future; this is the chief reason why I wished to see you here."

[69] This letter is printed in J. F. von Schulte, Der Altkatholicismus, pp. 268–69. In the above passage errors in spelling have been corrected.

to have been aroused by fear—fear of the concentration of arbitrary power in the Pope without the checks imposed by scientific theology. Once Newman saw that the definition left things pretty much as they were, the onus of interpretation remaining with the theologian, his fear was allayed.

Acton's case, however, was more complicated. In the first place he was not a theologian and had no deep appreciation of the science of theology apart from history. He tended to assign to history too exclusive a role in the determination of religious truth. Again, he held an exaggerated notion of the permanent character of the findings of critical scholars both in the field of natural science and in the humanities. He believed it was absolutely incumbent upon religious leaders to accommodate religious thought to the findings of science. But he failed sufficiently to take into account that what scientists teach today may be untaught by scientists of tomorrow and in a period of rapid transition a policy of patience and restraint might be the wisest one for religious leaders. By 1870 the liberal dogma of the perfectibility of man with the accompanying one of unrestricted liberty was beginning to take possession of his mind, and faint visions of a new earthly Kingdom of Liberty arose to tease his imagination. The policy pursued by Rome ran directly counter to all these things. The Roman System, Vaticanism, Ultramontanism—different names for the same thing—this was Acton's obstacle. He saw Infallibility as only a symptom of a far broader evil.

In a notebook containing reflections on the Vatican Council he set down some of the things in the Roman System that called forth his opposition.[70]

His most serious grievance against its supporters was their refusal to pay regard to history:

They refuse to be bound by the evidence of history . . . the antagonism is against historical science chiefly . . . The Roman authority is attacked by Scripture and Tradition. That is, by the historical sciences, and political. Against these his [the Pope's] bitterness is directed.[71]

Acton admitted that a purely scientific approach to religion was not sufficient:

To some extent the authority of religion over reason is essential to the existence of religion. At least of revelation. If all these truths could be

[70] CUL Add. Mss. 5542.
[71] CUL Add. Mss. pp. 32, 60.

ascertained, no revelation would be needed. If reason could demonstrate all truths, there would be no room for faith. As long as mysteries remain in religion, there are limits set to reason; there is a domain of imperative authority.[72]

But the Ultramontanes sought to extend the domain of imperative authority to everything:

They uphold the Trinity, which reason cannot prove a priori— with the same right they claim to govern every domain. They say the promise of Christ is ever present, fulfilled in the supreme ruler of the Church.

Their opponents rejected this:

The others say, he is bound, the whole Church is bound, by evidence. Her action must always be founded on sufficient reason. It is not sustained by revelation or illumination. It must be justified by proof. This proof it seeks in Scripture and Tradition.[73]

Acton could find no group that took their stand on principle alone: "The bishops being engaged in practical conflict, naturally are on the side of practical wisdom, not theoretical principle." The French liberals were no better; they "aspired to reconcile the Church with modern society not with science. It was to be connected with that which is change . . . not with that whose life is progress."[74] Döllinger himself was tainted: "Many by habit made concessions, defended, explained, ignored—even Döllinger."[75]

Acton believed an important work could have been accomplished by the Council if it had repudiated all past errors:

Two great powers, against which Trent fought, liberty in the state and truth of science, now capable of becoming the sure allies, the unfailing support of the Church . . . Time to abandon the unjust claims, and to acknowledge the just accusations.[76]

But unfortunately for the fulfillment of Acton's hopes, the current notions on liberty and on the all-embracing infallibility of science were the very things Catholic leaders feared as undermining Christianity, the evil spirits that had to be exorcised from society if it was to continue Christian.

[72] *Ibid.*, p. 39.
[73] *Ibid.*, pp. 39–40.
[74] CUL Add. Mss. p. 69.
[75] *Ibid.*, p. 41.
[76] *Ibid.*, pp. 62–63.

Acton saw two courses of action open to the enlightened Catholic and he attempted to follow both in turn. The first was to

prevent, by hook or crook, the definition of Inf[allibility]. In that nearly all the great minds agreed:—Döllinger and Ketteler, Kenrick and Newman, Dupanloup and Gratry . . . In this point of view were made all the practical negotiations: all the dilatory manoeuvers.

But there was another point of view:

to prevent it indeed if possible; but to obtain something else, whether prevented or not. To bring home to the consciousness of men that the Roman system is untenable, and imposed on its defenders the disastrous effects of a bad cause. To obtain the protest of the conscience; the resolution to condemn, abhor, and denounce the spirit of which Inf[fallibility] is but a manifestation—to reinstate [?] morality and truth—to proclaim and realize the internal reform of the Church, to turn against all that is unclean within, to embrace all that is good without. Believing that even the definition was an evil from which the immortal vitality of the Church would overcome and cast out in time; but that the hope of remedy, of reform, of reconciliation lay in the open acknowledgment of the faults and vices of the Roman system, of the political absolutism, the dread of freedom, the repression of literature, the arbitrary superiority over law, the Syllabus, the Inquisition.

In a word, it preferred the definition, accompanied by such a protest as would restore the honour and authority of the episcopate, rather than a patched up truce, and a victory over the Infallibilists.

How far this object was obtained, by what sequence of events the reluctant minority were driven farther in this direction, and how far the results thus obtained supply consolation and promise for the future of the Church, is the great leading question in the history of the Council.[77]

This was not an Acton writing to stir up an audience. These were the views of a deeply troubled man. He had a vision of an ideal Church which he believed was realizable here on earth. He saw and condemned the Roman System based on the pessimistic belief in the sinfulness of man and the need of restraints if, what Newman would call, man's wild living intellect were not to lead him to perdition. Acton had drunk deeply at the fount of liberalism and came to see restraints as accursed things which kept men enslaved. The Roman System was the antithesis to true liberalism. Acton's gaze brooded over the ages and he saw much that caused him grief. The Church, which should have led men along the road of progress, too often tarried along

[77] CUL Add. Mss. 5542, pp. 59–60.

the way and surrendered to the very evils it was meant to eliminate. The deposing power, the Inquisition and the disregard of human life and personal liberty, the claims to absolute authority, the arbitrary powers assumed or sanctioned, the restrictions on freedom of thought, all of these things were as so many blots that could only be removed by confession and repentance. But the Roman System, far from admitting past sins, attempted to sanctify them through the Syllabus. The papacy was a particular object of Acton's wrath not because he thought lowly of it as an institution but because he believed it was of Christ and was untrue to its origins. A Church "without a Pope, is not the Church of Christ," he taught his son in 1890.[78] The spirit of Christ was in the world, operating through His Church, leading men to freedom, but wicked or stupid Churchmen frustrated His designs and prevented their consummation. Acton could not abandon a Church which he firmly believed was a divine organization. His deep faith in the reality of Christ's presence in the Church and his distress at what he considered to be the abuses of its human representatives created a terrible conflict in his soul. One can but stand in awe at the depth of the faith which could withstand it.

It is not clear that Newman fully understood the nature of Acton's predicament, although Acton's public writings on the Vatican Council could hardly have left him in much doubt about his deep antipathy to Ultramontanism. While not knowing where Acton stood "as regards this sad Vatican question," Newman was confident he would not rebel. "There is only one locus standi," he wrote to Lord Blachford, "& I think in time he will see that."[79] But it was not until Gladstone's attack brought matters dramatically to a head in 1874 that Newman learned of Acton's true "locus standi."

Gladstone's decision to write on the Vatican Decrees four years after their promulgation at first sight appears an odd one. But things Roman were very much in his mind in the autumn of 1874. The conversion to Catholicism of his close associate, Lord Ripon, painfully reminded him of the ever present challenge of Rome. "How is it possible that such news can be true,"

---

[78] CUL Add. Mss. 4871. This manuscript is entitled "Conversations on Church History held with my Father at Tegernsee. Summer 1890."
[79] Newman to Blachford, 6 July 1872, Orat. P.C.

he distressfully wrote to Lady Ripon on August 21.[80] A September visit to Munich during the course of which he spent long hours in conversation with Döllinger stirred up new bitterness toward Rome. "It makes my blood run cold," he wrote to his wife, "to think of *his* being excommunicated in his venerable but, thank God, hale and strong old age."[81] In November he published a heavy attack on the Vatican Decrees on the grounds that they made it impossible for a Catholic who followed them to remain a loyal citizen.[82] By the end of the year 145,000 copies of the tract were in circulation.[83]

Newman had been permitted to see an advance copy of the pamphlet and in writing to A. P. de Lisle on November 6 he commented on it:

I am not at all sorry, that he is publishing such an expostulation as this is; it must turn to good . . . For myself, I consider he is misled in his interpretation of the ecclesiastical acts of 1870, by judging of the wording by the rules of ordinary language. Theological language, like legal, is scientific, and cannot be understood without the knowledge of long precedent and tradition, nor without the comments of theologians. Such comments time alone can give us.[84]

On November 12 Acton wrote to Newman:

By Mr. de l'Isle's permission Gladstone showed me your letter. He did not feel the full force of the argument you employ, but I think it is one he would feel the force of if it was put more fully before him. I don't know whether you will think it right to take any public or private opportunity of so putting it.[85]

Meanwhile Acton had decided to enter the lists himself to break a lance on behalf of his fellow Catholics. In a celebrated letter in the *Times* on November 9, 1874 he put the case against Gladstone.[86] He argued in a characteristic fashion. English Catholics might be trusted in spite of the letter and spirit of ecclesiastical laws since in many instances they ignored both.

[80] Gladstone to Lady Ripon, 21 August 1874. British Museum, Add. Mss. 44,444 (copy).
[81] J. Morley, *Gladstone*, ii, p. 121.
[82] *The Vatican Decrees In Their Bearing on Civil Allegiance* (London, 1874).
[83] J. Morley, *Gladstone*, ii, p. 127.
[84] *Life and Letters of A. P. deLisle*, ii, p. 42.
[85] Acton to Newman, 12 November [1874], Orat. D[uke of] N[orfolk] C[ollection].
[86] *Lord Acton's Correspondence*, pp. 119–24.

The Vatican Decrees did not increase the pretensions of Popes to civil obedience: they had made the extremest claims before 1870. Popes in the past had decreed the murder of excommunicates, the assassination of kings, absolved men from the duty of keeping faith with heretics, but throughout Catholics had remained loyal citizens. Why, then, should any new fulminations from the Vatican seriously disturb civil authority?

There was a certain grim logic in Acton's approach and Catholics might gain from it what consolation they could. But if it was the only answer to Gladstone's sweeping charges it left them devoid of intellectual integrity in any meaningful sense. No doubt many would have preferred to admit the truth of the accusation that they could not follow Rome and be loyal citizens if the only other alternative to abandoning their religion lay in an acceptance of Acton's peculiar brand. It is no wonder that many, smarting under Gladstone's attack, considered Acton's *tour de force* a betrayal.

The reaction of Lady Georgiana Fullerton, a sister of Lord Granville, was typical. The day Acton's letter appeared she wrote to Newman:

> This morning I have read poor Acton's letter in the *Times*. It has made me very unhappy and I thanked God with all my heart that his mother is not alive to witness his betrayal of the Church. But more than ever we all as [?] devoted children turn to you and call upon you to come forward and stand on the breach at this moment.[87]

A. P. de Lisle, a close friend of both Acton and Gladstone, wrote to the latter:

> If Lord Acton had announced his secession from the Barque of Peter, I shd understand the Line he is taking better than I do.[88]

And to Newman:

> I was shocked beyond what I can easily say at Lord Acton's Letter to Mr. Gladstone in the Times . . . There is no time to be lost—all my hopes, under God are centered in you—you are the only man to rescue the Church both from Foes and *Friends*.[89]

Newman, as always, sympathized with Acton and refused to judge him harshly. Alone, it would appear, among readers of

---

[87] G. Fullerton to Newman, 9 November 1874, Orat. D.N.C.
[88] *Life and Letters of A. P. deLisle*, ii, p. 92.
[89] De Lisle to Newman, 11 November 1874, Orat. D.N.C.

the *Times*, whether Catholic or Protestant, he endeavored to go beyond the obvious literal interpretation of Acton's letter to grasp what he really meant. He explained to a correspondent that Acton was "unlucky in his language, as not being a theologian" when he wrote that it was no matter what the Councils or Popes decree or do, for the Catholic body went on pretty much as it did, in spite of all. Acton meant (in Newman's opinion) that the Catholic Church has "its constitutions and its theological laws in spite of the excesses of individuals." The truth was that the Schola Theologorum was the regulating principle of the Church, and as lawyers and public officers

preserve the tradition of the British Constitution, in spite of King, Lords and Commons, so there is a permanent and sui similis life in the Church, to which all its acts are necessarily assimilated, nay, and, under the implied condition of its existence and action, such acts are done and are accepted.[90]

Acton may, and probably did, have something like the above in mind, but the plain reader, unaided, could never discover it.

Newman felt deeply for Acton at this period. He wrote to him, so related Lady Blennerhasset, "to congratulate him on his moderation and to say that historical truth must be given entirely and undisguised."[91] With due allowance for possible feminine exaggeration in the use of the word *moderation* it can at least be concluded that Newman's letter contained no reproach. Newman's sympathy was deeply appreciated by the hard-pressed Acton. At the time he was attacked by irate Catholics who challenged the accuracy of his historical statements, and, what was more serious, pressed by Manning for a declaration on his adhesion to the Vatican Decrees. On Friday, December 4, 1874 he wrote to Newman an important letter, opening with the revealing passage:

I did not write sooner to thank you for your kind and consoling letter, because I had much to say, and was constantly occupied with more than I could get through. You know, and I need not tell you, what the value of your sympathy has ever been to me, when I could think that I obtained it, and it could never be so valuable as now.[92]

[90] Newman to Blachford, 5 February 1875, Orat. C[opied] L[etters].
[91] "The Late Lord Acton," *Edinburgh Review*, April, 1903, p. 527.
[92] Acton to Newman, 4 December 1874, Orat. D.N.C.

After outlining his correspondence with his own Bishop and with Manning,[93] Acton endeavored to explain the exact state of his mind regarding the Vatican decrees:

The decrees have never been a difficulty to me, not because I have ever examined them and found that they approved themselves to my judgment but because, be they what they may, I am sure it will be all right, and if it is not evidently all right now, that is not my business. I take it that no interpretation holds that is inconsistent with tradition, and with former decrees. And if one does not see how the new and the old can be reconciled, time will show it, and the new will be digested and assimilated, and will be worked into what was there before. I feel no impulse to do this as well as I can for my own satisfaction, or to choose an interpreter. Indeed I have felt no more curiosity to read these decrees through than those of Trent, and know about them both only casually, very imperfectly, and partly at second hand. Therefore, just as I have kept aloof from the Germans, who think they ought to raise their voice and hand against the Council, I have gone through no process of study, comprehension and agreement with respect to the several propositions it lays down, I take them in the new state, without the least resistance, subject to the process they have to go through, and to the law of interpretation which upholds the continuity and consistency of doctrine; but I do not guess what the process will effect, and do not attempt to apply the law myself. I am in the same condition with regard to hundreds of canons of former Councils; and I daresay you know how little most of us, native Catholics, care to master details.[94]

There is no clearer statement of Acton's position available. It seems beyond doubt that the Vatican Decrees in themselves do not explain his opposition. His position was not that of Döllinger, who "asked to be allowed to appear before a board of bishops, and undertook to show that the new decrees have no foundation in Scripture or Tradition, and that they are incompatible with the constitution of the modern states of Europe."[95] Acton was not sure that Döllinger's pessimistic view of the future of the Church was justified: "Dans le doute, he wrote to him, "je m'abstiens de désésperer. Ich müsste viel

[93] For further on this see Lord Acton's Correspondence, pp. 151–53; Gasquet, Acton, pp. 359–70; "Gasquet and the Acton-Simpson Correspondence," C.H.J. vol. x, no. 1, 1950, p. 105.

[94] Acton to Newman, 4 December 1874, Orat. D.N.C.

[95] Quoted by Butler, Vatican Council, ii, p. 185. L. Kochan in his Acton on History (London, 1954), p. 26, identifies Acton's position with Döllinger's. On the same page he writes that Acton "had not agreed with the dogma of Infallibility—but he none the less accepted it." But he goes on to state on p. 31: "He did not on the other hand accept the new dogma."

klarer sehen als ich sehe um die Kirche aufzugeben die ich gerade durch Sie in ihrer Grösse kennen und lieben lernte."[96]
Why was Acton so reluctant to satisfy Manning? A passage in his letter to Newman on December 4, gives the answer:

If therefore I am asked whether I accept the decrees with a definite understanding and inward conviction of their truth, I cannot say either yes or no. But this is the question which the Archbishop—taking his letter and his pastoral together—wants an answer to. I certainly cannot satisfy him. I hope you will understand that, in falling under his censures, I act from no spirit of revolt, from no indifference, and from no false shame. But I cannot accept his tests and canons of dogmatic development and interpretation, and must decline to give him the only answer that will content him, as it would, in my lips, be a lie.[97]

Acton gave a further reason for his reluctance to give a categorical answer to Manning:

I have tried to avoid the crisis as long as I could, and have given every opening that I could find for the Archbishop to content himself. It is quite natural that he, on the other hand, should force on a catastrophe. In the last ten years I have collected a very considerable mass of historical materials, and I must try to avail myself of them. At every step I should be sure to encounter the same difficulties as now, and I cannot make any concession to danger without treason.[98]

A concluding passage in his letter to Newman revealed another anxiety:

But then I should like to put to you this question—Should you think ill, spiritually, of a penitent refused the sacraments without having denied or disbelieved the Decrees? If you would prefer to talk it over with me, pray telegraph early, and I can be with you on Saturday bringing the letters.[99]

It is not clear that Acton visited Newman. On Monday, December 7 he wrote to the latter: "I have only just time to thank you most sincerely for your two letters, which I received on returning home to-day."[100] Had he returned from a visit to Newman? It seems unlikely.

[96] Acton to Döllinger, 25 November 1874, Woodruff Mss. "In case of doubt I refrain from despairing. I should have to see much more clearly than I do as to give up the Church which it was you that taught me to know and to love in Her greatness."
[97] Acton to Newman, 4 December 1874, Orat. D.N.C.
[98] Ibid. [99] Ibid.
[100] Acton to Newman, 7 December 1874, Orat. D.N.C.

On December 9 he replied to what must have been a third letter from Newman:

> I think you will agree that the Archbishop's words are not the easiest he could use, in as much as my own bishop now asks me whether I accept the decrees or reject them. Now I certainly do not reject them, which is what the Council requires. Do you think that, consistently with what I have told you, I can honestly say that I accept them.[101]

Unfortunately none of Newman's letters to Acton during this exchange of correspondence is extant. His reply to Acton's question can only be conjectured. On December 16 Acton replied to his own Bishop:

> If you speak of the Council because you supposed that I have separated myself in any degree from the Bishops whose friendship I enjoyed at Rome, who opposed the decrees during the discussion, but accept them now that it is over, you have entirely misapprehended my position.[102]

From this reply there seems some justification for assuming that Newman told him he could honestly say he accepted the decrees.

The concluding paragraph of Acton's letter of December 9 revealed the heart of his difficulties:

> I can not understand why you think what I said of the Popes gratuitous. The papal power was the very thing in question and we were in danger of such declarations of its harmlessness as the bishop of Orleans gave of the Syllabus. It is the presumption in favour of papal acts, the tenderness for papal examples, that is the difficulty for Catholicism.
>
> I sometimes ask myself whether there is not here a point of fundamental difference which makes my efforts vain to understand the position of other Catholics.

Here is a foreshadowing of future isolation. Acton had begun to suspect that his view of Ultramontanism was not shared even by those who were one with him at the Vatican Council. The crushing sense of isolation so poignantly manifested in his letters to Mary Gladstone was not yet born, but its period of gestation had arrived.

Newman, in the meanwhile, had finally decided to reply to Gladstone's expostulation on the Vatican Decrees. His well known *Letter to the Duke of Norfolk* came out in January.[103]

---

[101] Acton to Newman, 9 December [1874], Orat. D.N.C.
[102] Shane Leslie, *Henry Edward Manning* (London, 1921), p. 233.
[103] Reprinted in *Difficulties of Anglicans*, ii, pp. 175–378.

It was a masterly production. Professor Laski's tribute to it bears repeating:

It remains with some remarks of Sir Henry Maine and a few brilliant dicta of F. W. Maitland as perhaps the profoundest discussion of the nature of obedience and of sovereignty to be found in the English language.[104]

That Newman did not explain the Vatican Decrees by explaining them away—Acton's complaint against Dupanloup's interpretation of the Syllabus—could in no way be better illustrated than by stating that the redoubtable W. G. Ward spoke cordially of the pamphlet in the ultra-orthodox *Dublin Review*.[105]

Newman's words on the German Catholic scholars who had rejected the Vatican Decrees are of especial interest:

It is a tragical event, both for them and for us, that they have left us. It robs us of a great *prestige;* they have left none to take their place. I think them utterly wrong in what they have done and are doing; and, moreover, I agree as little in their view of history as in their acts. Extensive as may be their historical knowledge, I have no reason to think that they, more than Mr. Gladstone, would accept the position which History holds among the *Loci Theologici*, as Catholic theologians determine it; and I am denying not their report of facts, but their use of the facts they report, and that, because of that special stand-point from which they view the relations existing between the records of History and the enunciations of Popes and Councils. They seem to me to expect from History more than History can furnish, and to have too little confidence in the Divine Promise and Providence as guiding and determining those enunciations . . . For myself, I would simply confess that no doctrine of the Church can be rigorously proved by historical evidence: but at the same time that no doctrine can be simply disproved by it. Historical evidence reaches a certain way, more or less, towards a proof of the Catholic doctrines; often nearly the whole way; sometimes it goes only as far as to point in their direction; sometimes there is only an absence of evidence for a conclusion contrary to them; nay, sometimes there is an apparent leaning of the evidence to a contrary conclusion, which has to be explained;—in all cases there is a margin left for the exercise of faith in the word of the Church. He who believes the dogmas of the Church only because he has reasoned them out of History, is scarcely a Catholic.[106]

Newman dealt at length with the questions of Conscience; the

---

[104] H. Laski, *Problem of Sovereignty* (London, 1917), p. 202.
[105] Ward, *Newman*, ii, p. 406.
[106] *Difficulties of Anglicans*, ii, pp. 311–12.

Syllabus of Errors, the Vatican Council, and the definition of Papal Infallibility—all questions in which Acton had a deep interest. But he wrote not a line to Newman in agreement or disagreement. Yet he believed Newman's *Letter* was "an important and successful product" of Gladstone's pamphlet.[107] And he made the significant comment to Lady Blennerhasset that "Newman's conditions would make it possible, technically, to accept the whole of the decrees."[108] The immense opinion he held of Newman is reflected in his comment to Gladstone on the latter's eloquent praise for Newman in his pamphlet, *Vaticanism:*[109] "No fault could well be found with your description of Newman. I myself remember calling him, in a speech which I made to Kenealy's[110] constituents, the greatest man our Church had had in England since the Reformation."[111]

Newman was anxious about Acton's position and writing to Simpson at the end of March he guardedly broached the subject:

I wish I heard something about Lord Acton. There were unpleasant words used of him in both Protestant and Catholic papers, when Gladstone's pamphlet came out, and then all notice of him ceased.[112]

Two weeks later he replied severely to a lady who evidently had written to him some hard words against Acton:

I do not think you should say what you say about Lord Acton. He has ever been a religious, well-conducted, conscientious Catholic from a boy. In saying this, I do not at all imply that I can approve those letters to which you refer.[113] I heartily wish they had never been written.[114]

Thus from the protracted Vatican Council crisis the harmony of the Acton-Newman relations emerged, on the surface, unaffected.[115] Newman apparently retained all his old affection for Acton, and he, on his part, found nothing in Newman's behavior

[107] Acton to Gladstone, 9 February [1875], British Museum, Add. Mss. 44093.
[108] *Lord Acton's Correspondence*, p. 155.
[109] W. E. Gladstone, *Vaticanism* (London, 1875), pp. 10–12.
[110] E. V. H. Kenealy (1819–1880), M.P. for Stoke-on-Trent.
[111] *Lord Acton's Correspondence*, p. 267.
[112] Newman to Simpson, 30 March 1875, Orat. D.N.C.
[113] An evident reference to Acton's letters to the *Times*. See *Lord Acton's Correspondence*, pp. 124–44.
[114] *Lord Acton's Correspondence*, p. 154.
[115] There is no foundation for the statement by G. Himmelfarb in her *Acton*, p. 31, that "long before the Vatican Council he [Acton] had assigned to him [Newman] the permanent label of enemy."

to diminish in any way his high regard for him. But at a deeper level their relations were profoundly altered. It took Acton several years to realize it, while Newman, it would seem, never became aware that any change had occurred.

To Newman the dénouement of the Vatican Council drama erased any lingering bitterness against the activities of the Ultramontanes before and during the Council. He saw in the moderate definition of Infallibility finally passed, a setback for the extremists. His own defense of the Vatican Decrees against Gladstone brought him a fresh expression of gratitude from the Catholic world. His credit never stood higher. Acton, on the other hand, had no consolations. To him the Vatican Council represented tragedy pure and simple. The minority Bishops, the last hope of rescuing Liberal Catholicism from oblivion, had to a man acquiesced in what was done in 1870. Döllinger, to whom he had always turned in time of grave indecision, was himself excommunicated. His own attempts to take a definite stand ended in a highly unsatisfactory compromise. He may have satisfied his Bishop, and his answers to Manning may have been sufficient to avoid excommunication but the whole episode could provide him only cold comfort. Ultramontanism in one form or another had triumphed.

VII. Acton as Critic of Newman

In the years after the contentions concerning the Vatican Council there is no evidence that Acton and Newman saw or heard much of each other. The final letter that passed between them appears to have been one written by Newman on January 23, 1877 thanking Acton for having sent him his recent article in the *Quarterly Review* and expressing the hope that Acton had duly received his thanks for a work he had sent him at an earlier date.[1] Ten years were to elapse before they met in person. At this final meeting, at Oscott on July 19, 1887, the aged Cardinal recognized his old friend "but was quite at sea, otherwise, and hopelessly weak."[2] If Newman had been told that the man for whom he had ever evinced sympathy and frequently defended had come to write of him as an "evil" man[3] and would one day refer to his religious teaching as "a school of Infidelity,"[4] he would have found it quite beyond his comprehension. Two more cruel imputations could scarcely be thought of.

How is Acton's remarkable tergiversation to be explained? Why should one, who in 1874 had turned to Newman as a trusted friend, a few years later write of his "deep aversion" for Newman?[5] The barest explanation is that Acton decided that Newman was an Ultramontane and all Ultramontanes were evil.

[1] Newman to Acton, 23 January 1877, Orat. P.C. The two works were: "Wolsey and the Divorce of Henry VIII," *Quarterly Review*, January 1877; and Dr. Nicholas Harpsfield, *Narrative of the Divorce* (edited by Acton).

[2] Acton to Gladstone, 20 July 1887, British Museum, Add. Mss. 44093.

[3] Acton to Mary Gladstone, 14 December 1880, British Museum, Add. Mss. 46239.

[4] Acton to Gladstone, 12 April 1896, British Museum, Add. Mss. 44094.

[5] *Letters to Mary Gladstone*, p. 107.

By 1879 Acton had developed into an inflexible judge who deemed it the duty of the historian to decide on the moral guilt or innocence of historical characters. The historian could make no allowance for time or place. If he tried to mitigate the guilt of those who had committed crime in the past he was as worthy of reprobation as the criminal he sought to excuse. A new factor was added to Acton's case against the Ultramontanes. By their unquestioning support of the Roman System they made themselves guilty of all the past crimes that could be attributed to that system. Of these crimes persecution in the name of religion dwarfed all others. The particular conclusions to be drawn from such reasoning were clear to Acton. Thus, for example, a Dominican or a Jesuit, the exemplar Ultramontane, "must be assumed to be living in sin."[6] And a Bishop like Dupanloup who defended the *Syllabus* with its approval of past papal acts was an immoral man.

The case of Bishop Dupanloup in particular was indirectly to prove of crucial importance in Acton's development. A eulogy on Dupanloup written by Lady Blennerhasset for the *Nineteenth Century* carried an introductory letter by Döllinger vouching for "the accuracy of the details and the truth of the appreciation."[7] The painful truth dawned on Acton that his revered Professor did not agree with him on the decisive issue of moral judgments in history. Acton was driven to admit that there was a serious weakness in Döllinger: he refused "to see all the evil there is in men."[8] "I am divided from him by a gulf almost too wide for sympathy," he despondently wrote to Mary Gladstone.[9]

In a long letter of supreme importance in understanding Acton's hostility to Newman he strove (unsuccessfully) to make Döllinger appreciate his standpoint.[10] He began by explaining that much reading of history had convinced him that a common vice in the world was the inclination "to defend one's cause by unfair or illicit means." With "infinite credulity and trust" he consulted and became intimate with many of the most eminent

[6] *Lord Acton's Correspondence*, p. 193.
[7] "Felix Antoine Dupanloup, Bishop of Orleans," *Nineteenth Century*, February 1879, pp. 219–46.
[8] *Letters to Mary Gladstone*, p. 2.
[9] *Ibid.*, p. 2.
[10] Acton to Döllinger, 16 June 1882, Woodruff Mss.

Catholics of his day. But invariably he found on studying things for himself that what they told him was, "on many decisive questions, false." He came "very slowly and reluctantly indeed to the conclusion that they were dishonest." And a special reason for their dishonesty was "the desire to keep up the credit of authority in the Church." They ignored the moral standard in history because "it is impossible honestly to apply a moral standard to history without discrediting the Church in her collective action." In order that "men might believe the Pope it was resolved to make them believe that vice is virtue and falsehood truth."

This infirmity, Acton continued, was not associated only with ignorance and want of talent. He perceived it "in the ablest, in the most learned, in the most plausible and imposing men" he knew—"for instance in Theiner, Newman, Hefele, Falloux." These men "who were outwardly defenders of religion," in reality were "advocates of deceit and murder." The "great point was that these men justified the things to which in the past the papacy stood committed. They wished men to think that those things had not happened, or that they were good. They preached falsehood and murder."

In Acton's mind Popes in the past through their intolerant policies sanctioned murder. Pius IX "covered with the white skull-cap of the Syllabus the overt acts of his predecessors, and invited the sanction of the Church for them at the [Vatican] Council." The conclusion was inescapable: "The papacy sanctions murder; the avowed defender and promoter of the papacy is necessarily involved in that sanction . . . No man defends the papacy who has not accommodated his conscience to the idea of assassination."

For Acton there was something peculiarly evil about Churchmen succumbing to Ultramontanism. They were not then "as other liars or other murderers." These latter went wrong from human passion but *in extremis* religion might convert and save them. In the Churchman there was no resource left: "He is dragged down by the best thing in him. What redeems others leads him to destruction. It is at his best, when he is swept and garnished that he takes the devil into his soul. He never repents."

Acton did not reserve his invectives entirely for the Ultramontanes. There were others as wicked: "Those who admire Mary Stuart, or Elizabeth, or Cromwell, or Lewis XIV, or

James II, or William III, or Napoleon, or Mazzini, or Carnot, that is, much more than half the educated world, have to go through similar defilement."

In another important letter to Lady Blennerhasset Acton gave, what is in some respects, a more coherent expression of the basis of his detestation of Ultramontanism.[11] He explained how, beginning his career as a sincere Catholic and a sincere Liberal, he renounced everything in Catholicism incompatible with Liberty and everything in Liberalism incompatible with Catholicism. Liberalism he identified with morality. To his study of history he brought the principle of the supremacy of the ethical standard and purpose. History, however, revealed to him that a great evil had entered the Church. Instead of always upholding the ethical standard the theory was accepted and carried into practice that much wrong might be done for the sake of saving souls. From the twelfth century onwards this tendency overspread Christendom and was sanctioned, encouraged, and employed by the papacy. The papacy "contrived murder and massacre on the largest and also on the most cruel and inhuman scale." The principle of assassination became a law of the Christian Church and a condition of salvation. Coming down through the centuries to modern times one found the papal party, out of reverence for the papacy, condoning its evil actions in the past. The papal supporters were infamous in the last degree. And because their motives were religious they were worse than those who acted from political or other motives, for they were guilty of sacrilege. The glorification of the papacy was really a scheme for the promotion of sin.

Acton's exposition of the case against the Ultramontanes seems such an over-simplification of complex historical and ethical issues that it is not easy to understand why it should have so forcibly gripped his mind as profoundly to affect the remainder of his life. "There is something alarming," he had written in 1862, "in the labor of distinguishing and comparing times and places, and of making due allowance for qualifying circumstances and conditions."[12] But by 1880 he condemned as immoral anyone who even made the attempt.

---

[11] *Lord Acton's Correspondence*, pp. 53–57. The Editors assigned this undated letter to February, 1879. G. Himmelfarb in her *Lord Acton*, p. 152, argues with considerable justification that it was more probably written early in 1884.

[12] *Essays on Church and State*, p. 42.

Newman could hardly escape Acton's condemnation. On May 12, 1879 (less than three months after Lady Blennerhasset's fateful article on Dupanloup) he was made a Cardinal by Pope Leo XIII. His twenty years of general agreement with Acton went for naught. In Acton's very first reference (at least in available sources) to the new Cardinal he categorized him as a very able but evil man.[13] And his notes leave no doubt that his gravamen against Newman was his Ultramontanism: "Nobody was ever more emphatically, more exclusively, an Ultramontane."[14]

In Acton's eyes the mark that clearly revealed the Ultramontane was intolerance and he believed Newman carried it. His notes abound with references to Newman as an abettor of persecution:

Tolerance of heresy offended Newman most of anything . . . Not an oppressor. But ready for oppression if it should effectually serve the truth which it is the mission of the Xn Church to teach, and the good which it is her mission to do . . . Observe that Newman in public disavowed persecution . . . His denial of persecution. Then, his secret opinion. So that he was not trying to present the Church in her true colours, but to present false ones . . . How Newman professed liberalism, when in fact he was in favour of the Inquisition.[15]

And both Lady Acton and Lady Blennerhasset give further testimony that the ground of Acton's condemnation of Newman was persecution.[16]

It would be unfair to Acton to dismiss cavalierly his hard judgments on Newman, and equally unfair to Newman to accept them unquestioned. Only a rather detailed review can show satisfactorily whether or not the facts support Acton's apparently deep-rooted conviction that Newman was an advocate of intolerance.

In studying Newman's views on religious toleration one is struck by the fierceness of his approach in his earlier writings. In spite of his disclaimer in the *Apologia* that "neither at this, nor any other time in my life, not even when I was fiercest,

[13] Acton to Mary Gladstone, 14 December 1880, British Museum, Add. Mss. 46239.
[14] CUL Add. Mss. 5666.
[15] CUL Add. Mss. 5511; 4990, 114; 5666; 4989, 187.
[16] Lady Acton to Lady Blennerhasset, 29 June 1904, Blennerhasset Papers, CUL Add. Mss. 7486, Item 54; Lady Blennerhasset to Wilfrid Ward, 4 March 1912, Blennerhasset Papers, CUL Add. Mss. 7486, Item 52, Envelope 21.

could I have even cut off a Puritan's ears,"[17] one cannot avoid the suspicion that in another age young Mr. Newman might well have been a hammer of heretics. The following passage from his *Arians of the Fourth Century* (first published in 1833) manifests the same intense zeal as led to the severe proscription of heresy in past ages:

Many a man would be deterred from outstepping the truth, could he see the end of his course from the beginning. The Arians felt this, and therefore resisted a detection, which would at once expose them to the condemnation of all serious men. In this lies the difference between the treatment due to an individual in heresy, and to one who is confident enough to publish the innovations which he has originated. The former claims from us the most affectionate sympathy, and the most considerate attention. The latter should meet with no mercy; he assumes the office of the Tempter, and, so far forth as his error goes, must be dealt with by the competent authority, as if he were embodied Evil. To spare him is a false and dangerous pity. It is to endanger the souls of thousands, and it is uncharitable towards himself.[18]

In a sermon on "Tolerance of Religious Error" (preached in 1834) he lamented the pusillanimous, gentlemanly toleration of his day:

We are over-tender in dealing with sin and sinners. We are deficient in jealous custody of the revealed Truths which Christ has left us. We allow men to speak against the Church, its ordinances, or its teaching, without remonstrating with them. We do not separate from heretics, nay, we object to the word as if uncharitable; and when such texts are brought against us as St John's command, not to show hospitality towards them, we are not slow to answer that they do not apply to us.[19]

Newman had no illusions about the popularity of his stern approach. In a parish sermon entitled "Christian Zeal" (1834) he acknowledged that his conception of zeal was labelled intoler-

---

[17] *Apologia*, p. 47.

[18] *Arians of the Fourth Century*, p. 253 (1833 ed.). A "Northern dignitary" on the basis of this passage accused Newman of wishing to re-establish the "blood and torture of the Inquisition." Newman countered in the *Apologia*, p. 47, that Arius was banished, not burned. In 1871 he wrote in his *Essays Critical and Historical*, i, p. 280, n. 1: "I have been unfair to myself in my Apologia, p. 47, ed. 2, in saying, in answer to Mr. T's charge, "Arius was banished, not burned," for there is nothing whatever, as above observed, about civil punishment in the passage in question. The notice of Arius's *banishment* occurs in a subsequent part of my volume, which throughout discountenances civil penalties for religious opinions as leading to hypocritical conformity."

[19] *Parochial and Plain Sermons*, ii, p. 280.

ance by the present age and intolerance was accounted the chief of sins; but he refused to admit that "there be an infallible token given to us to ascertain the superior illumination of the present century over all those which have preceded it."[20]

In the *Via Media*, published in 1837, he sternly rebuked those who

are reluctant to be confronted with evidence which will diminish their right of thinking rightly or wrongly, as they please; they are jealous of being forced to submit to one view of the subject, and to be unable at their pleasure to change; they consider comfort in religion to lie in all questions being open, and in there being no call upon them to act. Thus they deliberately adopt that liberty which God gave His former people in wrath, 'A liberty to the sword, to the pestilence, and to the famine,'[21] the prerogative of being heretics or unbelievers.

These freethinkers were anathema to Newman:

It would be well if these men could keep their restless humours to themselves; but they unsettle all around them. They rob those of their birthright who would have hailed the privilege of being told the truth without their own personal risk in finding it; and they force them against their nature upon relying on their reason, when they are content to be saved by faith. Such troublers of the Christian community would in a healthy state of things be silenced or put out of it, as disturbers of the king's peace are restrained in civil matters; but our times, from whatever cause, being times of confusion, we are reduced to the use of argument and disputation, just as we think it lawful to carry arms and barricade our houses during national disorders.[22]

On the principles underlying toleration one finds little in the writings of Newman. In his *Historical Tracts of St. Athanasius* (1843), however, he included an outline of what appeared to be the teaching of the Church Fathers on persecution. Since his own approach to a theological problem was generally the one he thought most in harmony with the early Fathers this outline probably reflected his own thinking on the subject:

The early theory about persecution seems to have been this,—that that was a bad cause which *depended* upon it, but that, when a *cause* was good, there was nothing wrong in using force in due subordination to argument; that there was as little impropriety in the civil magistrate's inducing individuals by force, when they were incapable of higher

[20] *Ibid.*, p. 384.
[21] "Jer. xxxiv. 17."
[22] *Lectures on the Prophetical Office* (1837 ed.), pp. 5–6.

motives, as by those secular blessings which follow on Christianity. Our
Lord's kingdom was not of this world, that is, it did not depend on this
world; but, as, subduing, engrossing, and swaying this world, it at
times condescended to make use of this world's weapons against itself.
The simple question was *whether a cause depended on force for its existence.*
St Athanasius declared, and the event proved, that Arianism was so
dependent. When Emperors ceased to persecute, Arianism ceased to be;
it had no life in itself. Again, all cruel persecution, or long continued, or
on a large scale, was wrong, as arguing *an absence of* moral and rational
grounds in the *cause* so maintained. Again, there was an evident *impropriety* in ecclesiastical functionaries using secular weapons, as there would
be in their engaging in a secular pursuit, or forming secular connections;
whereas the soldier might as suitably, and should as dutifully, defend
religion with the sword, as the scholar with his pen. And further there
was an abhorrence of cruelty natural to us, which it was a duty to cherish
and maintain. All this being considered, there is no inconsistency in
St Athanasius denouncing persecution, and in Theodosius decreeing
that "the heretical teachers, who usurped the sacred titles of Bishops
or Presbyters," should be "exposed to the heavy penalties of exile and
confiscation."[23]

Despite his stern approach as an Anglican it would be a grave
misunderstanding of character to see in Newman one who would
have sanctioned the use of any sort of physical compulsion in
exacting religious conformity in his own day. Nothing would
have been more repugnant to him. Though fierce in his denunciation of religious error he was always tender to the erring
individual.

As a Catholic practically all his references to toleration were
polemical and designed to answer Protestant accusations against
the Church.

In his first published work as an Oratorian, *Discourses to
Mixed Congregations* (1849), he briefly touched on religious
persecution:

All she [the Catholic Church] asks is an open field, and freedom to
act. She asks no patronage from the civil power: in former times and

---

[23] *Historical Tracts of St. Athanasius* (1843 ed.), p. 279, n.c. In 1881 Newman
re-edited *St. Athanasius* in two volumes under the new title *Select Treatises of
St. Athanasius.* The note just cited was incorporated into the text under the
heading "Use of Force in Religion" (ii, pp. 123–6). The passage remained substantially as written in 1843 with the addition of the following sentence: "So much
as to the question of principle, which even Protestants act on and have generally
acted; in this day and here, State interference would so simply tell against the
Catholic cause, that it would be a marvel to find any Catholic advancing it."

places she indeed has asked for it; and, as Protestantism also, availed herself of the civil sword. It is true she did so, because in certain ages it has been the acknowledged mode of acting, the most expeditious, and open at the time to no objection, and because, where she has done so, the people clamoured for it and did it in advance of her; but her history shows that she needed it not, for she has extended and flourished without it.[24]

Newman's *Lectures on the Present Position of Catholics* were delivered during the *Papal Aggression* hysteria in 1850. In the fifth lecture, "Logical Inconsistency of the Protestant View," after a withering attack on Dr. Achilli, a renegade Italian ex-priest who in public lectures held forth on the horrors of the Inquisition, Newman set out to show how illogical Protestants were in denouncing Popes as persecutors when Protestants had persecuted whenever and wherever they could in spite of their insistence on private judgment. He then spoke of "the utterly false view which Protestants take of the Inquisition, and of the Holy See in connection with it." He quoted the words of Dr. Balmez, a Spanish Catholic controversialist, that "the Roman Inquisition has never been known to pronounce the execution of capital punishment, although the Apostolic See has been occupied, during that time, by Popes of extreme rigour and severity in all that relates to civil administration." Newman added a cautionary note: "I am rather surprised that this is stated so unrestrictedly, *vide* Life of St. Philip Neri, vol. i.; however, the fact is substantially as stated, even though there were some exceptions to the rule."[25]

Acton undoubtedly had the above incident in mind when he wrote to Döllinger in 1882:

Newman says, no heretic was ever put to death in Rome, excepting one mentioned in the life of S. Philip, an exception that proves the rule. Here is the brutal liar, and the artful deceiver, who seems so scrupulous, and certainly does his work, the devil's work, best.[26]

Acton had forgotten that Döllinger himself had written the Preface to the German translation of Newman's *Lectures on the Present Position on Catholics* and had questioned none of Newman's statements. If, in Acton's eyes, Newman took a preposterous view of the Roman Inquisition in 1851 he might surely

[24] *Discourses to Mixed Congregations*, p. 253.
[25] *Present Position of Catholics in England*, p. 210.
[26] Acton to Döllinger, 16 June 1882, Woodruff Mss.

have granted him indulgence, since he, a recent convert, was simply relying on a Catholic authority whom even Döllinger, an ecclesiastical historian *ex professo*, did not appear to question on this particular point.[27]

As Newman's thought matured and his religious doubts were resolved he viewed the battle against infidelity with greater confidence. His lectures on University Education reflected this growing confidence. The young zealot who expressed the opinion that in a healthier society disturbers of the Christian conscience would be silenced or put out of it gave way to the maturer Newman who looked with disfavor on an age which did just that. The medieval age was seen as a period when "unbelief necessarily made its advances under the language and the guise of faith," and he expressed his preference for his own age "when universal toleration prevails" and the fight "was in the day, not in the twilight."[28]

During his association with Acton and Simpson in the *Rambler* period the question of persecution arose twice. On one occasion, in the course of a sympathetic letter to Acton, Newman made reference to Simpson's abrupt, unmeasured attack" on St. Pius V in his article on Edmund Campion.[29] He added the remark: "I don't wonder at a saying which I hear reported of a Dominican, that he would like to have the burning of the author." Years later this remark took on sinister undertones in Acton's mind and one finds related at least four times in his notes that a Dominican wanted to burn Simpson, and Newman was inclined to agree with him.[30]

A year later it was discussed at a more serious level. An article by Simpson[31] prompted a three-cornered correspondence on persecution. A. P. de Lisle, who steadfastly denied that "the Church as such, has any right whatever to the employment of *brute force* to back up any of her Laws,"[32] protested vigorously against Simpson's careless references to the Inquisition and his failure to make any distinction between the legislation of the Church and the legislation of Churchmen.[33] In writing to New-

[27] See *Lord Acton's Correspondence*, p. 82.
[28] *Idea of a University*, p. 287.
[29] Newman to Acton, 7 June 1861, Woodruff Mss.
[30] CUL Add. Mss. 4988, 197, 203, 205; 4989, 186.
[31] "Moral Law and Political Legislation," *Rambler*, March, 1862.
[32] *Life and Letters of A. P. de Lisle*, ii, p. 154.
[33] A. P. de Lisle to Acton, 5 March 1862, CUL Add. Mss. 4989 (original letter).

man some time later Acton commented on de Lisle's disapprobation:

> It seems to me a very difficult question to decide what can be said of the Church in matters of development, history, law, etc. Lisle Phillips, for instance, thinks us heretical for saying *the Church* approved of the physical punishment of heretics, and answered my quotations from the canon law by saying it was not the legislation of *the Church*. I do not believe he knew what he meant, but I suspect if this point could be made clear to people, much trouble, doubt and resentment would disappear.[34]

Newman's reply to Acton must be carefully noted as it became for him irrefragable proof that Newman was ready for persecution if it was to the advantage of the Church.[35]

> To take the instance of the 'physical punishment of heretics,' which you refer to, and to confine myself to Scripture. Is not the miraculous infliction of judgments upon blasphemy, lying, profaneness &c, in the Apostle's day a sanction of infliction upon the same by a human hand in the times of the Inquisition? I think it is. Yet on the other hand such infliction is not enjoined, and, in our Lord's words about Elias's bringing fire from heaven, is discouraged. That is, ecclesiastical rulers *may* punish with sword, if they *can* and it is *expedient*, or *necessary* to do so.
>
> The proposition, thus implied (I think) in Scripture, is all that the modern Church asserts. For I do not know anything more determinate on the subject (as far as my memory goes) than the condemnation (among the Propositiones damnatae) of Luther's assertion, 'Hereticos comburi est contra voluntatem Spiritus.'' Pius VI. has condemned the general denial of ecclesiastical punishments in the 'auctorem fidei.'[36]

This letter provided Acton with evidence enough, and more than enough, to brand Newman as the most wicked of men. But if Newman merited condemnation Acton himself could not escape a like fate. Had he not half a year earlier expressed pretty much the same sentiments to Simpson:

> To say that persecution is wrong, nakedly, seems to me first of all untrue, but at the same time, it is in contradiction with solemn decrees, with Leo X's Bull against Luther, with a Breve of Benedict XIV, of 1748, and with one of Pius VI of 1791.[37]

If Acton could escape the hangman on the plea that he eventually recognized his error, perhaps a similar plea might be

---

[34] Acton to Newman [? July 1862] Orat. P.C.
[35] CUL Add. Mss. 4989, 181, 186.
[36] Ward, *Newman*, i, pp. 639–40.
[37] Gasquet, *Acton*, p. 243.

entered on Newman's behalf. In the above letter to Acton he was obviously endeavoring to determine an authoritative teaching on the subject rather than thinking out a personal solution. When he learned of a more temperate teaching that had authoritative sanction he put it forward. Thus in his *Letter to the Duke of Norfolk* he followed the interpretation of Cardinal Soglia advanced in a work approved by Gregory XVI and Pius IX:

The opinion, says Cardinal Soglia, that the coercive power divinely bestowed upon the Church consists in the infliction of spiritual punishments alone, and not in corporal or temporal, seems more in harmony with the gentleness of the Church. Accordingly I follow their judgment, who withdraw from the Church the corporal sword, by which the body is destroyed or blood is shed.[38]

Newman concerned himself little about the speculative side of toleration. To him, the philosopher of the concrete, the practical side was of primary importance. Should the Church here and now practice toleration? On this question there was no doubt where he stood. To an inquiring Catholic M.P. he wrote:

As a fact, persecution does not answer. It goes against men's feelings; the feelings of the age are as strongly against it as they were once for it. The age is such, that we must go by reason, not by force. I am not at all sure that it would not be better for the Catholic religion everywhere, if it had no very different status from that which it has in England. There is so much corruption, so much deadness, so much hypocrisy, so much infidelity, when a dogmatic faith is imposed on a nation by law, that I like freedom better.[39]

Looking back on the intolerance of other ages, however, Newman refrained from outbursts of righteous indignation. For

a ruder people asks for a strong imperious teaching, armed with temporal sanctions, and such is good for it, whereas other ages reject it, and it would be bad for them. It was a good thing in the middle ages for men to be compelled to be Christian, and a bad thing now. I don't say the former way made more Christians in its day, but it was the way to make Christians, now it is not. Now it would but foster the worst hypocrisy, for men act from reasoning, not imagination.[40]

This realistic approach would have shocked a nineteenth-century Liberal, but one can see in it a more profound historical insight than that manifested in the latter's confident assumption that his own age was ethically superior to any previous one.

[38] *Difficulties of Anglicans*, pp. 291–92.
[39] Newman to Monsell, 17 June 1863, Orat. P.C.
[40] Newman to Allies, 22 November 1860, Orat. P.C.

Acton himself in 1862 regarded persecution as coming "naturally in a certain period of the progress of society":

At a certain point of mental growth, tolerance implies indifference, and intolerance is inseparable from sincerity. Thus intolerance, in itself a defect, becomes in this case a merit. Again, although the political conditions of intolerance belong to the youth and immaturity of nations, the motives of intolerance may at any time be just and the principle high.[41]

It would be difficult for the most liberal of Liberals to find any trace of intolerance in Newman's personal relations with non-Catholics. Never was there a person more sensitive to the rights of conscience, and more averse from the use of any sort of undue compulsion in leading one to the Catholic Church, whether that person was a lapsed Catholic or a prospective convert. Ironically Acton's notes charge him with a lack of zeal in making converts.[42] A passage in Newman's *Personal Journal* reveals his attitude to conversions and from it his deep personal aversion from any intolerance other than intellectual intolerance of error can be deduced:

To me conversions were not the first thing, but the edification of Catholics. So much have I fixed upon the latter as my object, that up to this time the world persists in saying that I recommend Protestants not to become Catholics. And, when I have given as my true opinion, that I am afraid to make hasty converts of educated men, lest they should not have counted the cost, & should have difficulties after they have entered the Church, I do but imply the same thing, that the Church must be prepared for converts, as well as converts prepared for the Church.[43]

In summary it seems clear that Acton's charge that Newman was offended by toleration of heresy most of anything must be ruled out of court. It was based on the rigid assumption that one who failed to condemn absolutely the intolerance of past ages was in favor of it in his own. If, on the other hand, it be a crime not to support toleration on principle but on the grounds of expediency, Newman with a host of Christian apologists down through the centuries stands justly condemned.

In the final analysis Acton's denunciations of Newman can only be understood in terms of advocacy. Acton was not the dispassionate judge, unmoved by any polemical considerations,

---

[41] *History of Freedom*, pp. 250–51.
[42] CUL Add. Mss. 4988, 119, 126, 132.
[43] *Autobiographical Writings*, p. 258.

carefully weighing the evidence before passing judgment. He
had a cause to plead and the case of Newman was used to add
weight to his plea. Acton had started out as a young enthusiast
to teach Catholics true wisdom, but they did not wish to learn.
They clung to their errors and preferred Ultramontanism to
Liberalism. Acton saw his predicament in terms of centuries of
growth. The pedigree of the modern Ultramontanes could be
traced back to the Middle Ages and intolerance was their distinguishing mark. The Inquisition became a symbol of all that
he opposed in the present order and memories of it called forth
all the bitterness that was rankling in his soul against the system
which had frustrated his life's work. Newman as a high-ranking
dignitary in the Church was nothing if not an Ultramontane.
Since religious intolerance was the supreme expression of Ultramontanism he had to stand condemned on that score. Newman
was sacrificed for the good of the cause.

Acton's notes in the Cambridge University library contain
many criticisms of Newman. He contemplated writing something on the Cardinal after his death and this undoubtedly
explains the special attention he devoted to him.[44] However, the
only notes that descend in any measure to a serious and dispassionate criticism of Newman's thought are those touching on
the theory of development as outlined in Newman's famous
Essay on the Development of Christian Doctrine, a work published
first in 1845 and again in a revised form in 1878. Surprisingly
one finds no criticism, favorable or otherwise, of Newman's
writings on education or of his investigations into the nature of
religious belief outlined in the *Grammar of Assent*. This latter
work in particular, one of Newman's most important, aroused
no interest whatsoever; indeed, Acton's copy in the Cambridge
library still has its pages uncut, suggesting the possibility that
he may never even have read the work.

Acton's special interest in the *Essay on Development* was
prompted by its profoundly historical character. "There is more
of the notion of history in it," one of his notes reads, "than in
any book of the time, more even than in Past and Present."[45]
When one recalls that he judged Carlyle's *Past and Present* "the

[44] *Lord Acton's Correspondence*, p. 76; M. Ward, *The Wilfrid Wards and the
Transition* (London, 1934), p. 249.
[45] CUL Add. Mss. 5666.

most remarkable piece of historical thinking in the language"
one can better appreciate his high regard for Newman's work.[46]
Several of his notes testify to the enormous influence he believed
Newman's *Essay* exercised:

> Dev.[elopment] did more than any other book of his time to make
> his countrymen think historically, and watch the process as well as the
> result . . . The greatest help to historic thinking that England had
> produced . . . He helped to make History essential to men who reasoned,
> and thought by logic, to determine truth. He raised it to a higher level
> and degree of authority. That is his leg.[acy] to men.[47]

It is not surprising that two months after Newman's death he
should write to the editor of the *English Historical Review*: "Was
not Newman worthy of a historian's niche?"[48]

The origins of Newman's theory of development tantalized
Acton. His notes reveal his efforts to trace its elusive pedigree.
Did it proceed from Lamennais? He was inclined to think that
it did, [49] but eventually came to the conclusion that it did not.[50]
Was not the idea of development a central one in Hegel's
philosophy?[51] But where was the evidence to link Newman with
the Hegelians? Acton finally fastened on Möhler, the Tübingen
theologian, as the most probable source.[52] But here again there
was little evidence. Acton hit upon the idea that Perrone, the
Roman theologian, in his textbook *Praelectiones Theologicae*,
re-edited in 1843, brought Möhler's theory to Newman's notice.[53]
But as Professor Chadwick has written: "there is no scrap of
evidence that Newman was reading, or was influenced by,
Perrone at this time."[54]

Acton appears to have confined his searchings for the origins
of Newman's theory almost exclusively to eighteenth and nineteenth century writers. And when he became convinced that
somehow or other Möhler was at the bottom of it he further
restricted himself to the period immediately preceding Newman's

---

[46] *Lectures on the French Revolution*, edited by J. N. Figgis and R. V. Laurence
(London, 1910), p. 358.
[47] CUL Add. Mss. 4987, 60; 5463; 4987, 11.
[48] Acton to Creighton, 27 October 1890, CUL Add. Mss. 6871.
[49] CUL Add. Mss. 5463.
[50] *History of Freedom*, p. 593.
[51] CUL Add. Mss. 5463.
[52] CUL Add. Mss. 5014, 350.
[53] CUL Add. Mss. 5666; 5463.
[54] O. Chadwick, *From Bossuet to Newman* (Cambridge, 1957), p. 113.

first explicit formulation of his theory in an Oxford sermon of February 1843.[55] Yet Newman had introduced the principle of development into his *Arians of the Fourth Century* written eleven years before the Oxford sermon.[56] Had Acton spent more time studying the writings of the Fathers or even carefully analyzing the *Arians* his search might have been more fruitful. The Platonic influence of the Alexandrian school had far more to do with Newman's theory of development than the writings of any German philosopher or theologian. Yet there was a point to Acton's quest. Though Newman may have been ignorant of German philosophy he was not completely outside the stream of the current philosophy of evolution unfolded in the writings of the Hegelians. One has only to come upon such phrases as "the warfare of ideas under their various aspects striving for the mastery, each of them enterprising, engrossing, imperious, more or less incompatible with the rest" to realize that Newman was a man of his century.[57] But it is impossible to determine to what extent, if any, a particular nineteenth-century writer was responsible for Newman's theory. Evolution was in the air in the 1830's and given Newman's cast of mind, his native genius, and his special pre-occupations, it was almost inevitable that he should work out some sort of theory on the development of Christian doctrine.

An early critic of Newman's theory attacked it as being offered as "the substitute for history, Creeds, Scripture, and consent of Doctors."[58] Recently it has been said that Acton, too, believed the general intention of Newman's *Essay* was to emancipate the Church from history.[59] Some of Acton's notes certainly seem to support this conclusion:

It [development] emancipated him from history, and made authority reigned [sic] . . . What he meant by development was *securus judicat*. It was the voice of the present Church superseding the study of the Past. Securus judicat orbis terrarum. Proceeds from Lamennais. Emancipates from the Past. Promotes authority.[60]

[55] *Oxford University Sermons*, pp. 312–51 (pp. 311–54 1843 ed.).
[56] See *Apologia*, p. 197; *Arians of the Fourth Century*, pp. 143–45 (pp. 158–60 1833 ed.).
[57] *Development*, p. 39.
[58] George Moberly, *The Sayings of the Great Forty Days* (3rd ed. London, 1846), preface p. xix.
[59] O. Chadwick, *From Bossuet to Newman*, p. 129 (see also, pp. 138, 144).
[60] CUL Add. Mss. 4990, 298; 5463; 4988, 100.

The above evidence notwithstanding it would be inaccurate to bracket Acton with the Moberlys and Kebles as one who believed that development in Newman's mind was an ingenious escape from history. Acton was far too good an historical critic to dismiss Newman's *Essay* in a superficial manner. His high opinion of its historical character would be inexplicable if he held that its main object was to prove history irrelevant to the subject at hand. Some of his notes suggest that he believed it was rooted in history. Thus in the following two abrupt, elliptical observations in which he penetrates to the heart of Newman's thought he shows that he has not misunderstood Newman's theory:

> Part of the great English reaction against the Revolution-led by Burke. Development broke through this. Not mere acceptance of the past—a lengthening chain. Growth, progress, assimilation [.] Look to the future as well as the past.[61]

> Idea of Dev. Therefore no revolution, everything accounted for by growth of a principle. So far, reign of the Past. Dev. a scheme which unites Past and Future—justice to both.[62]

Each phrase in the above observations is pregnant with meaning. It was Newman's vision of the organic continuity of the historical process that caused Acton to place him in the first rank of nineteenth-century historical thinkers.

There are other indications that Acton did not believe Newman's *Essay* to be a clever plea on behalf of Church authority. He pondered why Newman's work was welcomed so coolly by Rome and suggested the following answer:

> Part of the credit and authority which belonged to the Church teachers were taken from them and transferred to mere scholars. Theology was divided between the appointed teachers, and the independent scholar— the historian usurped the place of the prelate.[63]

Again:

> It [development] was expressly discarded, at Rome, in 1854. It was making the historian master of the Divine.[64]

In other words, Acton believed Roman authorities had no sympathy for Newman's theory because rather than having

[61] CUL Add. Mss. 4990, 282.
[62] CUL Add. Mss. 5463.
[63] CUL Add. Mss. 5463.
[64] *Ibid.*

effected an emancipation from history it (in their opinion) exaggerated its importance.

It has been shown that Newman played a part in reconciling Acton to the Vatican Decrees by bringing out that they could only be interpreted in harmony with the past traditions of the Church—to wit, by showing that in matters of doctrine history mattered very much. It is highly improbable that Acton had forgotten this in the 1890's.

Yet Acton was not altogether satisfied that development presented no threat to history: "Development, at first sight, is the reign of History. It could be made to dethrone History. The reign of the Present."[65] If development meant a constant upward progress, each stage superior to the preceding then it might easily be interpreted as the reign of the Present. Newman would then be bracketed with the German Idealists who saw in progress the law of history. It will later be seen that Acton himself approached far closer to this position than Newman. Newman's theory of development avoided on the one hand the extremes of historical Pyrrhonists as Manning and Brownson who believed religious truth depended on the present authority of the Church without reference to the past, and on the other hand, the Idealists who regarded the present as inevitably superior to the past. Newman through an historical inquiry satisfied himself that the Roman Church was substantially one with the Church of the Fathers. Having entered the Church he did not then turn his back on the past, as he would have had to do if his theory involved the reign of the present. Rather, throughout the remainder of his life he took his stand on the early Church Fathers. "The Fathers made me a Catholic," he wrote, "and I am not going to kick down the ladder by which I ascended into the Church."[66]

Development for Newman, as Acton admitted,[67] was not progress in the nineteenth-century sense of the term. It was not toward new forms; in so far as it meant progress at all it was toward a deeper understanding of old truths. There was a constant reaching back demanded to ensure that a development remained true to its origins. James Mozley misunderstood Newman's theory when he wrote: "So long as the idea goes forward

[65] CUL Add. Mss. 4906, 252.
[66] *Difficulties of Anglicans*, ii, p. 24.
[67] CUL Add. Mss. 5463.

at all, it is sure not to be wrong, the onwardness of the move-ment constituting its truth."[68] If this were Newman's meaning then development would mean the reign of the present. But for Newman the object of development, paradoxically, was preser-vation more than progression. A revelation received into a living community could not remain in a static form. The only alterna-tive to its development was corruption. Acton saw this clearly in 1863: "The development of doctrine is essential to the preser-vation of its purity; hence its preservation implies its develop-ment."[69]

Newman's insistence on the necessity of an infallible devel-oping authority might be taken to mean the reign of the present; but in Newman's mind its object was to preserve intact God's revelation to man, a revelation completed in Apostolic times. In his own words:

Infallibility cannot act outside of a definite circle of thought, and it must in all its decisions, or *definitions*, as they are called, profess to be keeping within it. The great truths of the moral law, of natural religion, and of Apostolical faith, are both its boundary and its foundation. It must not go beyond them, and must ever appeal to them. Both its subject-matter, and its articles in that subject-matter, are fixed. And it must ever profess to be guided by Scripture and by tradition.[70]

Although Newman modestly referred to his theory as "an hypo-theses to account for a difficulty"—to account for "the increase and expansion of the Christian Creed and Ritual" despite an original revelation that could not be added to—it was for him far more than an hypothesis.[71] It was a "principle," a "remarkable philosophical phenomenon, giving a character to the whole course of Christian thought."[72] It became for him (personally) an "ineffably cogent argument" for the "identity between the Catholic Church of the first ages and that which now goes by that name."[73]

Acton recognized Newman's potentialities as an historian but trained in the German school of criticism, where *facts* were all important and *definitive* history the desired goal, he had little

[68] J. B. Mozley, *The Theory of Development* (London, 1878), p. 33.
[69] *Essays on Church and State*, p. 38.
[70] *Apologia*, p. 253.
[71] *Development*, pp. 29–30.
[72] *Apologia*, pp. 198–99.
[73] *Difficulties of Anglicans*, i, pp. 395–96.

sympathy for Newman's use of theory and hypothesis in the interpretation of history:

> With great talent for history, he [Newman] had none of the historians leaning for things as we find them—for elaborately leaving them to tell their own tale. He wanted hypothesis, expedient, to give them interest.[74]

A further note expressed the same criticism:

> Certainty that whatever he really examined, he would speak with freshness and originality. The drawback was that he did not feel bound to examine everything he wrote about. He took much for granted, as settled by the principle of sustaining authority. He tested his Development on few topics, leaving the rest, as he said, to those who have time.[75]

Or more caustically: "He had his view. Let the facts shift for themselves."[76]

It would not be fair to Newman, however, to dismiss him as one who sacrificed facts to theory. He had no quarrel with those who stressed the importance of history:

> History is a record of facts and 'facts' according to the proverb, 'are stubborn things'. Ingenious men may misrepresent them, or suppress them for a while; but in the end they will be duly ascertained and appreciated.[77]

Newman distrusted mere theory. "Abstract argument is always dangerous," he wrote in his *Grammar of Assent*, "I prefer to go by facts."[78] To one of his lecturers at Dublin who sought advice on the philosophy of history he offered a caution against assuming laws in history.

> For myself, I cannot help thinking that laws are a sort of facts *in* the subject matter which is in question . . . First let us ascertain the fact, then theologise upon it . . . I can quite understand a Professor drawing religious conclusions from historical laws or ordinances, as from physical, but he must find his laws.[79]

Development recommended itself to Newman not as a plausible abstract theory but because he believed he saw it operating in history. It was an abstraction *from* history. A passage taken from his discussion of Papal Supremacy illustrates his approach:

[74] CUL Add. Mss. 5666.
[75] CUL Add. Mss. 4987, 14.
[76] CUL Add. Mss. 4990, 83.
[77] *Via Media*, i, p. 38.
[78] *Grammar of Assent*, p. 160.
[79] Newman to Allies, 16 November 1854, Orat. P.C.

It will be said all this is a theory. Certainly it is: it is a theory to account for facts as they lie in history, to account for so much being told us about the Papal authority in early times, and not more; a theory to reconcile what is and what is not recorded about it; and which is the principal point, a theory to connect the words and acts of the Ante-Nicene Church with that antecedent probability of a monarchical principle in the Divine Scheme, and that actual exemplification of it in the fourth century, which forms their presumption. Supposing there be otherwise good reason for saying that the Papal Supremacy is part of Christianity, there is nothing in the early history of the Church to contradict it.[80]

Whether one accepts this approach or not it cannot be dismissed on the grounds that Newman ignored the facts of history. It is doubtful if any of his contemporaries had more carefully studied the history of the early Church. Acton recognized this and noted that Duchesne considered him "l'homme de ce siècle qui a le plus étudié les Pères."[81] Newman, of course, went beyond the sphere of history proper in his *Essay*, but he was not making an historical investigation pure and simple. He was using history as one instrument among others to aid him in a personal predicament.

Acton believed that development in Newman's mind was the special prerogative of Christian doctrine. Thus one reads in his notes:

His devel. is a divine gift, as exclusive and supernatural a prerogative as Inspiration or prophecy[82] . . . What Lamennais claims for mankind in general, and Moehler for every great system in particular, he made an exclusive gift and the mark of a divine supremacy.[83]

In so far as a supernaturally guided authority was, for Newman, the ultimate guarantee against a false doctrinal development, Acton's remarks are true. But essential to Newman's theory was the notion that the ideas proceeding from revelation followed the same process as other ideas that took possession of the mind. To quote his *Essay:*

the increase and expansion of the Christian Creed and Ritual, and the variations which have attended the process in the case of individual writers and Churches, are the necessary attendants on any philosophy

---

[80] *Development*, p. 154.
[81] CUL Add. Mss. 5763, citing *Témoins*, p. 24.
[82] CUL Add. Mss. 5666.
[83] CUL Add. Mss. 5463.

or polity which takes possession of the intellect and heart, and has had any wide or extended dominion.[84]

Newman saw development operating in all fields involving mental activity. But in fields outside the doctrinal he saw no certain protection against false developments, i.e., corruptions. His pessimistic view of fallen man led him to reject the possibility of a Church's permanently avoiding corruptions without a divine *assistentia*. His conviction that the Church of Rome did avoid doctrinal corruptions became for him a proof of her divine guidance. In writing of the Church he never treated it as a natural organization confined within the limits of a purely historical structure. He considered it in its totality a divinely established and sustained organism. Since its activity was partly manifested in history, it could be the subject of historical investigation, but there would always remain an element which a purely historical criticism could never reach. His criticism of the Döllinger school of historians was, as has been seen, that they expected more from history than history could furnish. Although he believed his theory was strictly applicable only within a narrow field of doctrinal history, his observations on the process of development in the whole sphere of man's activity possess a depth and richness which have led thinkers so diverse as Matthew Arnold and A. N. Whitehead to acknowledge its influence on their thought.

In Acton's notes there are entries suggesting that for a period in the 1860's Newman "drew in" or virtually retracted his theory of development as expressed in 1845.[85] Writing in the *English Historical Review* in 1890 he was more cautious and stated that Newman "was inclined to guard and narrow his theory."[86] With a typically Actonian conjecture he attributed Newman's apparent trimming to the hostile reception greeting his article on "Consulting the Laity."[87] In both his notes and his published article he based his conclusions on two letters he received from Newman in 1862.[88] The following are the relevant passages:

[84] *Development*, p. 29.
[85] CUL Add. Mss. 5463; 5666.
[86] *History of Freedom*, p. 407.
[87] CUL Add. Mss. 5463. See above, p. 44.
[88] Newman to Acton, 8 July 1862, CUL Add. Mss. 5463 (extract in Acton's hand); 19 July 1862, Woodruff Mss., reprinted in Ward, *Newman*, i, p. 539.

1) What is meant by Development? Is it a more intimate apprehension, and a more lucid enunciation of the original dogma? For myself, I think it is, and nothing more. If I have said more than this, I think I had not worked out my meaning, and was confused. I think it is what an Apostle would have said when on earth, what any of his disciples would have said, according as the occasion called for it. If St. Clement, or St. Polycarp, had been asked whether our Lady was immaculately conceived, I think he might have taken some time to understand the meaning of the question, and perhaps (as St. Bernard) he might have to the end misunderstood the question; but if he did ever understand it, I think he would have said, 'Of course she was.' Whether the minute facts of history will bear me out in this view, I leave to others to determine. Accordingly, to me the words 'development in dogma' are substantially nothing but the process by which, under the magisterium of the Church, implicit faith becomes explicit:—
I should hold that the substance of the res credenda or dogma of Christianity was just what it was in the Apostles' day, and that the difference between the creed then and the creed now was only quoad nos— one of apprehension. I should like to say that the Church apprehends it more clearly; and I almost think that Bossuet countenanced such a notion. When I suggested it to Father Perrone, he disliked the idea. But what is the Church, as separated from Pope, Councils, Bishops and faithful?

2) As to the development of doctrine and action in the Church I should hold to Vincentius's account of it, who compares it to bodily growth, "ut nihil novum postea proferatur in senibus, quod non in pueris jam antea *latitaverit*," and says it is a false development "si humana species in aliquam deinceps *non sui generis* vertatur effigiem."

Did Newman in these two letters contradict anything he wrote in 1845? Was he, as Acton maintained, "adopting" the Vincentian Canon which he "rejected" in 1845 and again in 1878 on the re-editing of his *Essay?*[89]

The idea of development runs through all Newman's writings and an adequate treatment of these questions would demand a review of his writings from 1845 to 1878.[90] However, since

---

[89] CUL Add. Mss. 5463; 5666.

[90] Professor Chadwick in his recent work on development, *From Bossuet to Newman*, pp. 185–86, seems inclined to follow Acton. He refers to various passages in Newman's works from 1850 to 1874 which he considers difficult to reconcile with the 1845 and 1878 *Essay*. In every case the difficulty seems to turn on Newman's insistence that there can be no new additions to the deposit of faith. We believe that Newman made this assumption in writing his *Essay* and that it explains why he undertook the writing of it in the first place. Professor Chadwick

Acton appeared to have based his conclusions solely on the above two extracts the discussion will be confined to the points raised in them.

Is Acton's observation that Newman rejected the Vincentian Canon in 1845 and returned to it in 1862 an accurate one? This famous formula or canon was put forth by Saint Vincent of Lerins in the fifth century, and stated that revealed and apostolic doctrine is what has been held always, everywhere, and by all (*Quod semper, quod ubique, quod ab omnibus*).[91]

Newman, in his 1845 *Essay* (and again in 1878) sought a key to harmonize the doctrines of the early and later Church. He wrote:

It does not seem possible, then, to avoid the conclusion that, whatever be the proper key for harmonizing the records and documents of the early and later Church, and true as the dictum of Vincentius must be considered in the abstract, and possible as its application might be in his own age, when he might almost ask the primitive centuries for their testimony, it is hardly available now, or effective of any satisfactory result. The solution it offers is as difficult as the original problem.[92]

It must be noted that Newman did not reject the Vincentian Canon as an abstract truth. He simply did not consider it a satisfactory key to the evidence. His theory of development provided the key. Further, in his second letter cited above, he did not mention the Vincentian Canon but referred to an analogy used by St. Vincent, an analogy which appeared in both editions of his *Essay*.[93] Newman, *pace* Acton, did not *return* to St. Vincent in 1862. In so far as he was a Vincentian in 1862 he was one in 1845 and 1878.

Do Newman's statements, in his letter of July 8, that development was nothing more than "a more intimate apprehension and a more lucid enunciation of the original dogma," and that "the substance of the res credenda or dogma of Christianity was just what it was in the Apostles' day," constitute a drawing in or a narrowing of his original theory? The phrase, "If I said more than this, I think I had not worked out my meaning, and apparently takes the opposite view when he writes: "If it were established (for example) in Catholic theology that 'revelation ended at the death of the last apostle', Newman's theory could hardly survive without a restatement so drastic as to leave it almost unrecognisable" (p. 160).

[91] See, "What Says Vincent of Lerins," *Historical Sketches*, i, pp. 375–90.

[92] *Development*, p. 27 (p. 24 1845 ed.).

[93] *Development*, p. 172 (p. 58 1845 ed.).

was confused," might lead one to conclude that he had changed his position, until it is known that he had not re-read his *Essay* since he first published it seventeen years earlier.[94] The relationship of new developments to the original revelation or *depositum* is one of the most involved and difficult features of Newman's theory and a satisfactory discussion of it would demand a separate essay. At least it can be said that it is not at all clear that Newman's statements gainsaid anything in his earliest writings on the subject. They seem to imply no more than does the following passage from his first delineation of development in 1843:

> the doctrine of the Double Procession was no Catholic dogma in the first ages, though it was more or less clearly stated by individual Fathers, yet if it is now to be received, as surely it must be, as part of the Creed, it was held everywhere from the beginning, and therefore, in a measure, held as a mere religious impression, and perhaps an unconscious one.[95]

There seems to be absolutely no grounds for Acton's assumption that the delation to Rome of his 1859 article on "Consulting the Laity" prompted Newman to narrow his theory. Writing in the *Atlantis* one year earlier, in July 1858, Newman expressed sentiments similar to those in his letters to Acton:

> Every Catholic holds that the Christian dogmas were in the Church from the time of the Apostles; that they were ever in their substance what they are now; that they existed before the formulas were publicly adopted, in which, as time went on, they were defined and recorded; and that such formulas, when sanctioned by the due ecclesiastical acts, are binding on the faith of Catholics, and have a dogmatic authority.[96]

He had expressed himself in even more explicit terms in 1852:

> The notion of doctrinal knowledge absolutely novel, and of simple addition from without, is intolerable to Catholic ears, and never was entertained by anyone who was even approaching to an understanding of our creed. Revelation is all in all in doctrine; the Apostles its sole depository, the inferential method its sole instrument, and ecclesiastical authority its sole sanction. The Divine Voice has spoken once for all, and the only question is about its meaning.[97]

[94] O. Chadwick, *From Bossuet to Newman*, p. 187.
[95] *Oxford University Sermons*, p. 323 (p. 324 1843 ed.).
[96] *Tracts Theological and Ecclesiastical*, p. 333.
[97] *Idea of a University*, pp. 197–98. The last two sentences in the above quotation represent a slightly revised version appearing in later editions of Newman's University lectures.

What does seem to present a difficulty in interpretation is Newman's references to the knowledge of Saints Clement, Polycarp and Bernard. In his letter to Acton he made no distinction between the knowledge of the original dogma possessed by the Apostles and that possessed by the Fathers. It is this confusion which may have prompted Acton's scarcely justified remark that Newman thought "a divine of the second century on seeing the Roman catechism would have recognized his own belief in it, without surprise, as soon as he understood its meaning."[98] That this does not adequately represent Newman's thought on the subject can be seen from a paper written in 1868, and only recently published, in which he set forth "the view I have entertained for many years." After stating in an earlier section that "the Apostles were inspired, and the Fathers were not," he writes:

let then the words be taken, 'Spiritus Sanctus superveniet in te, et Virtus Altissimi &c—what person of the Blessed Trinity is meant by 'Spiritus Sanctus'? I conceive that an Apostle would have announced promptly, emphatically, "The Third"; so has answered the Church; but some of the earlier Fathers, I think, answered "the Second." Why do they say "The Second"? because they were not individually perfect theologians.[99]

The Achilles heel of Acton's entire hypotheses was the fact that Newman re-edited his *Essay* in 1878 substantially unchanged. Acton could only state that Newman went back to his former position but offered no explanations why he did so. If Newman's insistence in 1862 that development meant only a more intimate apprehension of the original revelation constituted a withdrawal and was prompted by fear of offending Rome then there were even stronger reasons why he should not reject this in 1878. The Vatican Council, in the constitution "On the Catholic Faith," declared that "the doctrine of faith which God hath revealed has not been proposed, like a philosophical invention, to be perfected by human intelligence, but has been delivered as a divine deposit to the Spouse of Christ, to be faithfully kept and infallibly declared."[100] Newman would certainly have

---

[98] *History of Freedom*, p. 407.
[99] "An Unpublished Paper by Cardinal Newman on the Development of Doctrine," *Gregorianum*, xxxix, 3 (1958), p. 594.
[100] Quoted by Butler, *Vatican Council*, ii, p. 267.

not reprinted anything in his *Essay* that appeared to go against the constitutions of the Vatican Council.

On the whole Acton's criticisms on development are disappointing. Though his notes abound with meticulously transcribed remarks of critics far less competent than himself, in his own comments he skirted many of the primary issues raised by Newman's *Essay*. He seemed to have given much thought to the theory of development but there is no evidence that he pursued a detailed course of research into either the genesis of Newman's ideas or their correct interpretation. Some of his conclusions appear to have been more the result of bold guesswork than of a careful review of the evidence. Yet Acton's conjectures are sometimes more stimulating than the cautious explorations of less gifted scholars, and can be ignored only at the risk of missing an exciting insight into a hitherto darkened or unexplored territory.

VIII. A Contrast in Ideas: Progress, History, Politics

It would be a serious error to attribute Acton's loss of sympathy for virtually all of his Catholic contemporaries solely to his hatred of Ultramontanism. Of equal importance in explaining his isolation was the increased influence on his mind of the liberal thought of his day. One cannot work one's way through the writings of the latter part of his life without being struck by the growing importance he assigned to nineteenth-century writers. He came to regard Rothe as "the greatest moral theologian of modern times."[1] His admiration for Vinet, Martensen and Thiersch was hardly less.[2] He saw George Eliot as a rival to Shakespeare and Dante.[3] From a militant young Catholic who stoutly maintained that the Church could not place trust in "the results of the political development of the last three centuries"[4] he developed into a defiant Liberal who passionately insisted that the Church's refusal to admit the superior character of modern Liberalism over all other political forms was a sin crying to heaven for vengeance. Leaving entirely aside the question of Ultramontanism it is hardly a cause for wonder that he should have lost intellectual sympathy for a Newman who stood out against most of the fondest notions of the century. A comparison of their respective approaches to some of the major

[1] G. E. Fasnacht, *Acton's Political Philosophy* (London, 1952), p. 242.
[2] Acton to Döllinger, 16 June 1882, Woodruff Mss.
[3] Letters to *Mary Gladstone*, pp. 43–44.
[4] *History of Freedom*, p. 210.

topics that most occupied Acton's mind in the 80's and 90's reveals a striking divergence.

If one idea could be chosen to represent the *Zeitgeist* of the nineteenth century it would probably be the idea of constant human progress. In the previous century such writers as Turgot and Condorcet believed they could enumerate the stages of development through which society had passed before emerging finally into an age of enlightenment. In spite of isolated protests the spirit of the new enlightenment swept victoriously into the nineteenth century and the generalizations of a superficial age were broadened and given a new respectability under a metaphysical mask called a philosophy of history. The story of mankind was interpreted in terms of an unfolding of a principle immanent in the historical process itself. In the new vision a worldly kingdom of perfection was seen as the end of history. Belief in providence became belief in progress.[5]

Now though Acton rejected the cruder expressions of idealist historicism he nevertheless fell very much under its influence. For him as for the Hegelians progress became a law of history. His conversion was far more than a reaction against Ultramontanism. As his thought matured his sense of the tragic element in history heightened and almost overwhelmed him. As has been the case with many other strong and original thinkers, the pettiness of man and his paltry achievements in the face of his lofty aspirations weighed heavily on his mind and drove him to seek a personal answer to the riddle of existence. The age-old Christian answer stressing the wretchedness of unregenerate man and holding out as his only hope a supernatural life perceived through the eyes of faith and only fully comprehended in a future heavenly existence no longer appeared adequate. His thought became secularized and he sought a meaning for the world in terms of temporal history. Turning his back on his earlier position he became an apostle of progress. "My theory," one of his notes reads, "is that divine gov.[ernment] is not justified without progress. There is no raison d'être for the world."[6] Acton came to believe that those who held that the ways of God were mysterious and beyond man's ken were really questioning God's rule:

---

[5] See Karl Löwith's *Meaning in History* (Chicago and London, 1957) ch. iv, and J. B. Bury's *The Idea of Progress* (London, 1920) p. 22.
[6] CUL Add. Mss. 5641, 55.

Providence means progress. Notion that God is active in history, that Christ pursues his work among men. That this action is not wasted . . . Not to believe in Providence is to question the divine government.[7]

Surveying history Acton concluded that its movement was toward liberty, and liberty meant "that condition in which men are not prevented by men from obeying their duty to God."[8] In a letter to Döllinger he put forth his theory:

there is a grand unity in the history of ideas—of conscience, of morality, and of the means of securing it. I venture to say that the secret of the philosophy of History lies there:—It is the only point of view from from which one discovers a constant progress, the only one therefore which justifies the ways of God to man.[9]

Acton believed that one could point to certain outward signs confirming progress as the law of history: to representative government, the extinction of slavery, the reign of opinion, the security of weaker groups, liberty of conscience.[10] All of these things showed that "the action of Christ who is risen on mankind whom he redeemed fails not, but increases."[11]

In contrast Newman, throughout his long life, remained virtually unmoved by the nineteenth-century cult of progress. "The country seems to me to be in a dream," he wrote in 1832, "being drugged with this fallacious notion of its superiority to other countries and times."[12] Nothing he learned in subsequent years caused him to alter his opinion. Current terms such as progress, liberalism, recent civilization, terms that seemed to arouse experiences akin to mysticism in many of his contemporaries, he dismissed as "the newspaper cant of the day."[13] His analysis of the prevailing optimism of his own time is probably better appreciated by a twentieth-century reader than by the University congregation to whom it was delivered over a hundred years ago:

Yet it is impossible not to observe, and it is useful to bear in mind, that mankind at large is not wiser or better than heretofore; rather, that it is an especial fault of the present day, to mistake the false security of the man of the world for the composure, cheerfulness, and benevolence

---

[7] CUL Add. Mss. 5011, 208; 4987, 55.
[8] CUL Add. Mss. 4969, 126.
[9] Acton to Döllinger, 22 September 1882, Woodruff Mss.
[10] *Essays on Freedom and Power*, p. 37.
[11] *Ibid.*, p. 36.
[12] Quoted by A. D. Culler, *The Imperial Intellect*, p. 81.
[13] Newman to Monsell, 5 February 1865, Orat. P.C.

of the true Christian; while all the varying shades of character between these two, though indefinitely more deserving of our respect than the former of them—I mean the superstitious, the bigot, the intolerant, and the fanatic—are thrust out of the way as inhuman and offensive, merely because their knowledge of themselves is more exact than their apprehension of the Gospel, and their zeal for God's honor more energetic than their love of mankind.

This in fact is the fault incident to times of political peace and safety, when the world keeps well together, no motions stirring beneath it to disturb the continuity of its surface, which for the time presents to us a consistent and finished picture. When the laws of a country are upheld and obeyed, and property secure, the world appears to realise that vision of constancy and permanence which it presented to our youthful imagination. Human nature appears more amiable than it really is, because it is not tried with disappointments; more just, because it is then its interest to respect the rights of others; more benevolent, because it can be so without self-denial. The warnings contained in the historical Scriptures, concerning the original baseness and corruption of the heart, are, in the course of time, neglected; or, rather, these very representations are adduced as a proof how much better the world now is than it was once; how much more enlightened, refined, intellectual, manly; and this, not without some secret feeling of disrespect towards the writers of the plain facts recorded in the Bible, as if, even were the case so bad as they make it appear, it had been more judicious and humane to have said nothing about it.

But, fairly as this superficial view of human nature answers in peaceful times; speciously as it may argue, innocently as it may experimentalize, in the rare and short-lived intervals of a nation's tranquility; yet, let persecution or tribulation arise, and forthwith its imbecility is discovered. It is but a theory; it cannot cope with difficulties; it imparts no strength or loftiness of mind; it gains no influence over others. It is at once shattered and crushed in the stern conflict of good and evil; disowned, or rather overlooked, by the combatants on either side, and vanishing, no one knows how or whither.[14]

"The stern conflict of good and evil"—Newman's Christian pessimism kept him far more of a realist than Christians who tended to ignore the doctrine that man was a fallen creature. A Gladstone might from Olympian heights proclaim the new gospel: "Above all things, men and women, believe me, the world grows better from century to century, because God reigns supreme, from generation to generation. Let pessimism be absent from our minds, and let optimism throw its glory over

[14] *Oxford University Sermons*, pp. 102–103.

all our souls and all our lives henceforth and ever";[15] and Acton might shout from the rooftops that to deny progress was to deny the divine government of the world; but Newman remained adamant and insisted that

it is our wisdom, both as to the world and as to Scripture, to take things as we find them; not to be wise above what is written, whether in nature or in grace; not to attempt a theory where we must reason without data; much less, even could we frame one, to mistake it for a fact instead of what is is, an arbitrary arrangement of our knowledge, whatever that may be, and nothing more.[16]

Newman had no sympathy for historians who turned to universal history to find a justification of God's ways to man. Apart from their ignoring the highly personal message of Christianity he denied that through historical investigation they could determine the designs of Providence. Providence "works beneath a veil, and what is visible in its course does but shadow out at most, and sometimes obscures and disguises what is invisible."[17] Christianity for Newman was grounded on faith in an *unseen* God, and faith was grounded on God's word, not on the findings of critical historians. "Let us be thankful for what He gives, without attempting to interpret His acts and to determine His purposes."[18]

Yet, as a cultured and highly sensitive Englishman, Newman readily admitted that much progress had been made in the acquisition of knowledge, and that in the development of his faculties and in his inventive capabilities man was "in his very idea, a creature of progress."[19] But as regards the cultivation of moral truth he insisted that the world ever remains in its infancy:

The religious history of each individual is as solitary and complete as the history of the world . . . When children cease to be born children, because they are born late in the world's history, when we can reckon the world's past centuries for the age of this generation, then only can the world increase in real excellence and truth as it grows older . . . 'As it was in the beginning, is now, and ever shall be,' such is the general

[15] Cited by Erik von Kuehnelt-Leddihn, *Liberty or Equality* (London, 1952), p. 12.
[16] *Oxford University Sermons*, p. 110 (p. 98, 1843 ed.).
[17] *Essays Critical and Historical*, ii, p. 190.
[18] Newman to Allies, 22 November 1860, Orat. P.C.
[19] *Historical Sketches*, i, p. 164.

history of man's moral discipline, running parallel to the unchanging glory of that All-perfect God, who is its Author and Finisher.[20]

While Acton maintained that "achieved liberty" was a fruit of advancing civilization,[21] Newman had no confidence that the movement of history was toward a stable society. As he wrote in his *Lectures on the History of the Turks:*

a huge conglomeration of destructive elements hangs over us, and from time to time rushes down with an awful irresistible momentum. Barbarism is ever impending over the civilized world. Never, since history began, has there been so long a cessation of this law of human society, as in the period in which we live.[22]

In Newman's mind the Church even less than civil society could expect long periods of calm. To a despondent friend he once wrote:

As to your question, the Church has ever seemed dying, and has been especially bad (to appearance) every 300 years. Think of it when the whole force of the Roman Empire was against it. Well, they triumphed, against all human calculations. Hardly had things got into shape, when down came the barbarians and all was undone and they had to begin again. Would not the prospect of the future look as terrible to St. Augustine or St. Leo (humanly) as it does to our generation? It is impossible to forecast the future, when you have no precedents, and the history of Christianity is a succession of fresh and fresh trials, never the same twice. We can only say, "The Lord that delivered me from the lion and the bear, He will deliver me from this Philistine." But we cannot anticipate the exact shape the conflict will take.[23]

And in the *Via Media* one again comes upon the same historical realism which somehow one does not expect from a Victorian:

But in truth the whole course of Christianity from the first, when we come to examine it, is but one series of troubles and disorders. Every century is like every other, and to those who live in it seems worse than all times before it.[24]

As Acton observed with implied condemnation:

N.[ewman] expected no great improvement of society . . . The only thing to work for is that men, living in maligno should die in the enjoy-

[20] *Parochial and Plain Sermons*, vii, pp. 248–49.
[21] *Essays on Freedom and Power*, p. 36.
[22] *Historical Sketches*, i, p. 12.
[23] Newman to Monsell, 30 April 1877, Orat. P.C.
[24] *Via Media*, i, p. 354.

ment of the resources of religion. To save, to reconcile the dying sinner
—all we can hope for.[25]

While Acton had visions of a liberal kingdom of freedom—
"End with the Kingdom of God, which is Liberty"[26]—Newman
did not believe that it was a safe thing to strive for such a lofty
goal. He had no confidence that a *Christian* civilization could
ever be realized, or was even desirable. To a correspondent who
had pointed out that "Catholic civilization . . . was the ideal
which the Church aimed at in the middle ages, and which she
worked into the laws, manners, institutions, public policy, and
public opinion of Europe,"[27] Newman replied:

> I do not see my way then to hold that 'Catholic civilization,' as you
> describe it, is in fact (I do not say in the abstract but in a world like this),
> is, or has been, or shall or can be, a good or *per se* desirable . . . Now,
> that it is the tendency of Christianity to impress itself on the face of
> society, I grant; but so in like manner it is the tendency of devotion to
> increase Church lands and property, and to multiply religious houses;
> but, as the state of the recipient (i.e. a given people, hic et nunc) may
> hinder the latter tendency from working well, e.g. may lead to secularity
> and corruption in the clergy, so may certain peculiarities in this or that
> age or place, interfere with the beneficial effects of the former; that is,
> it is not necessarily a good.
> St. John says 'Mundus totus in maligno positus est,' is this the decla-
> ration of an eternal fact? I think it is. If so, the world, though stamped
> with Christian civilization, is still in maligno positus.[28]

In Newman's mind the primary work of the Church was not
the reformation of society but the salvation of individual souls.
Surveying history he could see nothing that encouraged him to
alter his opinion:

> The state of great cities now is not so very different from what it was
> of old; at least not so different as to make it appear that the main work
> of Christianity has lain with the face of society, or what is called the
> world. Again the highest class in the community and the lowest, are not
> so different from what they would be respectively without the knowledge
> of the Gospel as to allow it to be said that Christianity has succeeded with
> the world *as* the world in its several ranks and classes.[29]

[25] CUL Add. Mss. 5511.
[26] CUL Add. Mss. 5504.
[27] Newman to Allies, 22 November 1860, Orat. P.C.
[28] *Ibid.*
[29] *Parochial and Plain Sermons*, iv, pp. 154–55.

Newman's realism was closely related to his eschatological approach to history. The doctrine of fulfillment and salvation, which in liberal thought was transferred to the temporal sphere, remained for him a goal to be achieved only in a future heavenly kingdom. In one sense the Incarnation marked the end of history, for Christ's second coming, the consummation of history, was ever at hand and the Christian ever close upon the next world. In a strangely fascinating passage in one of his parochial sermons Newman gave expression to his profoundly Christian concept of history:

But when the Christ had come, as the Son over His own house, and with His perfect Gospel, nothing remained but to gather in His Saints. No higher Priest could come—no truer doctrine. The Light and Life of men had appeared, and had suffered, and had risen again; and nothing more was left to do. Earth had had its most solemn event, and seen its most august sight; and therefore it was the last time. And hence, though time intervene between Christ's first and second coming, it is not *recognised* (as I may say) in the Gospel scheme, but is, as it were, an accident. For so it was, that up to Christ's coming in the flesh, the course of things ran straight towards that end, nearing it by every step; but now, under the Gospel, that course has (if I may so speak) altered its direction, as regards His second coming, and runs, not towards the end, but along it, and on the brink of it; and is at all times equally near that great event, which, did it run towards, it would at once run into. Christ, then, is ever at our doors; as near eighteen hundred years ago as now, and not nearer now than then; and not nearer when He comes than now. When He says that He will come soon, "soon" is not a word of time, but of the natural order. This present state of things, "the present distress" as St. Paul calls it, is ever *close upon* the next world, and resolves itself into it. As when a man is given over, he may die any moment, yet lingers; as an implement of war may any moment explode, and must at some time; as we listen for a clock to strike, and at length it surprises us; as a crumbling arch hangs, we know not how, and is not safe to pass under; so creeps on this feeble weary world, and one day, before we know where we are, it will end.[30]

Newman would have permitted a philosophy of history to the Jews:

It was otherwise with the Jews: they had a grant of this world; they entered the vineyard in the morning; they had time before them; they might reckon on the future.[31]

[30] *Parochial and Plain Sermons*, vi, pp. 240–41.
[31] *Sermons on Subjects of the Day* (Rivington, London, 1869), p. 10.

One of Acton's observations on Newman reads:

Note that Newman denies the divine government of the world. Providence does not manifest itself in history. The law of Progress is not the law of history.[32]

This criticism merely tells one that Newman in contrast to Acton resisted the allurements of nineteenth-century idealism.

In Acton's vision of the new order that was in the process of being born the role of the historian was pre-eminent. As guardian of "the conscience of mankind"[33] he had the sacred duty to direct the movement of the world toward liberty. It was his office to determine what told for or against freedom: "History sets up the historian as judge."[34] He was also to be executioner and should suffer no man, no cause "to escape the undying penalty which history has the power to inflict on wrong."[35] The function of the historian was so exalted that it required of him an absolute renunciation of anything which might hinder its proper exercise. The sober seriousness with which Acton viewed the role of the historian is strikingly illustrated by one of his notes:

Life is not worth living if one can do nothing for one's country, for religious truth and the relief of pain. Yet a historian must be indep.-[endent] of his pract.[ical] object. It takes a very exalted view of history to renounce all that.[36]

Acton attached enormous importance to the modern development of a science of history. To earlier men it had been only an instrument. It had not been recognized for what it could be: "a supreme master, and a sovereign guide."[37] Only in his own day had the discovery been made. Now when speaking *ex cathedra* the historian might claim infallibility for his judgments:

For men of equal competence, at a certain pitch of merit, there is no wide divergence possible. Their private theoretic opinions will remain. But their historical and moral judgment will be the same. The result is infallible, at a certain level.[38]

As a science, history was "an arbiter of controversy, a guide of

[32] CUL Add. Mss. 4987, 44.
[33] *Essays on Modern History*, edited by J. N. Figgis and R. V. Laurence (London, 1906), p. 383.
[34] CUL Add. Mss. 4914, 317.
[35] *Essays on Freedom and Power*, p. 48.
[36] CUL Add. Mss. 5014, 278.
[37] CUL Add. Mss. 5015, 70.
[38] CUL Add. Mss. 5015, 59.

the wanderer, the upholder of that moral standard which the powers of earth, and religion itself, tend constantly to depress."[39] And as a science its reign ought to be absolute: "Let not our religion, our politics, our philosophy react upon our history, but let history influence them."[40]

But eloquently as Acton might preach on the primacy of history there was one sacrifice he was not prepared to offer at its shrine: *Liberalism*. He remained to the end of his days an unrepentant doctrinaire Liberal, and his pleadings on behalf of objective history notwithstanding, his Liberalism colored almost everything he wrote. Yet he was not unaware that dogmatic Liberalism could be a pitfall to the historian:

Danger of liberalism to History. It has a dogmatic test. That is right which contributes to the security of Liberty. That is wrong which opposes it. No application of the time test. It is not a question of time and place. The propositions are absolute and universal. They must be taken or rejected. History knows nothing of dogmatic right or wrong. So it must stand independently of Rome. The formula must be generalized.[41]

In brief: if history must stand independently of the dogmas of Rome it must stand equally independent of the dogmas of Liberalism. It could subserve no cause.

Newman took a much humbler view of the definitive character of scientific history. He denied that the historian could achieve anything like the objectivity possible to the physical scientist:

Physical facts are present; they are submitted to the senses, and the senses may be satisfactorily tested, corrected, and verified . . . But it is otherwise with history, the facts of which are not present.[42]

Since the mere facts were not available the historian had to do the best with what was given him and look for aid from varied quarters. He had to make use of "the opinions of others, the traditions of ages, the prescriptions of authority, antecedent auguries, analogies, parallel cases" and the like.[43] Further, the historian himself by reasons of "the prejudices of birth, education, place, personal attachment, engagements, and party"[44] was

---

[39] *Essays on Freedom and Power*, p. 336.
[40] CUL Add. Mss. 5015, 61.
[41] CUL Add. Mss. 4908, 174.
[42] *Development*, p. 111.
[43] *Ibid.*, p. 111.
[44] *Development*, p. 76.

often so involved in the subject of criticism as to make it unlikely that he would achieve complete objectivity. Such being the case, who could say that history, past or present, was "secure from the possibility of a variety of interpretations."[45]

Newman, however, did not disregard the importance of history in religious inquiries. As an Anglican he lamented "the injury done to our whole view of Gospel truth by our ignorance of ecclesiastical history."[46] And as a Catholic he heartily concurred with Gladstone on the duty of maintaining "the truth and authority of history, and the inestimable value of the historic spirit."[47] But he insisted that Christianity was more than

a mere historical religion. Certainly it has its foundations in past and glorious memories, but its power is in the present. It is no dreary matter of antiquarianism; we do not contemplate it in conclusions drawn from dumb documents and dead events, but by faith exercised in ever-living objects, and the appropriation and use of ever-recurring gifts.[48]

From one point of view Newman had a deeper historical sense than liberal historians who were disposed to see the value of history too exclusively in terms of the present. For these history showed the superiority of the new liberal age over all preceding ages. Newman saw a sacred value in history apart from its relevance to the present:

As the Church is a sacred and divine creation, so in like manner her history, with its wonderful evolution of events, the throng of great actors who have a part in it, and its multiform literature, stained though its annals are with human sin and error, and recorded on no system, and by uninspired authors, still is a sacred work also; and those who make light of it, or distrust its lessons, incur a grave responsibility.[49]

On the claim so often made by many of the new critical scholars— and reiterated by Acton to the disparagement of Churchmen, Newman included—that they were the only honest inquirers who never sacrificed truth to religious advantage Newman wrote some thoughtful lines:

Much is said in this day by men of science about the duty of honesty in what is called the pursuit of truth—by 'pursuing truth' being meant

---

[45] *Ibid.*, p. 76.
[46] *Essays Critical and Historical*, ii, p. 250.
[47] *Difficulties of Anglicans*, ii, p. 309.
[48] *Grammar of Assent*, p. 488.
[49] *Difficulties of Anglicans*, ii, p. 309.

the pursuit of facts. It is just now reckoned a great moral virtue to be fearless and thorough in inquiry into facts; and when science crosses and breaks the received path of Revelation, it is reckoned a serious imputation upon the ethical character of religious men, whenever they show hesitation to shift at minute's warning their position and to accept as truths shadowy views at variance with what they have ever been taught and have held . . . An inquirer in the province of religion is under responsibility for his reasons and their issues. But whatever be the real merits, nay, virtues, of inquirers into physical or historical facts, whatever their skill, their acquired caution, their dispassionateness and fairness of mind, they do not avail themselves of these excellent instruments of inquiry as a matter of conscience, but because it is expedient, or honest, or beseeming or praiseworthy, to use them: nor, if in the event they were found to be wrong as to their supposed discoveries, would they, or need they, feel aught of the remorse and self-reproach of a Catholic, on whom it breaks that he has been violently handling the text of Scripture, misinterpreting it, or superseding it, on an hypothesis which he took to be true, but which turns out untenable.[50]

But on the question of the revelation of unedifying historical details Newman was in agreement with Acton. "Facts are omitted in great histories," he once wrote, "or glosses are put upon memorable acts, because they are thought not edifying, whereas of all scandals such omissions, such glosses, are the greatest."[51] In his major historical work, *The Development of Christian Doctrine*, so far removed was he from a policy of concealment that F. D. Maurice admitted: "The system Mr. Newman believes in is presented to us in its darkest form; all that can be said against it is anticipated."[52] But by always maintaining a high seriousness and carefully avoiding deliberate provocativeness Newman in his writings never stirred up the same degree of opposition and anger that greeted some of Acton's more sensational productions.

Nowhere does the fundamental divergence between the intellectual systems of Newman and Acton appear more manifest than in their views on the role of politics in human affairs. Here as in other fields the point of departure rested in Acton's proclivity to seek the realization of the ideal and Newman's patient resignation to the impossibility of fallen man's achieving any

---

[50] *Via Media*, i, pp. liii–liv.
[51] *Historical Sketches*, ii, p. 231.
[52] F. D. Maurice, *Epistle to the Hebrews* (London, 1846), Preface, p. liii.

great measure of perfection in this life. Politics for Newman were concerned with the political arrangements of sinful men and he believed it was a hazardous undertaking to attempt the establishment of a system on principles that assumed an ideal situation that never did or never could exist. He stressed the *practical* as the guide to correct political action to such an extent that Acton judged him to have divorced politics from morality altogether.

Acton, on his part, assigned politics a much loftier position in the moral order. From the time when he first gave serious thought to political affairs he regarded state absolutism as one of the greatest evils hovering over mankind. Liberty, meaning the reign of conscience, was man's protection against the encroachments of the State; "The State secures us against other enemies. Liberty secures us against the State."[53] The object of politics was to ensure that "men are not prevented by men from obeying their duty to God."[54] Hence the work of the politician was as sacred as that of the priest: "Politics as sacred as religion."[55] It was the duty of every true Christian to adopt Liberalism, "the theory which employs politics for the realisation of Liberty."[56]

Acton once wrote despairingly to Mary Gladstone:

The great bulk of cultured men in our day do not believe that politics are a branch of Moral Science. They think that politics teach what is likely to do good or harm, not what is right and wrong, innocent or sinful. If I say: 'I owe this man half-a-crown. He is sure to get drunk on it; shall I pay him'?

They will answer—Certainly; you must do your duty, in private life, and wherever the plain rules of morality or the applicable laws extend, regardless of consequences. But they do not admit a like obligation in politics.[57]

"The emergencies of practical politics," he noted elsewhere, "have introduced a false morality, and it is the mission of history to expose it."[58] Newman, he felt, was one of those who had to be exposed. He—along with such men as Burke, Maine, Stephen,

---

[53] CUL Add. Mss. 5606.
[54] CUL Add. Mss. 4969, 126.
[55] CUL Add. Mss. 5017, 184.
[56] CUL Add. Mss. 4969, 126.
[57] *Letters to Mary Gladstone*, p. 180.
[58] CUL Add. Mss. 5011, 80.

Dilke, Morley—was guilty of divorcing politics from morality, guilty of setting up a rival authority independent of religion.[59]

Newman, it is true, did not shrink from speaking of *expediency* as the guide of politics: "Political questions are mainly decided by political expediency, and only indirectly and under circumstances fall into the province of theology."[60] But for Newman, as for Burke, the term *expediency* had a very broad meaning. That he did not equate it with a narrow utilitarianism may be readily deduced from his savage attack on that doctrine in the *Tamworth Reading Room*;[61] and writing in the Dublin *Catholic University Gazette* in 1854 he repudiated the rule of expediency, taken in the sense of what is "useful," as a guide to a State in formulating its laws.[62] What he had in mind when stressing expediency as the guide to politics was a "refined expediency" based on man's *natural* powers of "ratiocination, judgment, sagacity, and imagination fully exercised, and the affections and passions under sufficient control."[63] Nevertheless, he believed that politics were above all a practical science and as such would suffer less than such sciences as ethics or metaphysics if separated from theology.[64]

Newman was far nearer to Augustine with his concept of a City of God versus a City of Man than to the medievalist who "accepted with confidence the things of the world."[65] Since the Church, having as its direct and prime aim "the worship of the Unseen God," was ever at war with a world which, through its social and political organizations, had the sole object of making the most of this life,[66] the Christian who participated in both could do so only by effecting some sort of compromise. Like the Augustinians he seemed to have "expected the secular state to betray a certain injustice."[67] Newman's approach can be seen in a letter he wrote to Monsell on the question of education without religion:

    [59] *Letters to Mary Gladstone*, p. 181.
    [60] *Historical Sketches*, i, p. xii; see also, *Via Media*, i, p.,xli.
    [61] *Discussions and Arguments*, pp. 254 ff.
    [62] *Historical Sketches*, iii, pp. 79–80; see also, *Apologia*, p. 296.
    [63] *Historical Sketches*, i, p. 166.
    [64] *Idea of a University*, p. 64.
    [65] Thomas Gilby, *Principality and Polity* (London, 1958), p. 10.
    [66] *Living Thoughts of Cardinal Newman* (London, 1948), pp. 148–49.
    [67] Thomas Gilby, *Principality and Polity*, p. 229.

Now you know that I, as most or all of us, am, as a matter of principle, utterly opposed to education without religion . . . And I have opposed projects tending that way for the greater part of my life. But now, if I was obliged to form a political judgment, I think I should concur in it, however grudgingly, and try to make the best of it, and make terms with the promoters of it . . . It is cowardly to abandon a principle which you uphold as good & true, because you have suffered one or two defeats in maintaining it—but surely the time may come, after a long warfare steadily carried out in successive great reverses and uniform disappointments of your hopes, when it is as unwise and as headstrong to continue the war, as it would have been in Austria not to make peace after Sadowa. It may be very well for the Holy See which is divinely intended to be the principle of immobility to continue its protests and to spurn the notion of concurrence or compromise; but that as little makes it its duty to forbid local hierarchies, according to their greater insight into local necessities, to act on their discretion, and as little justifies local hierarchies to refuse to political expedience what they cannot in principle originate or approve, what the Holy See cannot sanction, and must ignore, than it would have justified the Irish Hierarchy in 1829 and 1834 in refusing those concessions by which such great ecclesiastical & political advantages have accrued to Irish Catholics, the Holy See then, as it did, keeping silence.[68]

It would be a misunderstanding of Newman's political thought to read into it a sort of dualistic Manichaeism in which the Kingdom of Darkness was equated with the State and the Kingdom of God with the Church. He did not deny that there was good in civil society:

Good and evil go together in this world and its movements. I do not deny the good, but men in general deny the evil. The Apostles might have praised Rome for those virtues of its great men which St. Augustine recognises; but they simply call it Babylon and Apostate. I claim leave to follow the pattern of Apostles.[69]

The Christian resisted the world not because it was an unmixed evil, for in so far as it was from God it was good, but in order to possess higher realities beyond the temporal order. Religion was concerned with these "unseen" realities and as such "religion is higher than politics."[70] Politics were of the earth, and earth

[68] Newman to Monsell, 9 February 1868, Orat. P.C.
[69] Newman to J. G. Cazenove, 2 January 1867, Orat. Miscellaneous Papers, Collection 12.
[70] Newman to J. G. Cazenove, 2 January 1867, Orat. Miscellaneous Papers, Collection 12.

could never lead one to heaven: "Though I served the world ever so well, though I did my duty in it (as men speak) what could the world do for me, however hard it tried?"[71]

Acton saw in Newman's low view of politics a betrayal of Catholicism. He had visions of a kingdom of liberty administered by sacerdotal politicians guided by scientific historians. Liberal Catholicism was manifestly the only form of Catholicism consonant with the new order. But Newman opted for Ultramontanism. Acton came to believe that the key to Newman's whole life was opposition to Liberalism, political as well as religious.[72]

It is not surprising that Newman, who remained so unmoved by the eloquence of his liberal contemporaries, should have especially aroused Acton's ire. What is astounding, however, was Acton's conviction that his was the truly Catholic stand. Although he seemingly appreciated that most nineteenth-century philosophers were in effect seeking a rationalistic and humanistic basis for Western culture, he did not appear to comprehend clearly how perilously close he himself had drifted toward the secularistic philosophies he deprecated. This apparent blindness was due in no small measure to his lack of interest in philosophy proper. "With Acton history was irresistible," noted Tyrrell; "philosophy could be discounted."[73]

Acton allowed his vision of the other-worldliness of Christian fulfillment to become blurred. His liberal daemon told him that the *civitas Dei* and the *civitas terrena* could be reconciled if only politics were held to be as sacred as religion. But if it were once allowed that the law of politics was not identical with the Christian law then a rival power was set up claiming allegiance and a collision was inevitable. Then it could be said, "We live under a divided reign."[74] Newman, the traditional Christian, saw the conflict between the two kingdoms lasting until the end of time. But he believed the conflict would redound most to the benefit of religion under a tolerant constitutional system such as prevailed in England; "Indeed, I have a decided view that Catholicism is safer and more free under a constitutional *régime*, such as our own, than under any other."[75]

[71] *Meditations and Devotions* (London, 1953), p. 304.
[72] CUL Add. Mss. 4989, 42.
[73] M. D. Petre, *George Tyrrell* (London, 1912), ii, p. 359.
[74] *Letters to Mary Gladstone*, p. 182.
[75] *Discussions and Arguments*, p. 307.

Thus, paradoxically, the basis of Newman's Liberalism was the exact opposite of Acton's. He saw man as a fallen creature and regarded the hope of his perfectibility on earth as an insane dream. In practice the best social system was that one which left the Church free to exercise its office of reconciling the sinner to God. Ideally the state operating on Christian principles should actively assist the Church in its sacred functions, but in practice it was ultimately more to the advantage of religion if the state maintained a neutral tolerance.

To many modern observers Newman's pragmatic approach to politics offers a better safeguard to individual freedom than the idealistic approach of an Acton. Recent history has made modern man distrustful of theories that stress society at the expense of the individual. He would not be inclined to follow Acton in his criticism of Newman for being more interested in Saints than in societies or states.[76] Acton's political philosophy lends itself too easily as a prop to the theory that the individual exists for the state, a theory no one would condemn more roundly than Acton himself. If the movement of Universal History toward Utopia is all that matters then it might be expedient that the individual be sacrificed for the greater good. That Acton was not entirely free from contamination by the heresy against which he preached so earnestly is suggested by an interesting observation passed on him by his close friend, Arthur Russell:

Acton's mind is so vast, his serenity is so perfect that 50 years of anarchy in Ireland are to him a very short phase in the evolution of the island to perfection & happiness. But we who are engaged in *practical politics* while in a very inferior occupation we admit, have to consider also other things.[77]

Somewhat surprisingly it was the ascetical Newman, pursuing a monastic existence far removed from the world of practical politics, who retained the firmer grasp of the realities of political affairs. One has but to work his way through his lengthy correspondence with Monsell (a correspondence frequently touching on political questions of the day), to realize that Newman possessed an uncommon grasp of the art of government. Though he disclaimed any special knowledge of politics and in reference to himself spoke modestly of "the unreality of book-knowledge

[76] CUL Add. Mss. 4987, 80.
[77] A. Russell to Lady Blennerhasset, 30 August 1886, Blennerhasset Papers, CUL Add. Mss. 7486, Item 52, Envelope 1.

altogether in questions of fact,"[78] his political judgments were almost always accurate. Even on continental affairs he showed rare perception. Sir Rowland Blennerhasset, a widely travelled politician (and through his German wife well acquainted with German politics and scholars) once paid an unusual tribute to Newman's political acumen:

His wonderful instinct kept him strangely right in German politics. It was instinct for he knew no German, or nothing to speak of. Yet I always consider I owe him much as regards the little I know about Germany (.) It was not the facts he told one or the information he imparted. It was as well as I can express myself the method or habit of mind one got from him on looking at German affairs.[79]

One can but contrast the above praise with Lady Blennerhasset's severe strictures to Arthur Russell against Acton's political wisdom:

You mention Lord Acton. There is nobody who admires his extraordinary mental powers more than I do, nobody who has greater reason to be thankful to him for the intellectual good received at his hands. But as for politics, I believe in nobody who in regard to them has not assumed an open, direct and personal responsibility. There is no such thing as politics in an armchair and the most wonderful knowledge of books is no help towards the knowledge of men. In that way, and with due sense of his superiority in other ways I think that Lord Acton is at the beginning of his experiences in life and not in a position favourable to the experiment. There is perhaps nothing more dangerous than being fenced in morally by a hedge of superior specimens of the race, as for example the Athenaeum Club and then proceeding to judge or legislate for mankind standing behind the hedge.[80]

Acton's inability to construct a unified intellectual framework for his life's work in a large measure explains the frustrations and comparative sterility of his career. His *magnum opus*, a History of Liberty, could never be written until he had resolved the conflict between his Catholicism and his Liberalism on the one hand, and his Liberalism and History on the other. But though he failed to realize his life's ambition his legacy to mankind is not insignificant. He loved liberty passionately, possibly

[78] *Historical Sketches*, i, p. xi.
[79] R. Blennerhasset to Lady Blennerhasset, Blennerhasset Papers, CUL Add. Mss. 7486, Item 20.
[80] 3 September 1886, Blennerhasset Papers, CUL Add. Mss. 7486, Item 52, Envelope 1.

with a greater intensity than any man in history. Lesser men may point to serious flaws in his theories but the grandeur of his vision of freedom remains. When Western men cease to be stirred by such idealism their enslavement is not far removed.

One may regret his peculiar antipathy to Newman. But had Newman been aware of it he probably would have offered no reproach. Though fierce in his remonstrances to others he always demonstrated a marked forbearance toward Acton. He understood Acton better than most men and perceiving in him an immense depth of sincerity and moral earnestness was inclined to overlook more apparent failings. On Acton's part it is doubtful if in the innermost recesses of his heart there really existed aversion for Newman. Under the control of his liberal daemon he may have passed cruel and often unjust judgments on Newman, but there was another Acton. There was the loving father who cautioned his children against thinking ill of others—"not only wishing them well, but judging them favourably, making out the best case for them one can, understanding that others are wiser and better than ourselves, and have reasons for what they do beyond what strangers discover, who see only the outside"[81]—and who proudly presented his favorite daughter with the complete works of Newman as a Christmas gift five years after the death of the Cardinal.[82] One suspects this was the real Acton.

[81] Acton to his daughter Mamy, 14 August 1880, CUL Add. Mss. 4863. 19 (The uncompleted letter was apparently never sent). See also, Richard Acton's account of his father's deathbed advice to himself. *Times*. 30 October 1906.

[82] Acton to Gladstone. 28 January 1895, British Museum, Add. Mss. 44094.

Bibliography

A. *Unprinted Sources*
1) Newman manuscripts at the Oratory, Edgbaston, Birmingham. The
   following collection of Oratory letters have been utilized in the
   writing of the present work:
   a) *Personal Collections:* Acton, Allies, Blachford, Bowles, Monsell,
      Renouf, Simpson, Wetherell.
   b) *Various: Apologia* Collection, *Letter to the Duke of Norfolk*
      Collection, Oratory Letters (1868–75), Oratory School Begin-
      ning, *Rambler* Collection, Vatican Council Collection.
   c) Copied letters.
2) Acton Manuscripts, Anderson Room, Cambridge University
   library.
   The following manuscripts have been used:
   Add. Mss. 4862, 4863, 4865, 4901, 4906, 4908, 4909, 4914, 4916,
   4939, 4963, 4969, 4987, 4988, 4989, 4990, 5011, 5014, 5015, 5017,
   5018, 5395, 5462, 5463, 5468, 5504, 5511, 5542, 5606, 5609, 5641,
   5645, 5666, 5751, 6871 (Acton-Creighton Correspondence).
3) Acton papers in the possession of Mr. Douglas Woodruff. Of
   primary importance here are the collections of letters of a) Newman
   to Acton and b) Acton to Döllinger.
4) Blennerhasset Papers, Cambridge University Library (Add. Mss.
   7486). These papers are catalogued according to the various items
   in the collection. An item may consist of a single diary, a collection
   of press clippings, copybooks, or in some cases several bundles
   containing miscellaneous notes and letters.
5) Acton and Simpson Manuscripts at Downside Abbey. The most
   important part of this collection is the Acton-Simpson correspondence. Much of this correspondence has been printed in Gasquet's
   Lord Acton and His Circle and in the essential complement to this
   work, "Gasquet and the Acton-Simpson Correspondence" by A.
   Watkin and H. Butterfield.
6) W. E. Gladstone Correspondence and Mary Gladstone Correspondence at the British Museum.

7) Wiseman Correspondence in the Archives at Archbishop's House, Westminster.

8) Manning Correspondence in the Archives of the parish of St. Mary of the Angels. Bayswater.

B. *Printed Works of Acton and Newman*

1) *Acton:*[1]

Essays on Church and State. Edited by Douglas Woodruff. London, 1952.

Essays on Freedom and Power. Edited by Gertrude Himmelfarb. London, 1956.

Lectures on the French Revolution. Edited by J. N. Figgis and R. V. Laurence. London, 1910.

Lectures on Modern History. Edited by Figgis and Laurence. London, 1906.

Letters of Lord Acton to Mary Gladstone. Edited by Herbert Paul. London, 1913.

Historical Essays and Studies. Edited by Figgis and Laurence. London, 1907.

History of Freedom and Other Essays. Edited by Figgis and Laurence. London, 1910.

Letters from Rome (by "Quirinus"). London, 1870.

Lord Acton and His Circle. Edited by Cardinal F. A. Gasquet. London, 1906.

"Lord Acton's American Diaries." *Fortnightly Review,* November and December, 1921; January, 1922.

Sendschreiben an einen deutschen Bischof des Vatikanischen Concils. Nördlingen, 1870.

Selections from the Correspondence of the First Lord Acton. Edited by Figgis and Laurence. London, 1917.

Various articles and reviews in the *Rambler, Home and Foreign Review, Chronicle, North British Review.*

2) *Newman:*[2]

Apologia Pro Vita Sua (First publication 1864. Revised edition 1865).

[1] A list of Acton's writings is given in W. A. Shaw's *A Bibliography of the Historical Works of Dr. Creighton, Dr. Stubbs, Dr. S. R. Gardiner, and the Late Lord Acton* (Royal Historical Society, 1903). Shaw's section on Acton is reprinted with further additions in F. E. Lally's *As Lord Acton Says* and in the American edition of G. Himmelfarb's *Essays on Freedom and Power* (Glencoe, Ill., 1948).

[2] The standard edition of Newman's works (40 volumes) is that published by Longmans Green and Co. (1874–1921), with an index prepared by Joseph Rickaby, S.J. Where not otherwise indicated all references are to this edition. The dates of first publication and subsequent revised editions are given in parenthesis. For a more complete bibliography see H. Tristam and F. Bacchus, 'Newman,' *Dictionnaire de Theologie Catholique*, Paris, 1903–1949; and *Cardinal Newman-Studien*, 3rd vol., edited by H. Fries and W. Becker (Glock und Lutz, Nurnberg, 1957).

Autobiographical Writings, Sheed and Ward, London, 1956.
These writings extend over the period 1812–84.
Arians of the Fourth Century (1833 and 1871).
Development of Christian Doctrine (1845 and 1878).
Difficulties of Anglicans—
Vol. i —"Twelve Lectures" (1850).
Vol. ii—"Letter to Pusey" (1866).
Discourses to Mixed Congregations (1849).
Discussions and Arguments (1872). The Essays in this volume were
written between the years 1836–66.
Essays Critical and Historical. 2 vols. (1871). These essays were
written in the period 1828–47.
Grammar of Assent (1870).
Historical Sketches. 3 vols. (1873). The sketches were written
between 1824–72.
Idea of a University. New edition, 1947 (1852 and 1859).
Living Thoughts of Cardinal Newman. Presented by H. Tristam.
Cassell, London, 1948.
Meditations and Devotions. New edition 1953 (1893).
My Campaign in Ireland. Aberdeen, 1896. Printed for private
circulation only.
Oxford University Sermons (1843 and 1871).
Parochial and Plain Sermons. 8 vols. (1834–43).
Present Position of Catholics (1851).
Select Treatises of St. Athanasius. 2 vols. (1841–44 and 1881).
Sermons on Subjects of the Day (1842 and 1869). Rivington, London,
1869.
Sermons Preached on Various Occasions (1874). Burns and Oates,
London, 1887 (sixth edition).
Tracts Theological and Ecclesiastical (1874). These Tracts were writ-
ten in the period 1835–72.
Via Media of the Anglican Church. 2 vols. (1841–4 and 1881). Basil
Montague Pickering, London, 1877.

Papers and Articles by Newman:
"An Unpublished Paper by Cardinal Newman on the Develop-
ment of Christian Doctrine." *Gregorianum*, vol. xxxix, 3, 1958.
"Biblical Inspiration." *Nineteenth Century*, February, 1884.
"On Consulting the Faithful in Matters of Doctrine." *Rambler*,
July, 1859.

C. *Works on Acton and Newman:*
Auchmuty, J. J. "Acton's Election as an Irish Member of Parlia-
ment." *English Historical Review*, September, 1946.
Blennerhasset, Lady Charlotte. "The Late Lord Acton." *Edinburgh
Review*, April, 1903.
Butterfield, Herbert. "Journal of Lord Acton: Rome, 1857."
Cambridge Historical Journal, vol. viii, 3, 1946. "Lord Acton."

Cambridge Journal, May, 1953. *Lord Acton*. Historical Association Pamphlet. London, 1948.

Chadwick, Owen. *From Bossuet to Newman*. Cambridge, 1957.

Cowling, Maurice. "Mr. Woodruff's Acton." *Cambridge Journal*, December, 1952.

"Mr. Woodruff's Reply." *Cambridge Journal*, April, 1953.

Cross, F. L. *John Henry Newman*. London, 1933.

Culler, A. D. *The Imperial Intellect*. New Haven, 1955.

Fasnacht, G. E. *Acton's Political Philosophy*. London, 1952.

Fitzsimons, John. "Acton: The Wavy Line." *Blackfriars*, October, 1952.

Himmelfarb, Gertrude. *Lord Acton: A Study In Conscience and Politics*. London, 1952.

Hutton, R. H. *Cardinal Newman*. London, 1891 (2nd edition).

Kenny, Terrence. The Political Thought of John Henry Newman. London, 1957.

Lally, F. E. *As Lord Acton Says*. Newport, Rhode Island, 1942.

Kochan, Lionel. *Acton On History*. London, 1954.

Mathew, Very Rev. David. *Acton: The Formative Years*. London, 1946.

McGrath, Fergal, S. J. *Newman's University: Idea and Reality*. London, 1951.

Tedder. H. R. "Lord Acton as a Book Collector." *Proceedings of the British Academy*, 1903–1904. vol. i.

Thurston, H., S. J. "Was St. Charles Borromeo a Murderer?" *Tablet*, 29 July 1905.

Various Authors. *John Henry Newman: Centenary Essays*. London, 1945.

Ward, Wilfrid. *The Life of John Henry Cardinal Newman*. 2 vols. London, 1912.

Watkin, A. and Butterfield, H. "Gasquet and the Acton-Simpson Correspondence." *Cambridge Historical Journal*, vol. x, 1, 1950.

Woodward, E. L. "The Place of Lord Acton in the Liberal Movement of the Nineteenth Century." *Politica*, September, 1939.

D. *Other works cited.*

Aubert, R. *Le Pontificat de Pie IX*. Paris, 1952 (vol. 21 of *Histoire de l'Église*, edited by A. Fliche and V. Martin).

Brownson, H. F. *Orestes A. Brownson's Middle Life*. Detroit, 1899.

Bury, J. B. *The Idea of Progress*. London, 1920.

Butler, Dom. Cuthbert. *The Life and Times of Bishop Ullathorne*. 2 vols. London, 1926. *The Vatican Council*. 2 vols. London, 1930.

Butterfield, Herbert, *Man on his Past*. Cambridge, 1955.

Cornish, F. W. *The English Church in the Nineteenth Century*. 2 vols. London, 1910.

Denzinger, H. *Enchiridion Symbolorum Definitionum Et Declarationum De Rebus Fidei Et Morum*. Freiburg, 1952 (28th ed.).
Döllinger, J. I. "A Letter addressed to the Archbishop of Munich" (28 March 1871). Authorized translation, London, 1881.
Declarations and Letters on the Vatican Decrees (1869–1887). Authorized translation Edinburgh, 1891.
The First Age of Christianity and the Church. Translation, London, 1866.
The Pope and the Council (by "Janus"). Authorized translation, London, 1869.
Elliott-Binns, L. E. *Religion in the Victorian Era*. London, 1936.
Gilby, Thomas. *Principality and Polity*. London, 1958.
Gladstone, Right Hon. W. E. *The Vatican Decrees in their bearing on Civil Allegiance*. London, 1874. *Vaticanism*. London, 1875.
Hales, E. E. Y. *Pio Nono*. London, 1956 (2nd ed.).
Halévy, Élie. *Victorian Years* (1841–95). London, 1951. (vol. iv of *A History of the English People in the Nineteenth Century*).
Kuehnelt-Leddihn, Erik von. *Liberty or Equality*. London, 1952.
Laski, H. *Problem of Sovereignty*. London, 1917.
Lathbury, D. C. *Correspondence on Church and Religion of William Ewart Gladstone*. 2 vols. London, 1910.
Leslie, Shane. *Henry Edward Manning*. London, 1921.
Liddon, H. P. *Life of Pusey*. 4 vols. London, 1893.
Löwith, Karl. *Meaning in History*. Chicago and London, 1957 (4th ed.).
Manning, Cardinal H. E. *The Temporal Power of the Vicar of Jesus Christ*. London, 1880.
Mascall, E. L. *The Recovery of Unity*. London, 1958.
Maurice, F. D. *Epistle to the Hebrews, with a preface containing a review of Mr. Newman's Theory of Development*. London, 1846.
Moberly, George. *The Sayings of the Great Forty Days . . . with an examination of Mr. Newman's Theory of Development*. London, 1846 (3rd. ed.).
Morley, John. *The Life of William Ewart Gladstone*. 3 vols. London, 1903.
Mozley, J. B. *The Theory of Development*. London, 1878.
Pattison, Mark. *Memoirs*. London, 1885.
Petre, M. D. *Autobiography and Life of George Tyrrell*. 2 vols. London, 1912.
Purcell, E. S. and De Lisle, E. *Life and Letters of Ambrose Phillips de Lisle*. 2 vols. London, 1900.
Schulte, J. F. von. *Der Altkatholicismus*. Gissen, 1887.
Sickel, Theodor von. *Römische Erinnerungen*. Wien, 1947.
Snead-Cox, J. G. *The Life of Cardinal Vaughan*. 2 vols. London, 1910.

Unsigned Articles. "The Italian Revolution—its Causes and Character." *Dublin Review*, May, 1860.

"Döllinger and the Temporal Power of the Pope." *Dublin Review*, May, 1861.

"The Oratory School." *Tablet*, April 18 and May 2, 1959.

"The Patrimony of St. Peter." *Edinburgh Review*, July, 1860.

"Pius IX and the 'Civiltà Cattolica.' " *Dublin Review*, October, 1866.

"Rome and the Four Last Popes." *Saturday Review*, April 3, 1858.

Various Authors. *The English Catholics 1850–1950* (edited by the Rt. Rev. G. A. Beck). London, 1950.

Vincentius of Lerins. *The Commonitorium* (edited by R. S. Moxon). Cambridge, 1915.

Ward, Maisie. *The Wilfrid Wards and the Transition: I The Nineteenth Century*. London, 1934.

The Wilfrid Wards and the Transition: II Insurrection versus Resurrection. London, 1938.

Ward, Wilfrid. *The Life and Times of Cardinal Wiseman*. 2 vols. London, 1897.

William George Ward and the Catholic Revival. London, 1893.

Index

Index

Achilli, Dr. G., 148
Acton, John Emerich Edward Dalberg, 1st Lord, 4; early history, 6–7; assists Newman in Ireland, 10–13; on Catholic University in England, 14–16, 20–21; helps found Oratory School, 17–20; contributes to proposed Oxford Mission, 23; parliamentary career, 17, 45, 46n.96, 50, 68, 71–73, 77, 99; joins *Rambler*, 28; on English Catholics, 30, 31; on Buckle, 31; on *Rambler* and *Dublin Review*, 32–35; on *Atlantis*, 35; Jansenist controversy, 36–39; on the Catholic Press, 40–42; editor of *Rambler*, 46–51; XYZ controversy, 52, 53; on unpopularity of *Rambler*, 53, 54; on Temporal Power, 65, 67–77 *passim*, 80, 100, 102; on Pius IX, 66, 67, 142; on Napoleon III, 61, 68, 72, 73; on the modern state, 69; changes *Rambler* to *Home* and *Foreign*, 80–82; on Munich Brief, 88, 89; stops *Home and Foreign*, 89; his influence on the *Apologia*, 91–93; with the *Chronicle*, 102–107 *passim;* on papal infallibility, 111–112, 114, 117, 125, 131–139;

on the Vatican Council, 116, 117 and n., 125 and n., 126–130; his opposition to Ultramontanism, 140–144, 153, 167; on Newman's intolerance, 148, 149, 150, 152, 153; on Newman's *Essay on Development*, 153–166; on Progress, 168–169, 172, 173, 175; on History, 175, 176, 177, 178; on Politics, 178–180, 182–184

Marie (Arco-Valley), Lady, his wife, 50n.
Marie (de Dalberg) later Countess Granville, his mother, 6, 7, 50, 66
Richard, his son, 130, 185n.
Mamy, his daughter, 185n.

Allies, T. W., 32 and n.28, 113
Amherst, Francis, Bishop of Northampton, 117
Antonelli, G., Cardinal, 66, 77, 78, 80
Arianism, 147
Arnold, Matthew, 161
Arnold, Thomas, 20, 83
Atlantis, see Newman
Aubert, Professor R., 4n.7, 97n.3
Auchmuty, J. J., 46n.96
Augustine, St., 36, 180
Austria, 58, 59, 62, 73